Down to Earth

About the Author

Sharad Joshi is the National President of the farmers' organisation Shetkari Sanghatana, which describes itself as the only truly liberal party in India. He is Member of Parliament (Rajya Sabha) since 1984. A former bureaucrat and UN technocrat, he turned farmer in 1980s. His work for farmers and rural women and also in the field of promotion of enterprise, technology and economic reforms provided new dimensions in the understanding of the Indian agricultural problems.

Down to Earth

SHARAD JOSHI

ACADEMIC FOUNDATION
NEW DELHI

www.academicfoundation.com

First published in 2010
by

ACADEMIC FOUNDATION
4772-73 / 23 Bharat Ram Road, (23 Ansari Road),
Darya Ganj, New Delhi - 110 002 (India).
Phones : 23245001 / 02 / 03 / 04.
Fax : +91-11-23245005.
E-mail : books@academicfoundation.com
www. academicfoundation.com

Cataloguing in Publication Data--DK
Courtesy: D.K. Agencies (P) Ltd. <docinfo@dkagencies.com>

Joshi, Sharad Shankar.
Down to earth / Sharad Joshi.
p. cm.
ISBN 13: 9788171888429
ISBN 10: 8171888429

1. Agriculture--Economic aspects--India. 2. Agriculture and state--India. 3. Agricultural credit--India. I. Title.

DDC 338.10954 22

Typeset by Italics India, New Delhi.
Printed and bound in India.

Contents

Section III
Environment

Section IV
Technology

Section V
Marketing

Section VI
Exit Policy for Agriculture

Section VII
Economic Reforms

Section VIII
Farmers' Allies and NGOs

Section IX
WTO

Section X
Budget

Section XI
Case Studies

Introduction

I became a farmer, towards the end of 1977, by purchasing a piece of land admeasuring about 23 acres in the village Ambethan in *taluka* Khed of Pune district of Maharashtra. This dry land farm was used essentially for experiments in marshalling of groundwater and examining the economics of various crops that could be produced in Maharashtra. The fact remains that farming became my only source of livelihood.

The ban on the export of onions, which was my main crop, brought down the wholesale prices where farmers could not afford even to take them out of the ground. Thus began the farmers' movement reclaiming the freedom of access to markets and to technology. I was probably the only farmer activist with background in Economics, Statistics and various languages including English and French, apart from acquaintance with half a dozen Indian languages.

The agitation forced on me imprisonment over two dozen times and hundreds of criminal prosecutions. It also imposed on me the responsibility to explain the economics of agriculture in India.

I have had occasion to write for various periodicals including the *Deccan Herald, Business India, The Times of India* and various sundry newspapers including *The Indian Express, The Economic Times* and *The Organiser* as also in various e-periodicals.

I owe it to the large community that has an interest in Indian agriculture to make available to them writing in a suitable form.

I am beginning by bringing out a compilation of my selected writings for *The Hindu Business Line* where I have been writing the column "Down to Earth" regularly without fail since April 1998. These articles have particular importance as they relate to the relatively more recent issues in agricultural development. To make the selection more contemporary, I have included in this selection only articles published since 2002.

I would like to acknowledge the contribution of Mr. Barun Mitra of Liberty Institute and Mr. Sanu Kapila, Publisher, Academic Foundation for bringing out this publication.

I hope the scholars and others interested in Indian agriculture would find this representation of the non-official, if not the anti-official, position on agricultural issues interesting.

Sharad Joshi

I

Agriculture

1 Indian Agricultural Policy in a Nutshell

An Introduction

A large number of researchers and scholars who wish to study agriculture in India are intrigued by the extreme penury of the farmers and the low levels of productivity. It surprises them that the peasantry of a country so well endowed in water resources and sunlight should be so miserably placed.

It was only as late as in 1990 that the documentation of the World Trade Organization (WTO) clearly established that the government of India imposed a negative subsidy on Indian farmers. In the WTO parlance, the term 'negative subsidy' has a specific meaning. It refers to cases where the income received by the farmer by the sale of his proceeds is less than the income he would have received in a hypothetically free market where the government does not intervene in any manner.

On the other hand, 'positive subsidy' refers to cases where the farmers receive an income that is higher than what they would have received in a hypothetically free market, thanks to the intervention of the government.

The central and the most essential fact about Indian agriculture is that it suffers from both the caprices of nature and the tyranny of governmental interventions.

It is astonishing that most learned reports and books on Indian agriculture skillfully avoid referring to this central fact.

For years, all economists and agronomists have held that the poverty of the farmers and the low productivity of agriculture in India are interconnected and are both caused by the illiteracy, wasteful expenditure and large incidence of alcohol and other vices amongst the farmers. It is strange that this calumny persisted for long decades of the British rule as also the first five decades after Independence.

The farmers and the agriculture are the source of all wealth and multiplication thereof, at least in the physiocratic sense. In the peasant idiom, "if a farmer sows one seed the crop is hundred- or even a thousand-fold."

How come the one industry where there is an actual physical multiplication suffers from the most serious deprivations?

Practically, every regional language in India has a proverb that maintains that agriculture is the best of all vocations; trade comes only second and service is the least honourable of all. The proverb persists even though the reality has turned upside down, particularly after Independence. Now a job, particularly the government service is the most prestigious and agriculture almost the passage to poverty, indebtedness and suicide.

Even though the learned economists and the erudite scholars refuse to recognise the fact of the negative subsidy in agriculture, there was abundant evidence of the social recognition that agriculture was the most arduous of all vocations.

Children of farmers, who had the good fortune of getting higher education, systematically preferred jobs and turned their backs on the parental lands. Daughters of non-agrarians have, for decades, clearly expressed their reluctance to be married into agricultural families. The life of a farmer housewife is a continuous misery, comparable to life imprisonment. Now, even the farmers' daughters indicate a clear preference for grooms in non-agricultural vocations, be they even menial.

The instruments of intervention that the government of India used were simple but lethal.

Until as late as 1960s, government imposed a compulsory levy on the food grains produced by the farmers. If a farmer had produced less quantity than was required to be given as 'levy', he was required to make up the difference by purchasing the food grains in the open market at higher prices and delivering them to the government at lower levy prices. If he failed to discharge his 'levy' obligations, he risked being handcuffed and paraded in public places in great ignominy.

All transport, storage, trade, processing and export of agricultural produce were severely restricted if not totally banned. This was done by raising the boggy of consumers' interest and the obligation on the part of the government to ensure food security.

The government did put up a show of ensuring remunerative prices by introducing a system of Minimum Support Prices (MSPs); but manipulating to make them work not as minimum prices the farmers should ever receive but as the signal of the maximum prices the traders need to pay for the agricultural produce.

The government did not need to depress the prices of each of the hundreds of agricultural commodities. It could depress the agricultural economy in general and keep the farmers permanently 'needy' by depressing artificially prices of just about a dozen commodities.

These anti-farmer policies were sought to be justified by various arguments:

1. The desirability of low-cost economy;
2. The need to promote industry by keeping prices of wage goods and raw material low;
3. Need for comprehensive consumer protection; etc.

This is a brief summary of the essentials of the state policy on agriculture. And, all that I have written in last 30 years was essentially a commentary on the various methods used by the government to exploit the 'Bharat' to the benefit of the 'India'.

---

24 November 2009.

2 No Big Deal for Farmers

"Not a paisa will be paid to the farmers above the minimum support price (MSP) fixed for cotton by the Central government." This was the declaration by Dr. N.P. Hirani, the Chief Administrator of the Maharashtra Cotton Producers' Marketing Federation—the supreme body presiding over the ill-famed Maharashtra Cotton Monopsony Procurement Scheme.

The scheme came to be called Maharashtra Cotton Monopoly Procurement Scheme due to penury of economic diction on the part of its architects. The Central government has not as yet announced the MSP for this season, though the cotton sowing is long over in Maharashtra. The MSP per quintal for the standard variety H4 last year was Rs. 1,850; the current market prices in Madhya Pradesh vary between Rs. 2,150 and Rs. 2,300; the futures quotations both in India and in New York show an ascending trend.

It is evident that a marketing scheme working on commercial principles will be able to pay a price much above the MSP. It would appear that the government is calculating to make up for a substantial chunk of losses accumulated over the last three decades.

Mr. Jayant Patil, the Maharashtra Finance Minister, had announced in his March 26 Budget the state government's decision to wind up the monopoly (monopsony?) procurement scheme. The Chief Minister has apparently rolled back that decision and proposes to continue the scheme with two changes.

One, the entire operation will be carried out at the MSP and nothing but the MSP. Two, technically it will no more be a monopsony as the government intends to authorise certain traders, spinning mills and the Cotton Corporation of India (CCI) to purchase cotton as agents of the Federation on identical terms and conditions. There is one difference. The Federation has not completed payments for the last year's purchases, but the agents will be under obligation to make payments within 48 hours of delivery.

The persecution of the cotton producers in Maharashtra is going to become worse as they will continue to struggle under a virtual monopoly without any advantage in consequence of conceding monopsony.

Cotton producers of Maharashtra have suffered for the last three decades under a tyranny called monopoly. In fact, it is a monopsony scheme which forbids free market, storage and transport and the government has the exclusive right; no one else, no trader, not even the CCI, which is entrusted with the responsibility of ensuring that the market price does not fall below the MSP fixed by the Central government, is permitted to enter the cotton market.

The scheme was launched in 1971, when the prices in the international markets were comparatively much higher than in India, with the objective of ensuring ready availability of lint to the textile mills in Mumbai at the world's lowest prices without exposing themselves to the vicissitudes of the cotton market or incurring substantial inventory costs. The scheme succeeded eminently in achieving this objective, albeit concealed.

Corruption and inefficiency ran rampant in the scheme. It employed huge staff full-time round the year for an essentially part-time and seasonal exercise and consequently, incurred astronomical administrative costs. Throughout the three decades of its existence, it achieved consistently low cotton/lint conversion ratio.

Its grading staff, which enjoys the discretionary authority to fix the quality grade and hence, the price payable to the farmers, lives in lavish ostentation that would put to shame even a minister or a major industrialist.

The ruling party machinery milks the scheme of crores of rupees. Those on the Lint Sales Committee are still more opulent and manage to show in accounts sale prices substantially lower than those obtained by even petty traders.

No wonder the scheme has consistently failed in achieving its formally stated objective of ensuring for cotton producers the highest possible share of the lint price and prices higher than in other parts of India. For 27 of the 30 years it was in operation, it paid farmers prices that were substantially lower than those prevailing in neighbouring Gujarat, Madhya Pradesh and Andhra Pradesh.

The cotton marketing centres at Barhanpur in MP and at Adilabad in AP prospered through massive arrivals from Maharashtra. The cotton producers of the Vidarbha region preferred to transport their cotton in bullock carts or hired trucks to Barhanpur in the hope of obtaining better prices and escaping the compulsory deductions on account of the price fluctuation fund (25 per cent), the capital cess (5 per cent) and repayment of loans from cooperative institutions (40 per cent) that together could be as much as 70 per cent of the sales proceeds at poor monopoly (!) prices.

The transport across Maharashtra's border was treated as smuggling, and police personnel extorted huge amounts of money from the farmers. So lucrative were the postings at the checkposts that they carried price tags of lakhs of rupees.

So much for the oppression caused by this notorious scheme. It was also stupid because it did no good to the government either. The state fisc had to carry a whopping burden of hundreds of crores of rupees every year. The state has lost over Rs. 2,300 crore till date.

The non-Congress opposition demanded, at one point, that the scheme be scrapped and supported agitations with that objective. The BJP and the Shiv Sena, when in the opposition, wanted it scrapped but changed their stand and convinced themselves of its virtues soon after they came to power in Maharashtra.

The BJP-led NDA wants the monopoly scheme abolished; the Maharashtra BJP and Mr. Bal Thackeray want it to continue. All parties demand vociferously better returns for farmers when in the Opposition and resort to brutal repression once in power. The farmers' movement has agitated for the termination of the scheme; thousands have gone to jail and several have died in unprovoked police firing.

The PDF government under Mr. Sharad Pawar had conceded that the guaranteed price under the Monopoly (!) Scheme—the price paid at delivery—should be at least 20 per cent higher than the MSP, which stood last year at Rs. 1,850 for the standard H4 variety. The principle was generally observed till 2000-01.

Last year, the Maharashtra government suddenly decided that the guaranteed price would be 20 per cent less than the MSP. The decision was simply illegal. But the government protested fiscal incapacity. The payment of even the MSP for the cotton delivered has not been completed to date.

Everyone thought the state government had learnt the lesson, however belatedly, and would wind up the multi-folly scheme at the first possible opportunity. As mentioned earlier, the Finance Minister had even made an announcement to that effect. Now the Maharashtra Chief Minister, Mr. Vilasrao Deshmukh, has possibly started seeing some political and financial advantages in continuing with the scheme. The situation has improved since last Diwali. Most of the unsold stocks of lint have been disposed of and the lint prices are climbing.

The Chief Minister does not wish to let go of the hen that has laid golden eggs for politicians for three decades. He wants to continue the monopsony without any price premium. This cannot be. It is clear that the farmers will be forced to organise Rythu Bazaars for cotton in Maharashtra or take their cotton to the neighbouring Andhra Pradesh, where Mr. Chandrababu Naidu is going in for Rythu Bazaars in a big way.

---

12 September 2002.

3 The Great India-Bharat Divide

"The Government is determined to bridge the divide that separates 'India' and 'Bharat'," screams a news item, quoting the Prime Minister, Mr. Atal Bihari Vajpayee. I wish I had taken out, in 1978, a copyright on the 'India *vs* Bharat' syndrome. I could be getting substantial sums by way of royalties and I would not need to slog for wages and honoraria.

In 1978, some years after I became a practising farmer in the small village of Ambethan in Pune district of Maharashtra, I had put forward the idea of a neo-colonial exploitative relationship between the two notional entities 'India' and 'Bharat'. Since then, a large number of people have used that expression often to mean things they had not intended.

I made it clear right at the outset that these were not geographical entities, and had no territorial frontiers. 'India' and 'Bharat' are notional entities and I tried to define them as clearly as I could, at that point of time.

'India' is that notional entity, largely Anglicised and relatively better-off, that had obtained the succession of colonial exploitation from the British; while 'Bharat' is largely rural, agricultural, poor and backward that was being subjected to colonial-like exploitation even after the end of the Raj.

Many have erroneously interpreted the expression to denote the urban-rural divide. That was far from my mind. In fact, I made it explicitly clear, even in those early stages, that the relatively opulent segment of the rural society that derived its incomes from non-agricultural activities under State-protection were a part of 'India' while the slum dwellers and the footpath occupants of cities were, in fact, refugees from 'Bharat' to 'India' in search of livelihood.

The basic purpose in enunciating the 'India *vs* Bharat' was to do away with, as suggested by Michael Lipton (*Why Poor People Stay Poor*), all traces of geopolitical character from Marx's "town and country divide", German ideology, as also Mahatma Gandhi's diatribe against the townspeople who, he said, will have to answer before God for their sins against the rural people while bringing out, as starkly as possible the dual character of Indian society and wide chasm between the agricultural sector and the industry in British India. Like Ambedkar, I needed to bring out the iniquity of the Hindu caste system without driving them to ferociously anti-Hindu Islam.

Chaudhary Charan Singh's *Asli Bharat* had a predominantly budgetary connotation. He brought out assiduously, with the data compiled by the Secretariat, that the budgetary allocations for the countryside had been, over a period, extremely unfair and unjust. The step-motherly treatment of the countryside by successive finance ministers has resulted in low income levels and poor infrastructure—roads, railway network, telephones, post office, medical services, schools, electricity and all in the countryside. Charan's *Asli Bharat* is essentially a budgetary concept, quite different from the 'Bharat' in the 'India-Bharat' syndrome which is based on skewed trade relationships enforced through draconian laws.

It is more than 25 years since the idea of 'India-Bharat' was put forth and became the basis of today's farmers' movement in India. Now that the Prime Minister has specifically referred to the 'India-Bharat' contradiction, it is worthwhile clarifying what made me formulate this expression for dualism in the economy.

By 1978, I had come close to the realisation that, despite hard work in my chosen vocation, my academic and administrative background as also the considerable funds I had drawn from my UPU provident fund, I was fighting a losing battle and was sinking, season by season, into losses and possibly into debt. I had not still fully realised the deliberate viciousness of the anti-farmer price policies of the Indian state.

It was at the time, that a young boy who worked on my farm at the then prevailing minimum wage rate of Rs. 3 per day managed to get a job in a Japanese collaboration factory Dai-ichi in nearby Pimpri-Chinchwad industrial area. At the end of one month, having received his first salary packet, he came to see me, eyes full of tears. "Here on the farm, I slogged from morning to evening, had hardly any time for a sip of water and I got 3 pieces per day. In the factory, all of us smoke *bidis* behind the machines most of the time and I get at the end of a month 10 times as much! What kind of a phenomenon is that?," he wondered.

At about the same time, I saw, in a literacy night class I ran for those who worked on the farm, a little girl who had put her slate in her lap and was trying to copy the alphabets I had written on the blackboard, with utmost seriousness, serenity and concentration. The very next day I happened to visit a festival organised in my daughter's school. It was all fun, fanfare, games, shopping, refreshments, balloons, festoons, fire-crackers making in all for extreme hilarity. Little children were throwing away rupee notes as if they were scraps of paper. "Which was the true India I had returned to from Switzerland?," I asked myself. "The one in which the little girl was trying to learn her first alphabets in a dimly lit squalid room in Ambethan or this festival in Pune that an English-medium Convent school was organising?"

It suddenly dawned on me that Ambethan and other villages, on the one hand, and Pimpri-Chinchwad and Pune, on the other, were worlds apart and had little in common between them. Countryside people migrated to cities in search of jobs exactly as the non-resident Indians settling abroad for quantum hikes in remunerations. Not a bit of funds that was wasted on festivities in urban schools could become available to provide blackboards in village schools.

I had tried to explain what was churning my mind to my wife who in her enthusiasm mentioned the crass inequity of the situation to her sister, an affluent urban socialite. The reaction of the latter was simply stunning. "But, you know sister; these farmers do not mind living like that. They are so used to it, you know!" That clinched the thing for me.

Not only was there the horrendous cleavage between the two notional entities, but there was further, a wall of apathy, indifference, unconcern and insensitivity. The predators had hardened their hearts to the miseries of their preys. It was this lack of sensitivity that convinced me that for all practical purposes the two notional entities were two separate nations, in spite of the fact that they shared a common flag and national anthem.

I have put the genesis of the 'India *vs* Bharat' expression to bring out all the dimensions of the divide. Since 1978, the chasm has further widened in, at least, two more dimensions added. First, the digital divide is keeping the informatics revolution in the field of communications away from the countryside. Second, the government is deliberately blocking the flow of technology, particularly biotechnology, into agriculture while allowing it to reach the urban sectors almost without any restrictions.

The Prime Minister has not spelt out what specifically he intended to do to bridge this divide between 'India' and 'Bharat'. The Budget day is fast approaching and the debate on the Kelkar Committee report has included serious suggestion of an agricultural income tax. It would be crassly unfair if one tries to suggest that the Prime Minister would be thinking of endorsing agricultural tax to put 'Bharat' out on a par with 'India'. That would be ridiculous since the respectable farm community has always wanted the pleasure and the privilege of paying income tax as also an income to pay them on.

If the Prime Minister is contemplating increases in the budgetary allocations for infrastructural development or development plan projects such as the rural road development plan or linking of rivers, he may not be able to go far because the fiscal limitations of both the Central and the state governments would make progress in that direction extremely tardy. The incremental budgetary allocation can be nowhere near the net losses inflicted on 'Bharat' through negative subsidies. The measures that are really required to be taken for removing the 'India-Bharat' divide, as I highlighted it 25 years back, will be as follows:

1) Abolish all restrictive and monopoly regimes in agricultural sector including both the access to inputs and the post-harvest treatment of agricultural producc;
2) Abolish the Essential Commodities Act, the Food Corporation of India and the Genetic Engineering Approval Committee (GEAC);
3) Pending reparations to farmers for damages caused them over the last 20 years on account of anti-farmer trade policies estimated by the Task Force on Agriculture at Rs. 300,000 crore, put a moratorium on all coercive recoveries from farmers on account of loan recoveries, electricity dues, etc.;
4) Improve budgetary allocations for a day-to-day networking between 'India' and 'Bharat' including roads, waterways, railways and electronic communications.

Measures of this type will take far more courage for the Prime Minister than what was required to do a 'Pokhran'. The *Hindutva* front has been far too much preoccupied with the Partition; it has shown little concern for the 'India-Bharat' divide which happened at about the same time. Now that the Prime Minister has shown an awareness of this reality, will he be able to muster the necessary courage to do his second 'Pokhran' that will blast most post-Independence socioeconomic and political institutions of their foundations?

---

12 February 2003.

4 A Genuine *Kisan* Manifesto

The Swatantra Bharat Party (SBP) will be holding its first national convention in Mumbai from May 26 to 28, 2003. The SBP is only a registered party, and not a recognised national party.

It has not yet been allotted a reserved electoral symbol. As a registered party, it has a preferential claim on the electoral symbol of an airplane. It has no representation, at present, in Parliament or in any of the State Assemblies.

The SBP has a fair share of control in the Panchayat Raj institutions of two districts in Maharashtra—Chandrapur and Gadhchiroli and a substantial presence in the *taluka panchayats* of Rajura, Korapana, Varora, Kurkheda, Samudrapur and Jalana.

As far as numbers go, the SBP is clearly a lightweight party. One wonders that it came to exist at all. Section 29(A) of the Representation of the People Act, 1989, clearly lays down that to be registered, any political party must, through an affidavit, swear allegiance to the tenets of secularism, democracy and socialism.

The SBP, as a staunch liberal party, had moral compunctions about swearing allegiance to socialism. Wedded as it is to the tenets of freedom of the individual, a plural polity and a market-driven economy, it filed a writ petition challenging the validity of Section 29(A) which has been pending in the Bombay High Court for years.

No one knows why the petition does not come up for hearing.

At academic level, however, the SBP enjoys an enviable clout and prestige. It enjoys the support of all the farmers' organisations in the country that stand for freedom of access for the farmers to markets and to technology.

The SBP spokesmen played a major role in the national debates on economic reforms, the Dunkel draft before the signature on the WTO agreements at Marrakesh as also on validation of genetically modified seeds and food in India.

It had published before the 1998 elections an electoral manifesto that was editorially described as the only sensible manifesto by an economic daily. On the agenda of the Mumbai national convention will figure the party's draft electoral manifesto of 2004 (*http://www.shetkari.in*).

What will go down in history is the fact that the plenary session of the national convention is expected to be attended by over a million farmers from all over the country.

That is creditable for the party which inherits the mantle of the economic philosophies of the erstwhile Swatantra Party, founded by C. Rajagopalachari, which Pandit Nehru, and later, Indira Gandhi succeeded in cleverly branding it as the party of the princes and of capitalists.

At one time, the Swatantra Party was the largest in Opposition and most of its MPs came from rural constituencies. It is also a historical fact that Nehru's attempt to bulldoze the collectivisation of Indian agriculture was frustrated largely because of opposition from the Swatantra Party. All farmers as also the nation at large owe the erstwhile Swatantra Party a debt of gratitude.

Had Nehru's attempts at collectivisation of Indian agriculture succeeded at the Nagpur Congress 1959, India would have been, along with the erstwhile USSR, in a critical food situation and not what it is today—a food-surplus country prepared to exporting food grains.

The SBP has succeeded in rubbing out the vicious propaganda campaign against the old Swatantra Party equating liberalism with feudal capitalism.

This time, this liberal party has come up essentially on the groundswell of support by those farmers and farm labourers who live by agriculture. The cooperative lobby, the sugar barons and their ilk, of course, continue to keep a distance from the SBP as they have inevitably to stand by the party in power.

Whatever the future electoral performance of the SBP, its contribution to the debate on economic reforms will forever stand recognised as exemplary. Further, the Mumbai convention of the party is attaining significance because of the large gathering of farmers expected.

The farmers will throng Mumbai from all over the country at their own expense for transport, lodging and boarding.

The last two items will mean surviving on home-packed food and sleeping under the open sky, wherever they can. They will enjoy none of the facilities offered on similar occasions by political parties.

Compare this with what is happening in Madhya Pradesh. After the debacle of the Congress(I) in the Gujarat elections, the MP Chief Minister, Mr. Digvijay Singh, has sworn to seek revenge in the ensuing elections in his state. The BJP could not let that go unchallenged. It has been organising farmers to agitate against what it calls the miserable performance of the Digvijay Singh government on the situation of roads and electric supply in rural MP.

BJP now plans to hold a massive *kisan* rally to launch its electoral campaign. Instructions have been issued to district units to mobilise farmers on a massive scale and have them transported to the site of the rally, well-fed and dressed in apparel appropriate for a *Hindutva kisan* rally.

The Congress president, Ms. Sonia Gandhi, has been itching to have a really massive *kisan* rally somewhere in the country, preferably in Delhi itself.

She has approached, though without much success, quite a few *kisan* leaders for support for the purpose. Now the Congress and its president need to have a *kisan* rally in Madhya Pradesh to match BJP's. The sooner the better.

Unfortunately for the party, the performance of the Digvijay Singh ministry has been so lacklustre, if not dismal, that the peasantry is most likely to turn a cold shoulder to the party chief's attempts to mobilise them as a demonstration of their support to the Congress. The party needs a demonstration of farmers' support.

So, it has been decided (*Daily Bhaskar,* February 13, 2003) that a rally will be held not in MP but in the predominantly tribal Chhattisgarh, where issues concerning commercial agriculture matter little and not as a *kisan* rally but as a felicitation rally for the party president, Ms. Sonia Gandhi.

That is understandable as for the Congress party, its president remains the only trump card.

The farmers' organisations that stand by the SBP advanced in the 1980s the thesis that the government was deliberately imposing negative subsidies on the farmers.

They have frequently led massive agitations against interventions calculated to depress commodity prices by governments of diverse parties—the Congress, the Janata and the BJP. They were the vanguards of what has now been recognised as movement for remunerative agriculture prices.

All political parties, including the ruling BJP-led NDA, the Congress party as also the Third Front parties give an important place, in their programmes and electoral manifestos, in ensuring remunerative agricultural prices without specifying what precise measures they intend to take in that direction other than continuing the systems in place relating to minimum support prices, administered prices and food procurement.

That precisely is where the electoral manifesto (2004) of the SBP is likely to mark a significant difference. Those who initiated the demand for remunerative prices do not even make a reference to the minimum support prices and the procurement of agricultural produce through governmental agencies.

In fact, the SBP manifesto promises the scrapping of all governmental bodies and legislation for market interventions, including the Food Corporation of India (FCI), the Genetic Engineering Approval Committee (GEAC) and the Essential Commodities Act, and the introduction of a system free of governmental shackles for warehousing of agricultural produce with a 70 per cent advance on delivery with receipts that will be negotiable instruments under the relevant laws.

Furthermore, the SBP, conscious of the fiscal constraints of any government in the country, does not even mention increases in the budgetary allocations or subsidies to farmers.

On the contrary, it promises a moratorium on all coercive recoveries of loans, electricity dues as also other taxes. The SBP manifesto does contain programmes for instauration of modern marketing, grading/testing laboratory network as also abolition of the rural-urban digital divide. The

SBP's draft manifesto provides good guidelines on most issues relating to economic reforms that are bothering the pundits in the ruling and in the Opposition parties—interest rates, convertibility on capital account, and so on.

It also contains a number of prescriptions that are certain to provoke bitter controversies, such as abolition of all systems of reservations in jobs and opposition to a common civil code, stable government, reservations in legislature for women and abrogation of Article 370.

The SBP has little prospect of coming to power in the near future. Its objective in launching the manifesto is obviously academic.

If the Mumbai convention of the SBP succeeds in launching nationwide debate on the issues of agricultural development in the era of WTO and biotechnology, as also on the modalities of economic reforms, that by itself would be a major achievement.

---

26 February 2003.

5 Is Rajnath Singh Tilting at Windmills?

"Rs. 250-crore seed scheme to be launched soon": Agriculture Minister, Mr. Rajnath Singh, July 16.

"Farm credit rate cut to 9 per cent": Finance Minister, Mr. Jaswant Singh, July 16.

"The cut will apply to cooperative loans as well": Mr. Rajnath Singh, July 16.

"Rs. 600-crore package for sugarcane growers": Prime Minister in consultation with Agricultural and Finance Ministers, July 17.

The Lok Sabha elections must be approaching fast. Otherwise, the farmers would not receive this much attention in less than 48 hours. But, then, the farmers have witnessed such drama in the past and look askance at this kind of attention. They have more reason to be suspicious this time because if the top leadership of the ruling NDA is talking "Ayodhya Temple", the second rank seems charged with distributing 'handouts' to the farmers.

Unfortunately, for the ruling alliance, the farm package has so many holes. Their authors are perhaps not tuned to the ground realities. Let us leave the seeds to the birds and examine the credit rate ceiling and sugarcane price.

- The farm credit rate ceiling of 9 per cent. It is not everyday that the Finance Minister addresses a Press conference with the Minister of Agriculture. Mr. Rajnath Singh must have substantial clout in the Cabinet to have managed that. Pity that the announcement, though well packaged, had so little substance.
- If fixing a ceiling on the interest rate of farm credit and sticking to the quota of 18 per cent for priority loans are not a return to the pre-1994 era of administered interest rates, one wonders what it is? In the reforms era, Mr. Jaswant Singh has brought in contrived rates of

interest for senior citizens and housing sector. His July 17 declaration is only a confirmation that in the banking sector, the government is backtracking to the old days of controlled interest rate regime. This will certainly lend itself to creating a black market in credit. The loans may get diverted to non-farm purposes.

- At present, just about 2 per cent of the farm credit is extended at a single digit rate of interest. All that the Finance Minister proposes is to eliminate one link in the chain of intermediaries. It is unlikely that mere elimination of the apex banks will bring down the cost of credit to below 10 per cent.
- The network to which the scheme is applied meets only 45 per cent of the over Rs. 40,000 crore extended as crop loans. The crop loans generally cover only 80 per cent of the cultivation cost. Thus, even on paper the advantage can conceivably reach the farmers to the extent of only about 35 per cent. In spite of Mr. Rajnath Singh's hopes, it is unlikely that the cooperative network will accept to implement the scheme. It is not specified if the RBI is being directed to extend its line of credit to NABARD. Unless NABARD gets a finance of at least Rs. 2,500 crore over and above the present Rs. 6,500 crore, the scheme will not even take off.
- The talk of using the postal network was only at conceptual level. No detailed scheme was presented. The reasons are obvious. Bringing in the post office will mean additional cost to the exchequer or at least an additional line of credit. The Finance Minister is out to show generosity to farmers only if it does not pinch the exchequer.

There is a much bigger substantial fault, which goes to the core of the scheme. An administered rate of interest of 9 per cent in the housing sector makes sense because the returns are in double digit. That is not the case in agriculture. The Finance Minister thinks that he has done a magnanimous act by cutting the farm credit interest rate to 9 per cent. The Minister of Agriculture should have told him that the Commission for Agricultural Costs and Prices (CACP) computes into its calculations a rate of interest that ranges between 2 per cent and 3 per cent only (See Table 5.1). If the farmers get a price that covers an interest cost only 2-3 per cent, reduction of the rate to 9 per cent is an exercise in futility.

Table 5.1

Showing Realised Rates of Interest on Crop Loan for Some Crops

Sr. No.	*Crop*		*Rs. Per Hectare* CACP Cost of Cultivation	*Crop Loan*	*Interest Cost in CACP Calculations*	*Realised Rate of Interest on the Crop Loan % p.a.*
1.	Paddy		7063	7500	224.47	3.0
2.	*Jowar*	Hybrid	5929	5000	95.79	1.9
3.	*Bajara*	Hybrid	5124	4500	89.99	2.0
4.	Groundnut		10365	8000	186.15	2.3
5.	Cotton		10374	8000	196.79	2.5

The Cane Package

More controversial will be the declaration of the Rs. 600-crore package for sugarcane growers. It *reeks* of parochial politics. The idea is that the Centre should divert money from the Sugar Development Fund to the benefit of cane producers in Uttar Pradesh, Uttarakhand, Haryana and Punjab where the state governments declare state advised prices (SAPs) substantially higher than the SMPs for sugarcane.

The cooperative and the government sugar mills in these states have agreed to pay the higher SAP; they have no choice in the matter. The private mills have made it clear that they can, at most, manage to pay the SMP. The Prime Minister, in consultation with the Finance and Agriculture Ministers, now proposes to use Rs. 600 crore from the Sugar Development Fund to meet the difference between the SMP and the SAP. The Sugar Development Fund draws its resources from a cess on sugar collected from all the states. To use it for the benefit of only four states will certainly provoke sharp reactions from Gujarat, Maharashtra, Karnataka and Andhra Pradesh. These are the states, which are normally penalised for higher productivity through fixation of lower prices for levy sugar!

The Prime Minister's decision is tantamount to the replacement of the SMP fixed by the Centre by the SAP fixed by individual states. The four southern cane-producing states would now have a lower assured price for the cane in addition to a lower levy price for the sugar. Gujarat, Karnataka and Andhra Pradesh do not have the system of SAPs. The cane producers there would be penalised because the governments in their states have scrupulously followed the spirit behind the fixation of the SMP and desisted from announcing a parallel SAP.

The case of Maharashtra is even more bizarre. The state government is dominated by cooperative sugar barons. The Government thought that it was doing good to the cooperative sugar factories by permitting them to pay the farmers a price lower than the SMP. Maharashtra, in fact, has a negative SAP in the sense that it is lesser than the SMP. In the just-ended season, the SMP for good factories in southern Maharashtra works out to around Rs. 1,000 per tonne, while the SAP is as low as Rs. 560 per tonne.

But for the fact that the Maharashtra government, blackmailed by the sugar cooperative barons, fixed an SAP lower than the SMP, the cane growers in Maharashtra would have got at least the SMP under the Prime Minister's Rs. 600-crore package.

The cooperative movement in Maharashtra stands completely exposed. The government of Maharashtra will have to fork out much more than Rs. 170 crore that it is offering the financial institutions to stave of seizure of government property.

How is the Rs. 600 crore going to be used? According to the explanation given by the officials, the amount will not be paid in cash to the farmers but will be used for improving the productivity and the quality of sugarcane and sugar. This would be the first case where a cash subsidy is being converted into a 'Green Box' subsidy. This is something the rich countries have been doing since Marrakesh. If India does it, nobody can object because the amount comes not from the budgetary source but from the Sugar Development Fund, which is contributed by the cane producers themselves.

Mr. Rajnath Singh certainly thought he was strengthening BJP's electoral muscle. But was he?

---

23 July 2003.

6 Let's Start from the Scratch

The election drums can be heard loud and clear. Some time back, the Union Agriculture Minister, Mr. Rajnath Singh, called me to fix a meeting urgently. "Elections could be very close," he said, "and I need to launch programmes that will start showing results in three months time." Brave words! But the meeting never happened.

I had devoted a whole column to listing out the kind of things I would do if I wanted to make Indian agriculture world-class. Mr. Rajnath Singh, probably, was never shown my proposals. After a month or two, he made the surprising announcement of allotting Rs. 600 crore to bridge the gap between the state advised price (SAP) and the statutory minimum price (SMP) for sugarcane in Uttar Pradesh, Haryana and Punjab. Understandably, there was a howl of protest, particularly from the southern states that have been fixing the SAP way below the SMP under the pretext of observing the norms of fiscal prudence. The scheme was rolled back quickly. Then the Minister, along with his Finance counterpart, announced at a Press conference that the rate of interest for crop loans will not exceed 9 per cent. There was no tangible benefit reaching the farmers from that. None was expected. The whole scheme became something of a joke when it came out that the maximum rate of interest computed into the works of the Commission for Agricultural Costs and Prices (CACP) never exceeds 2-3 per cent.

Then, on August 15, the Prime Minister announced from the Red Fort the setting up of a *kisan ayog*. But nothing further has been heard about it since.

The reactions of the Prime Minister and the National Democratic Alliance (NDA) become very clear when there is a clearly perceived threat to national interest. This has been often noticed in relation with Pakistan. Recently, it was in evidence in relation to the whole of the West and its peoples. The Prime Minister took personal initiative to help build G-21 that made so much brouhaha at the Fifth Ministerial Conference of the WTO at Cancun.

The issues at Cancun were fairly simple. In 1995, at Marrakesh, the WTO members, both rich and poor, made certain commitments on opening up their systems. The implementation was far from uniform. The poor countries, of course, expect to increase their exports but are not unaware of disadvantages of increased imports.

The rich countries, on the other hand, have for fairly substantial reasons been unwilling to wind up their decades-old systems of elaborate and massive subsidies to their farmers.

How could India play the game so as to make the rich countries honour their Marrakesh commitments and not play diversionary tactics by diluting the agenda? The Task Force on Agriculture appointed by the Prime Minister (2000-01) had recommended that the best option for India would be to insist on maintaining the sanctity of the Marrakesh agreement.

Sooner or later, one by one, the rich countries would have to fall in line. If the rich countries are seen dragging their feet, the developing nations could propose an international commission for inspection of the factual situation on agricultural subsidies and try to improve the WTO system by making it less pedantic and legalistic. Evidently, under the Prime Minister's instructions, the Commerce Minister, Mr. Arun Jaitley, took the *swadeshi* stance at Cancun where liberalisation and globalisation have suffered a temporary setback. But the Vajpayees and Jaitleys have made it look, at least in the national Media, as if they are heroes!

That the least developed countries (LDCs)—highly sceptical of G-21 and particularly of India—staged a walkout and that quite a few African countries were about to distance themselves from G-21 when the US started on the sidelines negotiations on cotton, shows the risks involved in jingoistic fervour.

Clearly, the NDA was keen on showing that it had made a fight of it at the WTO negotiations and not surrendered abjectly, as the Congress had done on the eve of Marrakesh agreements. The Americans were prepared to react softly as India's bellicosity comes with the US presidential elections on hand.

After Cancun, the scene turns again on the domestic front.

Mr. Digvijay Singh, the Congress Chief Minister of Madhya Pradesh, did a *volte-face* and changed his position on farm electricity tariffs since the last Assembly elections. Now he has announced complete waiver of power bills for the last three years for less than 5HP motors, and free one-point connections to scheduled castes and scheduled tribes.

At the other end of the spectrum, the Gujarat Chief Minister, Mr. Narendra Modi, is not bothered about electricity tariffs. Last month he let loose his police on farmers who wanted to organise a rally to protest against hike in electricity tariffs. Now, even before the farmers are out of hospital, and on the eve of the Khedut Samaj's grand rally (today), he has further hiked electricity tariffs. Back to Mr. Rajnath Singh, who has promised a crop insurance policy that would protect the farmers against both the loss of crops and the loss of income. This is a matter that has been thrashed out on numerous occasions over the years.

Even excluding natural calamities and enemy acts, the risk coefficient in Indian agriculture is so high that the statistically computed premium will be around 12 per cent of the gross domestic product (GDP). If Mr. Rajnath Singh wants to include income losses due to price fluctuations also, the quantum of premium may go up to 18-20 per cent of GDP.

If the insurance is sought to be offered through a colossus of a corporation on the lines of automobile insurance, that would make a dream project for the *babus*; but the farmers will probably get nothing out of it.

Agriculture has taken the centre-stage in international trade. No government in India can afford to play around with agricultural policies in the hope of winning some gullible votes. It is high time we wiped clean the slate of farm policies and start drafting a new plan and new architecture with new ambition.

---

2 October 2003.

7 National Commission on Farmers, at Last

Nearly six months after the Prime Minister made the announcement, the National Commission on Farmers has been set up to prepare the roadmap for sustainable development of agriculture and optimising its contribution to growth and development of the economy, particularly improving the income and standard of living of farmers. But how much headway will it make?

Appointments of committees are routine business for any government. Committees are appointed, day in and day out, whenever the governments wish to know facts, or whenever it wishes to hide them or put the issues on back burner or just push matters under the carpet. There is a standard format for the announcement of their appointments. The notification begins by declaring solemnly that the subject for which the committee is being appointed has been engaging the attention of the government in recent years/for a long time/for quite some time/or any expression that suggests that the government has not suddenly woken up to the gravity of the matter.

It is rather extraordinary that the appointment of the National Commission on Farmers (NCF) should have taken nearly six months after it was proclaimed by the Prime Minister himself from the ramparts of the Red Fort in his Independence Day speech. During the long interval, there was considerable speculation that the delay was due to the fact that the Prime Minister had suggested that it should be a Constitutional commission on par with the Election Commission or Vigilance Commission with overriding authority on matters concerning farmers. That understandably would take some time since it would call for an amendment of the Constitution.

When Ms. Sushma Swaraj announced the setting up of the Commission, she highlighted that the NCF was to go into the farmers' grievances (*Daily Hitvada,* January 21, 2004). That would call for a huge administrative set-up and powers comparable to those of the Vigilance Commission. She went on to add that the NCF will help in preparing the road map for sustainable development of agriculture and optimising its contribution to growth and development of the economy, particularly improving farm income, standard of living of farm households and make Indian agriculture globally competitive. So the emphasis is on farmers rather than on the agriculture.

That sets the NCF apart from the Standing Advisory Committee (SAC), which was to draft a National Agricultural Policy, as also the Task Force on Agriculture (TFA) charged with making Indian agriculture world-class in the context of the WTO commitments; both bodies, like the NCF, were headed by a chairman of the rank of a Cabinet Minister.

One little odd thing. Ms. Sushma Swaraj, in the same Press session, also announced the new policy permitting private traders to intervene in the grains market without the intermediary of the Food Corporation of India (FCI). That could mark the beginning of the end of the FCI, which has been a major instrument of the government's farm policies. One cannot but wonder why such a ponderous decision could not be deferred till the NCF had deliberated on it and formulated its views in one of the first interim reports.

Why the inordinate delay in setting up the NCF? Why did the announcement come on the eve of the Lok Sabha elections? Is it just a poll gimmick setting up a two-year committee when the government is not certain to stay that long? So many questions that would normally make me ignore the whole matter. This one occasion I could not, as Mr. Sompal Shastri is designated as the Cabinet-rank Chairman of the NCF.

Mr. Sompal Shastri is not only a close friend of mine but also a highly respected expert in agriculture. Even as it is, he is a Member of the Planning Commission and has been Minister of State in independent charge of Agriculture with additional charge of the Ministry of Water Resources. He has been a member of both houses of Parliament and has worked on innumerable committees concerning agriculture. The sheer comprehensiveness of his knowledge and the command of vast array of facts and figures at his fingertips are impressive. He is articulate in a number of languages including English and Hindi. We have held common positions on most subjects relating to agriculture. Both of us cherish Sir Chhotu Ram as a messiah of farmers.

Anything that affects Mr. Sompal Shastri is of deep concern to me. So I got on the Internet to see the actual notification of the Ministry of Agriculture dated February 10, 2004. The reading of the document made a number of pieces fall in place. First, the NCF is not a Constitutional commission; it is just another report-writing committee with the difference that its mandate tilts towards the situation of the farmers, rather than the state, and growth of the farm sector.

All the same, the focal point of its mandate remains "Improving the economic viability and sustainability of diversified agriculture including horticulture, livestock, dairy and fisheries and doubling the farmers' income...alleviate poverty and impart viability and attractiveness to farming as a remunerative and rewarding profession."

The development of agriculture is driven by the technology, infrastructure and economic incentives. The emphasis of all governmental policies and of the terms of reference of most committees on agriculture has been on the first two: technology and infrastructure to the near-exclusion of the third, that is, economic incentives. This was in stark contrast to the almost exclusively economic character of the demands of the farmers' organisations. The terms of reference of the NCF represent a better balance between the physical and the economic engines of agricultural growth.

The timing of the declaration of the setting up of the NCF was certainly influenced by the advent of elections. The announcement itself of the creation of a National Commission could help make up the deficiency of 'feel good' factor in agriculture, to which even Mr. L.K. Advani confessed.

All eyes will be on Mr. Sompal Raghuvir Singh Shastri, Member, Planning Commission, now NCF Chairman, enjoying the rank of a Cabinet Minister. There is little that he can do as Chairman of the NCF that he could not have done in his earlier position. The new assignment has a lot of distinction and trappings but also some treacherous traps.

---

3 March 2004.

8 From Fragmented Fields to Food Factory

The NDA Agenda visualises India as the 'Food Factory' of the world. But this is easier said than done, as there are a lot of barriers at the production and processing levels. High standards are expected of processed food and India has no network of laboratories to certify quality. The transition from small fields to a food supplier to the world is no easy task.

The National Democratic Alliance (NDA) released its Agenda for Development, Good Governance, Peace and Harmony on April 8, 2004. That was rather late in the day to permit any fruitful debate, during the electoral campaign, on the vast range of subjects and issues it covers. The newspapers headlined the item "Ram Mandir included in the NDA agenda". In fact, there is no mention of the temple in the over 50 pages of the Agenda document. The only reference figuring in paragraph 57(2) reiterates the well-known twin approach of consensus-cum-judiciary on the Ayodhya issue.

Agriculture, on the contrary, covers over 15 pages (Chapters 5, 6 and 7). The Media, both print and electronic, paid scant attention to the agricultural agenda of the alliance that, according to many a poll and forecast, is most likely to form the next government at the Centre.

The Agenda formulates a new seven-pronged strategy with a view to making India an "Economic Super Power". As for agriculture, it visualises India as the 'Food Factory' of the world.

Agriculture is the provider of food, fuel and fibre. Making India a food factory of the world, that is, supplier of food grains, pulses, oilseeds, their derivatives, fruit and dairy and poultry products would obviously be a pipedream.

The Agenda spells out numerous schemes for raising the production in agriculture, horticulture, dairy, poultry and fisheries; it would still obviously fall short of becoming the food factory of the world.

Since consumers the world over demand mainly processed food, any country with ambitions of becoming a global supplier of foods would have to plan to become a major processor.

The NDA believes that "the food-processing industry can make our rural economy vibrant in the same manner that IT has made our national economy prosper". It proposes to raise the percentage of the value of agricultural produce processed from 2 to 10 in coming five years. The handicaps are exhaustively enumerated: fragmentation of land, inefficiency, low quality standards and inadequate logistic support.

As regards the fragmentation of holdings, the NDA proposes legislation to enable leasing of land (Para 5.11). However, Para 12.2 explicitly excludes private investments in the nature of corporate farming.

While some reservations about corporate sector's entry into agriculture are understandable, farming through corporations of farmers formed through conversion of land and labour into equity could play a major role in providing fillip to food processing.

The food processing industry requires large quantities of water. In these times of water shortages, it would be difficult to launch any ambitious programme of enhancing food processing capacity. Even in the long run, a food processing industry that is vulnerable to vicissitudes of monsoons and water availability can scarcely hope to be a global player.

On the demand side, the consumers are increasingly becoming conscious of quality, sanitary and phytosanitary standards. Most food, as harvested in tropical countries including India, is substandard. Scanning for such unhygienic ingredients as E. Coli and aflatoxins involves a major effort.

The fact is that the farm community, at large, is ignorant of the exacting standards of the global market. Worse, it has no access to laboratories that can test and certify its products in the light of specifications in different countries.

Before one can seriously contemplate becoming even a minor food factory of the world, one will have to plan for an extensive network of well-equipped food laboratories within easy access of all villages.

The NDA Agenda recognises this deficiency and provides for a Unified Food Law to be enacted within the first six months as also an independent Food Regulatory Authority, also within six months, that will be responsible for setting and enforcing standards for all food products.

The NDA Agenda also proposes a dairy industry development plan within the first six months and promises to set up an expert committee to suggest ways to minimise wastage and damage along the food chain.

Some of the more serious problems relating to the food processing industry have received scant attention in the NDA Agenda. The food processing industry is dependent on availability of food surpluses. "Eat what you can and can what you cannot," describes the present stage of food processing in India. So, first, the food processing industry must command a supply of raw materials as also the varieties and quality thereof.

The cooperative sector in the sugar industry has failed to produce satisfactory results in spite of abundant government funding. Contract farming is not seen as a solution as the entry of corporate sector is frowned upon. Further, contract farming would presuppose a judiciary that decides cases on farm contracts in less than 30 days. Farmers' corporations would appear to be the only feasible solution. But that does not even find a mention in the NDA's Agenda.

The most important question on the demand side is which market would the food processing industry cater to? At present, the food processing industry produces Western-type foods that are consumed by a small consumer class in India.

In this area, they face difficult competition from foreign manufacturers which have long experience of manufacturing these items. The food processing industry in India would need to make a quantum switch to indigenous food products that would be consumed even by the upper- and middle classes and consumers at large abroad.

The menu card of the NDA is certainly appealing but will the alliance get the mandate to be the chef in Delhi?

---

28 April 2004.

9 Unchanged Quarter Century for Farmers

Farmers' agitations in the present epoch started over a quarter century back in Tamil Nadu, with Narayan Swamy Naidu's bullock cart blocking roads in protest against farm power tariff hikes and seeking their rollback.

Farm power is free now in Tamil Nadu, Andhra Pradesh and Maharashtra. But the farmers, crushed under the burden of debt, still commit suicide in large numbers. Indian agriculture continues to be a gamble in the monsoon and suffers from poor infrastructure. What has a quarter century of farmers' movement to show by way of gains and what are the losses to the farm community?

The movement concentrated on reduction of input costs for the first half-decade. It was only with the onion agitation in 1980 that it developed a comprehensive economic theory. "Remunerative prices for agricultural produce" came up as a single-point prescription for agriculture's malady and general poverty.

Remunerative prices were to be obtained through elimination of all governmental interventions in the commodity market.

Till such time as the State adopts the necessary level of liberalisation and economic reforms, it must ensure a minimum support price to make up for the price-depressing effects of its interventions: restrictions on exports, domestic movement, processing, storage, etc., and non-commercial imports of farm commodities.

General poverty arose out of the fact that the economy's main activity, agriculture, was a losing proposition. This, in turn, was directly attributable to the government's policies that depressed agricultural prices.

The formulation of the 'remunerative price' theory was straightforward and simple, and captivated the hearts of peasant masses that participated in large numbers in the farm agitations from Karnataka to Punjab and from Gujarat to Uttar Pradesh.

However, the economic pundits and the politicians protested vehemently. They cried:

- "Remunerative prices for agriculture are tantamount to subsidising the rural rich at the expense of the urban poor."
- "Remunerative prices will benefit only the rural rich and not the landless poor."
- "Agricultural losses are due to the long chain of intermediaries that needs to be eliminated so that, side-by-side with remunerative prices for farmers, the consumers will get the produce at reasonable prices."
- "Free markets for agricultural commodities can produce shortages and food insecurity and eventually, even starvation."

The opposition of all the establishment economists notwithstanding, the farmers rallied in ever-larger numbers to the call of remunerative prices. The agitations produced immediate gains in the form of increase in support prices.

- The Chakan agitation (1980) got the onion farmers a support price of 60 paise a kg in the place of the mere 7 paise they were getting at that time. The constant reaction of onion producers to all attempts at restricting export of the commodity ensured a price of Rs. 3-5 a kg now.
- The tobacco "Rasta Roko" at Nipani (1981) was a terrible setback. The tobacco growers got little to show for the 13 dead in the SRP firing.
- The Maharashtra-wide blockade of milk (1982) was also a failure. The farmers could not stop the supply of milk beyond three days and the government remained stubborn.
- The sugarcane agitation centred in Nashik district (1980) succeeded in hiking the statutory minimum price (SMP) of sugarcane from Rs. 180 to Rs. 300 per tonne.

- The agitation against the Maharashtra State Cotton Monopoly Procurement Scheme, which required the growers to sell their produce exclusively to the State dragged on for 18 years and ended by vanquishing the monopoly procurement scheme. The guaranteed price of cotton was Rs. 700 per quintal in 1986. Now growers get around Rs. 3,000 per quintal.

Apart from the concessions wrested by the thrust of farmers' agitations, the demonstrated clout of farmers' opinions and unity had its political consequences and the MSPs continued to increase year after year. In the decade since 1990-91, the procurement price of wheat went up by 258 per cent, that of coarse cereals by 215 per cent, of *arhar* by 275 per cent, of cotton by 270 per cent and the SMP of sugarcane by more than 300 per cent.

The sheer strength of agitations and the political clout of the farm lobby were supplemented by yet another major development. The historic fall of the Soviet Union and the shift to the market paradigm ensured a successful culmination of the Uruguay Round of GATT negotiations.

The Agreement on Agriculture (AoA) of the WTO endowed a large number of benefits to farmers in India.

First, there was a clear vindication of the fact that the farmers here suffered under heavy negative aggregate measurement of support (AMS). Second, the abolition of quantitative restriction (QRs) took away all incentives for the political decision-makers and the bureaucracy to order imports in the nature of dumping.

In 1996-97, the quantum of negative AMS for 14 major crops in India was Rs. 113,000 crore. Since 1998, the indications are that the AMS has actually turned positive. That does not mean the Indian agriculture is no more a losing proposition. The AMS is probably positive; that is, the prices in India are not lower than those prevailing in the international referral market.

But it also does not mean that the prices are higher than the costs. Since 1995, the domestic costs have increased while the international prices have remained low.

The gains of the farmers' movement on the price front were too modest when compared with the swelling costs and farmers continue to fall into debt, and death traps.

However, the gains of this movement on the doctrinal front are spectacular:

- There is a universal acceptance that India has had a long regime of price-depressing policies that need to be reversed.
- There is a clear understanding that there is little conflict between the interests of the landless labourers and those of the landholding farmers. The wage rates increase much faster than farm produce prices.
- There is also a realisation that the local chain of intermediaries is not the cause of the gap between the consumer and the producer prices. The India-Bharat syndrome is the more significant cause of the chasm and can be corrected by overall liberalisation and market reforms.

At the end of a quarter century of struggle, the typical farmer is as badly indebted as he was at the beginning but stands vindicated and cleared of all charges of being indolent, ignorant and incompetent.

---

1 September 2004.

10 Maharashtra Farmers, a Crossed Lot

The paddy farmers of the Gadchiroli district of Maharashtra are in a quandary. They are receiving, as assistance from the government, crossed cheques for sums as small as Rs. 50. They are totally in the dark about how to process these paper elephants.

Suicides by and malnutrition deaths of farmers in the Vidarbha region of Maharashtra have been in the news for quite some time. The developmental backlog of that region has been patent for a much longer time. The *modus operandi* of the neo-colonial exploitation of Vidarbha are depressing prices of the prime produce cotton and paddy, paltry compensation for the resources such as coal and electricity, and the grossly inadequate budgetary allocations for the development of water resources and infrastructure. The loss to the farmers of Vidarbha on account of inadequate prices over the last 30 years is put at around Rs. 33,300 crore. The budgetary backlog over the last 40 years is about the same. The million-dollar question is: How will the Maharashtra government compensate for all this?

In the pre-election flush of populism, the Congress-NCP government, under Mr. Sushil Kumar Shinde, had announced a special assistance package for Vidarbha. It included a grant of Rs. 20 crore to paddy growers with holdings of less than two hectares at the rate of Rs. 295 per hectare. The sum was apportioned between the various paddy-producing districts of the region. The share of Gadchiroli district came to a mere Rs. 2 crore. The district administrations had specific instructions to make payments to individual peasants only through crossed cheques, to ensure that the amount reached the intended beneficiary alone. If Rs. 2 crore were to be divided among about 1,00,000 paddy farmers of Gadchiroli district, the average endowment per head works out to less than Rs. 200. The minimum for an individual peasant is Rs. 50 and the maximum Rs. 590.

"Remember this is a crossed cheque in your own name," the poor payee was told.

"You cannot get cash for it over the counter of the bank on which it is drawn. You will have to deposit it in your account; if you do not have an account, you will have to open one. You will, henceforth, be a proud holder of a bank account."

When a poor, often uneducated, farmer takes the cheque to the nearest post office or the bank, he is told that it can be cashed only at one of the branches of the bank, on which the cheque is drawn.

The peasant drags himself to the appropriate counter in the bank, where he learns that for opening an account he has to fill an application form with the recommendation from an existing account holder in the same branch and has to make an initial deposit, in cash, of Rs. 200 at least.

"Is not a cheque from the government as good as cash?" he wonders.

"By no means," he is told bluntly. "First, the cheque amount is less than the minimum required to open an account (in most cases). Further, there have been instances in the recent past of government cheques issued to cotton farmers being dishonoured for lack of funds."

Further, he is told that he has to attach two passport size photographs to the application for opening an account, as proof of identity.

"Where can I get them?" he asks.

"Go to any nearby studio. These days, you get instant photos in any digital studio for as little as Rs. 30 (three-four copies). Attach two to the application and you will have a couple spare for future use," is the kind advice.

So, to realise a cheque for Rs. 50, the poor farmer realises that he has to spend at least Rs. 250. And, at the end of the day, there is no guarantee that the government cheque will be honoured.

A poor paddy peasant from the economically most-backward tribal district, on whom is dependent his family, gets a relief assistance of less than Rs. 100, and to lay his hands on it, he has to spend Rs. 300.

---

10 November 2004.

11 Farmer can Look to Greener Pastures

A number of eminent people have talked about a second agricultural revolution that is set to happen in India. Some have called it a second Green Revolution; others the Rainbow Revolution that will include white, blue and yellow too. Very simply, the next revolution would mark a qualitative change in agricultural technology and the marketing of farm commodities.

All agricultural production hitherto was based on the realisation of the traits of nature-given seeds or those selected on the basis of some traits from a variety produced by multiplication or combining desirable traits of two or more different varieties.

Now, with the advent of genetic engineering, the seeds of tomorrow are more likely to be produced by manipulating the genes. This new technology might reverse the trend set by the Green Revolution that was based on the abundant use of water, pesticides and fertilisers.

As regards the marketing of farm commodities, gone are the days when one dreamt of self-sufficient villages or nations. Transport, communications and information technology have facilitated the globalisation process.

Agricultural production in the days to come must not only be competitive and find markets abroad, but also keep the geographical advantage in one's own country. There are many who feel that the farmer, given the handicaps he faces in respect of the size of holding, the extent of capitalisation and the paucity of infrastructure, would find it difficult to enter the new era of genes and the WTO. Not that the hurdles are insurmountable.

India has abundant sunshine, ample water resources and a hardy peasant class—factors that will prove decisive in the long run. The handicaps posed by social and political institutions will vanish, sooner or later, and the farmer can soon prove himself to be second to none in the world community. While this does not mean that the farm community does not possess the wherewithal to face this futuristic kind of agriculture, those who are diffident about tackling new technologies and pessimistic about the future of farming in such a scenario will not be able to make the best of their natural advantages.

What do we do to change the mindset of the farmer? First, there has to be a massive education drive to convince the farmers that their backwardness is entirely due to a set of artificially contrived anti-farmer policies and that, in spite of the stranglehold of governmental regulation, they are quite capable of handling the global challenges.

The grape farmers of Maharashtra have shown that it can be done. That many of the successful farmers in the OECD countries are of Indian origin is proof enough. But there is more to it than that.

Agriculture in India has been a closed economy for centuries. Those born in farmers' families depend on agriculture for their livelihood. Every member of a farmer family takes the first possible opportunity to leave farming and the countryside and settle down in a non-agricultural environment.

Experience has shown that farmers who have opted out of agriculture have made a better living for themselves while many of those who stayed back have become impoverished and indebted. The closed character of agriculture is largely due to governmental restrictions in many regions on non-farmers entering the sector.

Those who make a living out of agriculture sometimes find no escape. They are also denied access to new investments and capital.

The Green Revolution of the 1960s overcame this problem in a rather fortuitous manner. The switch from a cultivation practice based on home-grown seeds and cattle manure to one based on hybrid seeds, fertilisers and pesticides was not easy. Even at that time, a large number of farmers wanted to quit agriculture. From this community, sprang a number of leaders demanding abolition of landlordism and the tenancy system. They succeeded beyond measure and that was how the anti-tenancy and anti-*zamindar* legislation came into effect.

The Green Revolution of the 1960s was preceded by a programme that acted as an unintended 'golden handshake' or voluntary retirement scheme for tired farmers. The qualitative switchover involved in the new WTO-based revolution in farm technologies and genetic modification is even more drastic. The proportion of farmers who are apprehensive of the new world of agriculture is increasing.

Clearly, there must be some way by which those who find themselves trapped in agriculture are offered an escape route, giving way to those who feel confident of tackling the more technical and mechanised cultivation system.

It will not suffice to allow a few large corporations to acquire substantial landholdings; they may not be able to cultivate land even as efficiently as the farmers of today. What is needed is the setting up of an active and efficient land market that can bring about liberalisation in the farm sector and ensure freedom of entry and exit.

It would appear that most of the properties offered for sale are suitable for farmers wanting to establish opulent farmhouses. If some arrangements are evolved to encourage farmers to come forward with offers of sale and for the intending buyers to register their requirements, a very healthy and booming market can develop.

A great new opportunity has come up without any design. A proposal to bring about a convergence of the Forward Markets Commission (FMC) and the Securities and Exchange Board of India (SEBI) is now under contemplation and scrutiny. The major difficulty in bringing together these two regulators is that they have fairly diverse fields of activity and functions.

The objective of the commodity futures markets is price discovery and risk management while the stock exchanges ensure orderly investments. If instead of trying to converge the commodity futures markets and the stock exchanges, one could attempt bringing together the land market and the stock exchanges; the former could flourish at the rates at which the commodity futures market is exploding—350-400 per cent annually.

The country is on the threshold of a second agricultural revolution. One essential precondition of a smooth revolution is to facilitate the exit of one class and the entry of another, enthused by the challenges of the new era. The development of a land market will not only reinforce agriculture to accept the challenges of the new revolution but will also provide the substantial investments required for bringing it about.

---

16 November 2005.

II

Credit

12 Agricultural Credit, Farmers' Indebtedness and Suicides

An Introduction

The East India Company came to the Indian subcontinent at the end of a period of great turmoils in Indian history. The invaders from across the borders, local robbers, thugs and Pindaris ruled the roost. The trade was financed by the moneylenders who had developed their own system of the communication network. Actual transfer of funds and gold or silver was fraught with risk. The traders had evolved over time, the instrument of *hundis*, the equivalent of the bills of exchange. The traders and the moneylenders enjoyed great respect and prestige over distant territories. They maintained their own unofficial armed constabularies which were often used for plunder.

This network of moneylenders and credits was used by the local princes as also the traders. It had little links with the domain of agricultural credit. The village moneylender used to be a village artisan on par with any other of the 12 types of artisans: the cobbler, the ironsmith, the coppersmith, the carpenter, the potmaker etc.

With the advent of the British rule, formal civil and police administration and the introduction of the system of revenue payable in cash, the traditional moneylenders came under severe stress. Few traditional moneylenders had resources large enough to meet the requirements of payment of even a year's land revenue for a handful of farmers. This brought in the emergence of a new type of moneylenders essentially belonging to higher castes. The earlier moneylenders belonged to the same castes as the tillers of the land themselves.

It was an old practice in the villages and in the countryside that while most trading took the form of mutual exchanges and barter, the religious rituals involved some kind of a cash offering, howsoever meagre, to the village priest. The village priest and his kin, with their traditional thrift had accumulated funds although meagre in absolute terms, sizeable by the standards of those days. The land revenue system also resulted in the down gradation of the actual land tillers who became wage earners or crop sharers. Only some of them, particularly those belonging to the warrior castes, were made the *zamindars*.

The establishment of the British administration marked the abolition of the hegemony of the robbers, thugs, Pindaris etc., as also of the traditional system of land revenue and of money lending. The village that traditionally was governed in a sovereign manner by the local *panchayat* became a fractured entity with distinct lines drawn between the tillers of the land, the *zamindars* and the moneylenders.

The advent of the British also ushered in an era of policies resulting in cheap primary commodities and expensive manufactured goods all deliberately calculated to benefit the metropolitan country. The traditional systems of irrigation fell into disuse and in spite of certain measures taken by the colonial government to improve irrigation in certain areas, agriculture became more dependent on the vagaries of monsoons than it ever was.

Agriculture that is subject to the caprices of nature, on the one hand and the tyranny of the State on the other became a highly risky and unprofitable vocation. It became increasingly difficult for the village moneylender to meet the demands for accommodation of the tillers for production, consumption as also payment of government dues. The more unscrupulous of the moneylenders must have evidently tried to take advantage of the situation by questionable practices, crooked accounting, high rates of interest and coercive expropriation of property at the first sight of default in repayment. The local *zamindars* and the moneylender bore the brunt of unpleasantness caused by the policies of the colonial government. Soon, there surfaced revolts by the peasantry against both of these institutions. The better organised urban moneylenders' network was not entirely unhappy about this development. Money lending in villages had become more lucrative than the meagre margins earned by the urban moneylender. The resentment against the village leadership was shared by the urban bourgeois which had nothing to do with agriculture and, in fact, antithetical interests. The resentment and the revolts of the peasantry met with a positive response in the nationalist independence movement. Abolition of *zamindars* and suppression of the *sahukars* became a very popular plank in the political platforms of the Indian National Congress as also other diverse political and social reform outfits.

The colonial government could not remain a silent spectator to the development of this conflict. It introduced, following upon the Deccan riots, some State-sponsored schemes of credit like the *taqavi* loans and ushered in the institution of cooperative societies. It would have been inimical to the interests of the colonial government to make the cooperatives genuinely autonomous as was the practice in the countries of origin of the cooperative movement. The cooperative network in India, on the other hand, was closely monitored and regulated by government appointed registrars.

Very soon after Independence, both *zamindars* and village moneylenders became extinct. There was little gain for the peasant personally or for the agricultural vocation in this development. The only beneficiaries were the urban society. In the system of *zamindari* and *sahukari*, the extraction of surplus from the farmers remained in the villages and, directly or indirectly, was used in the villages themselves, particularly in the years of famine and drought. In a few cases, they were used for village festivities and sundry festivities.

The informal moneylender, somehow, attracted both the ire and hatred from the ruling classes as also the urban bourgeoisie. Its replacement by the formal sector cooperative societies and even the commercial banks did not bring about any improvement in the situation of the farmers. The Green Revolution brought about a quantum jump in the productivity and the production of agriculture. The farmers continued to be debt-ridden nevertheless. It was quite obvious that the misery of the farmers was entirely unrelated to the form and structure of the credit institutions or land tenure. The root cause went much deeper and was to be found in the economic policies followed by the post-Independence government of deliberately siphoning the agricultural surplus to urban industry through an armory of instruments that could depress agricultural prices.

Theoretically, every farmer who borrowed money from the cooperative societies became a member of the cooperative society and could be considered as one of its owners thereof. The cooperative administration did not treat the farmers as part owners but as loanees from whom the loans had to be recovered no matter by what means.

The cooperative institutions continue, till date, to charge exorbitant rates of interest, compounding them, in many cases every quarter or every six months. This is strictly against the instructions issued on this subject by the highest court in the land as also by the Reserve Bank of India. This practice resulted in the amount of the sum getting multiplied many times within a very short time.

A large number of farmers got so deep in indebtedness and were so badly humiliated by the recovery agencies and officers that they found it preferable to have recourse to suicide.

The purpose of any credit is to help the receiver to tide over temporary difficulties. If the difficulties are not temporary but secular and built into the system of vocation then, there is a case for outright grants or subsidies and not credit. Agriculture which works under a situation of negative subsidies cannot confer any benefit from any system of credit. In particular, the cooperative or corporate institutions, as they have an urban culture and character, are inappropriate in the farm sector because they are largely dominated by bureaucracy and politicians.

The highly statised cooperative structures introduced by the colonial government, became highly politicised in the hands of the politicians after Independence. Registration of the societies, its rules, elections, dispute settlement all passed into the hands of the Registrar who finds it difficult to flaunt the instructions from the political authority well nigh impossible. The cooperatives lost all their autonomy. The fact that in the cooperative all members have one vote made offices in these bodies passages to political power.

The cooperative primary societies charge extortionist rates of interest and deploy cruel methods to secure repayment of loans. Statistics on farmers' suicides reveals that the incidence of suicides is very substantial in loanees of cooperative bodies.

All agricultural loans in India are both illegal and immoral. They are illegal under the Indian Contract Act which declares as void all contracts where a party to the contract itself takes active measures to prevent performance by the other party. A government which follows policies deliberately calculated to depress agricultural prices and keep agriculture a losing vocation has no legal or moral right to demand repayment of the loans.

There is yet another aspect. The total amount of losses caused to the farmers' community because of the sustained policies of keeping agriculture a losing proposition is calculated at over Rs. 15,000 crore per year. Compared with this astronomical figure, the volume of total indebtedness of all the farmers together is only a fraction of the losses caused to the farmer through negative subsidies on the agricultural vocation. The only rational and logical course for resolving the problem of agricultural indebtedness is to treat the problem on an analogy with the problem of transfer payments in the international finance. Unilateral payments are not possible unless they are facilitated by appropriate trade stipulations.

Any scheme of loan relief or waiver that discriminates between types of loans, lending agency is *ipso facto* illogical and malicious.

The farmers' movement, at an early stage of its 'loan waiver' campaign, offered their willingness to withdraw the agitation if the government could provide adequate assurance that the policy of negative subsidies will be discontinued for all times to come.

The problem of agricultural credit is essentially the problem of making agriculture a remunerative activity. Till such time as it becomes one, no gimmickry about the structure of credit institutions is likely to produce any results.

Offen there has been some talk about the microfinance institutions. These institutions are unlikely to be helpful. In fact, the experience is that microfinance institutions are formed by the kind of people who would generally form non-governmental organisations (NGOs) and would be more interested in getting the easier subvention from the government. Once they have pocketed it, they continue to practice money lending more or less on the same lines as the old world village moneylender, charging very high rates of interest and using brutal methods for recovery.

The correct solution to the problem would be that the politicians get rid of their mental blocks caused largely by caste politics about the village moneylender, create a system of registration and licensing for carrying out that profession and reintroduce the system of *daam duppat* that put a ceiling on the total amount of interest at the original sum borrowed. This system lapsed into disuse after the passing of the central legislation on banking business.

The government is doing exactly the opposite. It is trying to outlaw all loans given by the private moneylenders. This has disastrous consequences. In many regions, the private money lending is more in the form of credit given to farmers for their domestic provisions and agricultural inputs. Threats pronounced by certain politicians against private money lending have the result of drying up the last source from which the farmer could hope to get credit. The remedy is worse than the disease.

Any rational policy on agricultural credit must firstly try to ensure that the agriculture becomes a paying vocation, that there is adequate provision for risk bearing in one form or another and abandonment of the political prejudices in favour of the so-called formal credit institutions as also the feelings of chronic hatred of a particular caste.

---

24 November 2009.

13 Politics of Farm Interest Rates

When a fortnight back the Finance Minister, Mr. Jaswant Singh, announced a ceiling of 9 per cent on interest on crop loans by banks, it made a big splash in the Media—both electronic and print. Compared with that Media blitz, the announcement on the same subject by the Prime Minister on July 28 received scant attention.

Mr. Jaswant Singh was addressing a Press conference along with the Agriculture Minister, Mr. Rajnath Singh. The Prime Minister, on the other hand, was addressing an impromptu meeting of farmers who were escorted by the Agriculture Minister, as a sort of delegation. Lack of adequate prior arrangements could be one reason why the Prime Minister received a rather muted treatment, particularly from the print Media. The government television, of course, could not be faulted. It covered the event of the Prime Minister making the announcement word by word hesitatingly slow.

Another reason for the inadequate coverage of the Prime Minister's announcement was, probably, that the journalists had difficulty in grasping the precise substance of it. The Finance Minister had already announced a ceiling of 9 per cent for crop loans up to Rs. 50,000. Now the Prime Minister was saying that agricultural loans up to Rs. 2 lakh would carry a rate of interest below the prime lending rate. So what was the difference?

Obviously, a larger number of farmers would now benefit. It was not clear if the Prime Minister was extending the concession to crop loans by all financial institutions, including the commercial and the scheduled banks. The reference to prime lending rate could mean that the scheme was being extended to all commercial banks.

The Prime Minister dwelt relatively long on advising the farmers to ensure that the benefit of this concession actually reaches them and to form vigilance committees for that purpose.

Two questions arise: One, what would be the correct rate of interest for crop loans in view of the situation of agricultural productivity and risks involved due to climatic and marketing vicissitudes? Two, can lending rates vary between various types of lenders?

This brought to my mind a historic of phenomena. During the British Raj, towards the end of the 19th century, the issue of indebtedness of the agriculturists was weighing largely on the government because of the revolts in various villages of Poona and Ahmednagar districts (the Deccan riots). On the recommendations of an inquiry committee into the causes of the riots, the Deccan Agricultural Relief Act, 1879 was passed. In 1881, on the recommendations of the Famine Commission, public funds were provided for land improvement works and the Deccan Agriculturists' Relief Act was extended to other provinces. Public funds became open to farmers for *taqavi* loans. The Punjab Alienation of Land Act was passed in 1901 (Sir Chhotu Ram Act).

In the same year, the Government of India introduced the Cooperative Bill. Eventually, the British government passed the Usurious Loan Act, which recognised the traditional practice of *daam duppat* or *dvaigunya*. Though this principle was embodied in Section 16 of the Madras Debt Conciliation Act, 1936, Section 39 of the Bombay Agricultural Debtors' Relief Act and Section 30 of the Deccan Agriculturists' Relief Act, 1879, it has since then ceased to have any application.

In 1938, the pre-Independence Congress government, apparently at the initiative of the All India Kisan Congress, passed the Agriculturists' Debt Relief Act of 1938, which was known as 'Rajaji Act' after C. Rajagopalachari. Section 13 of this law laid down that in any proceeding for recovery of a debt, the court shall scale down all interest due on any debt incurred by an agriculturist so as not to exceed a sum calculated at 6.25 per cent per annum, simple interest. This meant that an interest charge of one pie per rupee per month simple interest or 1 anna per rupee per annum simple interest. The law empowered the government to alter or fix any other rate of interest from time to time.

The pre-Independence Congress considered that a rate of interest above 6.25 per cent per annum would be usurious. Further, it made no distinction in the interest rates to be charged by different types of lenders.

Although the original purpose of the legislation was to suppress extortive practices of private moneylenders, the law prescribed the same parameter for all lenders including banks.

In the early years of Independence, the situation of agriculture in India was calamitous. All the same, Parliament enacted the Banking Regulation Act, 1949 which was amended in 1984. The newly introduced Section 21A of the Banking Regulation Act, which took effect on February 15, 1984, had the effect of denying the farmers the protection extended by the 'Rajaji Act'. It said: "Notwithstanding anything contained in the Usurious Loans Act 1918 or any other law relating to indebtedness in force in any State a transaction between a banking company and its debtor shall not be reopened by any court on the ground that the rate of interest charged by any banking company in respect of such transaction is excessive."

In 1951, the Constitution was amended to abridge the fundamental right to property and specifically to deny farmers recourse to law on the grounds of encroachment of a fundamental right given by the Constitution.

Now the 1984 amendment to the Banking Regulation Act blocked the farmers' access to courts of law for exercising their privilege under an earlier legislation. Banks could henceforth charge any rate of interest and not bother about even the traditional practice of not to let the total interest charge exceed the principal. However, the Andhra Pradesh High Court held that the 1984 legislation was *ultra vires* the Constitution since agricultural debt is a state subject and the 1938 state law could not be restricted or passed over by Parliament. The Supreme Court upheld the amendment of 1984. Later on, the Andhra Pradesh High Court observed in a 1988 case that the burden of indebtedness cannot change with the type of money-lenders.

In independent India, agriculture is becoming a losing proposition because of the vicissitudes of nature and the tyranny of government policies. Farmers manage to pay interest charges of about 2-3 per cent as computed by the Commission for Agricultural Costs and Prices. (See Chapter 7). The Finance Minister and the Prime Minister think that they are doing a great favour to the farmers by fixing a ceiling on rates of interest at 9 per cent.

The principle of *daam duppat* has been cast aside and even the protection given by 'Rajaji Act' as also 'Sir Chhotu Ram Act' have been done away with. Do we need a recurrence of the Deccan riots to make the government see reason?

---

6 August 2003.

14 Death is Better than Debt

The number of farmers' suicides in Maharashtra is fast approaching the double century mark. The incidence of suicides is particularly high in the Vidarbha region, blessed with fertile black cotton soil and rivers that run with plenty of water for much of the year. The region grows around 15 per cent of India's cotton production. It is famous for its distinctive variety of oranges and abundant forests and mineral wealth.

Farmer suicides all over India are mainly the result of chronic indebtedness—the inability to clear debts and pay interest accumulated over years.

Once a family starts on economic decline, other complications follow—family disputes, illness, alcoholism, and so on. In areas where the lending institutions are from the organised sector, the recovery officers, fully armed with legal powers, take recourse to highly coercive measures to "extort" loan repayment.

Chronic indebtedness, its consequences and the inability to suffer the humiliation of the recovery methods used by lending institutions push the farmers to suicide, from Andhra Pradesh to Punjab.

But last year was an exceptionally good year for Vidarbha. The cotton crop was good and farmers received unprecedented good prices, thanks to the suspension of the Maharashtra State Cotton Monopoly Procurement Scheme.

The soyabean crop was plentiful and fetched as high a price as Rs. 1,900 a quintal. Why should such a year of plenty followed by a spate of suicides?

One explanation is that the recovery officers must have smelt a great opportunity to force recoveries. "Farmers have the money," they must have thought. It is only a matter of getting the money out of them. The coercive pressure they brought to bear on them meant humiliation at it worst and consequently, the suicides.

Recently, I visited the family of a suicide victim in Anandwadi village near Ashti, in Wardha district. In the course of my brief stay there, newspapers carried reports of five suicides by farmers in Wardha, Amaravati and Yavatmal districts. It was not possible to visit all the affected villages. I chose to visit Anandwadi because of its proximity to Ashti.

Ashti is emblazoned in the chronicles of India's freedom movement in an incident associated with a modern-day saint, Tukadoji.

On August 16, 1942, the ryots there attacked the revenue office as also the police *chowki*, and ransacked and set fire to both premises. Six people were killed on the spot in police firing and four later in the hospital. Ten freedom fighters were sentenced to death and 55 to life imprisonment. Fortunately, India's Independence came before the sentence could be carried out.

In my earlier visits to Ashti, I have seen the militancy of the farmers who obviously considered it their duty to continue the tradition of the 1942 episode of Ashti. That a farmer living so close to Ashti should have preferred suicide to revolution struck me as rather extraordinary.

The bereaved family lives in a *pucca* stone house, which was a sign of prosperity in the pre-Independence era. Now it has fallen into disrepair. Grass and plants are growing out of crevices in the walls. The new rich in the village live not too far away, in RCC houses with a decent coat of paint.

The bereaved family in Anandwadi consists of the father, the mother and an elder brother and sister, both married with children, and the victim's pregnant wife.

The family has 14 acres. It has institutional outstandings of around Rs. 70,000, besides a large number of loans taken from friends and other farmers as also from loan-sharks at exorbitant interest rates.

The private moneylenders had really not even attempted to make a recovery. The family is held in respect. In this particular village, there was no question of any pressure being exercised by recovery officials of banking institutions or the Maharashtra State Electricity Board (MSEB).

The farmers' organisation is strong. In recent months, its activists have thrown out bank recovery officers as also MSEB wiremen.

The original amount of the bank loan of the victim's family was a mere Rs. 10,000. Accumulated interest over the years had swelled the principal seven times. But there was no real pressure to repay.

The disabled father had handed over the family agriculture to the younger son (the victim) as the elder was mentally incapable of taking any responsibility.

The victim had managed to get his elder sister married a couple of years earlier. He got married just four months back. Neither the indebtedness nor the family responsibility was too burdensome by the standards of his society. Then, what could have driven this young farmer of 30 summers to suicide?

Question No. 1: The victim was a competent young farmer. What happened to the handsome earnings of last year? Some inquiry brought out that last year's money just disappeared in the large pit of accumulated debts and family needs.

Preference was given to loans taken from family friends and neighbours. That is consistent with the social mores of the village society. There was not much left that could be spared for the organised banking institutions.

Question No. 2: The young man must have asked himself, "Why am I the one carrying this burden of the past and responsibilities of the future alone? The father and the elder brother have escaped since mental disease has put them beyond the pale of concern. Why should I not put myself beyond all these worries by cutting off the organ that causes concern?"

He could not, at will, turn lunatic. But he could certainly end it all by a swill of pesticide that is handy in any farmer's house.

There is a heart-rending verse by Bhartruhari, poet laureate of Vidarbha, that translates thus: A poor man, in similar circumstances, goes to the burning *ghat* and, envying the peace of a dead body lying there, requests it to exchange places if only for a moment; but the shrewd corpse, knowing full well that the death is preferable to poverty, just does not budge.

---

16 September 2004.

15 Farm Loan Straitjacket Loosened

The basic cause of farmer indebtedness is that agriculture is a losing proposition. To blame are the various government measures that depress farm prices and deny the farmers the advantage of a free market.

The farmers of Maharashtra see a new dawn of freedom. The state government has agreed, in principle, to pass a law, and in the intervening period, issue an ordinance bringing two major changes *vis-à-vis* loans to farmers.

It will stop all measures to deprive the farmers of their land on account of their inability to repay loans. It will also provide that the amount of accumulated interest on an agricultural loan shall not exceed the principal. The state government undoubtedly deserves praise for this bold move.

However, it is necessary to understand how the system traps the farmer in indebtedness. The basic cause of farmer indebtedness, of course, is that agriculture is a losing proposition. To blame are the various measures taken by the Centre that have had the effect of depressing agricultural prices and denying the farmers the advantage of a free commodity and input market. That makes all agricultural loans both void in law and immoral in public policy. Add to that, the various methods used by banks.

Discussions on agricultural credit consider the proportion of credit extended by the organised sector as one of the indices of the health of the credit system. The presumption is that private lenders are villains and the organised sector banks paragons of virtue. The unregulated operations of the private moneylenders include a number of invidious practices, especially usurious rates of interest. These *sahukars* also use harsh and unscrupulous means for securing the repayment of loans and interests.

Officially, private money lending has been abolished. Yet, it continues to be the main source of agricultural credit. While all those in authority appear to presume that rooting out private money lending is a desirable goal, there is little realisation that the organised sector banks are hardly any better.

In a recent case, a regional rural bank lent Rs. 97,000 to a farmer for the purchase of tractor. By the time the bank went to the court for realisation, it had grown to a hefty Rs. 19 lakh. What rates of interest are the organised sector banks permitted to charge? This is governed by the directives of the Reserve Bank of India, issued under Section 21 of the Banking (Regulation) Act, 1949.

The RBI has issued a series of circulars from March 14, 1972 to September 15, 1984, often contradicting one another. But one recognised principle has been that the agricultural loans stand on a different footing.

Farmers get their income on the sale of crops, generally once a year and therefore, the repayment schedule should be fixed so that the payment is demanded only when the farmers have funds. The compounding of interest is, therefore, ruled out as far as farm loans are concerned.

Maharashtra recognises another principle. The amount of principal together with the rate of interest cannot exceed double the principal, called *daam duppat*. This principle is also recognised by some of the high courts in peninsular India.

Unfortunately, even in Maharashtra, the principle applies only to crop loans given by cooperative banks. There is no limit on the interest that can accumulate on term loans or long-term credit for developmental purposes.

Primary cooperative credit societies circumvent this regulation by a farcical drama every year before the onset of the monsoons. Farmers who have not been able to repay the crop loans taken the previous year become ineligible for fresh loans. If the previous loan is carried over to the next year, the amount of interest, over a period, could exceed the original principal. This is not allowed to happen.

Some officials of the societies carry on money lending businesses on the side. On paper, they lend the farmer an amount equivalent to what is due or what has to be paid to make him eligible to receive a fresh loan. The previous year's loan is, thus, 'closed' and there is no question of accumulation of interest exceeding the principal. The principle of *daam duppat* is thus brought to a nought. It is said that most banks also charge farmer rates of interest that are higher than those prescribed. Further, they compound the interest by adding the amount of interest to the principal every quarter. Thus, the debts of farmers soon assume crushing proportions.

Why does the RBI or the Centre not take any punitive action against the defaulting banks?

The rub lies in Section 29A of the Banking Regulation Act which precludes courts from opening for scrutiny loan contracts merely on the ground that the rate of interest is excessive; it is alleged that this provision was included by vested interests in the banking administration.

A farmer approaching a bank for loan is in dire need of money and therefore, ready to sign on the dotted line without looking at the fine print of the agreement.

Once the agreement is signed and the loan extended, the farmer cannot go to a court of law to question the validity of the contract even if the terms are unreasonable and therefore, voidable.

In the erstwhile state of Mysore, there existed a Usurious Loans Act, 1918 which permitted the courts to open contracts of farmers' loans to examine the reasonableness and fairness of the terms. A question was raised whether Section 29A overrides the provisions of the Usurious Loans Act, 1918.

Obviously, the new Section cannot have overriding effect in its application to agriculture. It refers generally to 'debtors'. Section 29A contains a provision similar to Article 31A and Schedule IX of the Constitution inasmuch as it denies farmers the right to approach the courts of law. In this context, the Maharashtra government's latest move may be the first step to loosen the straitjacket that the farmer has been bound in for centuries.

---

20 April 2005.

16 The Moneylender Surfaces Again

For those who thought that the controversy about private moneylenders was a thing of the past, there is news. There have been several suicides among the cotton growers in the Vidarbha region of Maharashtra. Even those in high places are intrigued as to why so many farmers in Vidarbha, in particular, have taken the extreme step. They further wonder why Yavatmal is the region that is witnessing such terrible desperation.

While the experience all over Vidarbha is that the farmers are driven to suicide in desperation at the extractive methods used by the cooperative bank officials, Yavatmal has a different story to tell. Yavatmal used to be district of *ijaradars*—petty landlords—who held about a hundred acres of land. It is understandable that some *ijaradars* lent money to the farmers in the village. Some ex-*ijaradars* probably do so even today. While private moneylenders have mostly disappeared, there are about 100,000 registered moneylenders in Maharashtra. Some of them, probably, operate in Yavatmal.

In other districts also, farmers do go to private moneylenders and borrow money. The private moneylenders are in no position to use coercive methods to recover their loans. The Maharashtra government is actually asking the farmers not to repay these loans. In any case, what the moneylenders can do is innocuous compared with the kind of methods that are used by the cooperative or commercial banks.

The leaders of ruling coalition have decided, nevertheless to lay the blame for the high incidence of suicides in Yavatmal on the private moneylenders there. They have dug out a couple of cases where farmers allegedly took loans from the private moneylenders. Not only the government authorities, including the Deputy Chief Minister, but also a well-known TV channel, have been devoting a lot of time to indicate that the prime reason for the farmers' desperation were the brutal methods used by the private moneylenders to recover their loans.

It is remarkable that this accusation does not stick. Even the TV channel was embarrassed when in front of their cameras, ordinary farmers made it clear that the government officials were joining hands with some of the distressed farmers to convert transactions of sale into loan operations and that the purchasers in the particular cases were hardly in position to lend thousands of rupees to any farmer whatsoever. Indeed, to a perceptive observer, the alleged 'moneylenders' looked more like landless labourers trying to acquire some land through a straight purchase.

At the dawn of Independence, 'private moneylenders—*sahukars*—and their operations' were big issue. In the heyday of socialism, private moneylenders and *zamindars* became the prime targets of political rhetoric. Nobody talked of agriculture being a losing proposition. The entire blame for peasant misery was put on the devious practices of the moneylenders and the *zamindars*. The two institutions were suppressed expeditiously.

It was quite clear that even after the abolition of private moneylenders, agriculture continued to be a losing proposition. Farmers continued to be heavily indebted and often driven, in desperation, to suicide. The abolition had one notable result. The agricultural surplus, instead of remaining in the countryside, started moving to the urban areas. That, to all evidence, was the real motive.

Are private moneylenders the main cause of the farmers' misery? Among the invitees at a recent seminar on the challenges in agriculture, were a large number of executives who represented the financial institutions and the Maharashtra government. Surprisingly, the farmers themselves went unrepresented, as pointed out by Dr. S.K. Goel, the Maharashtra Agriculture Commissioner.

Though there was nobody to speak for the farmers, as such, a number of participants representing the financial sector pointed out that the private moneylender has his own place and justification, and could be better regulated in order to improve the resources available for agriculture and to augment investment in the farm sector. Remarkably, the participants included Mr. Nachiket Mor of the ICICI Bank who, coincidentally, hails from Yavatmal. Mr. Mor and others observed:

"Agriculture is being starved of genuine homegrown credit institutions. Those who had a certain financial capacity have been scuttled out in the 1950s and are being further targeted now. Further, the exit policy for agriculture does not permit any new enterprise or finances to come in the field of agriculture, even for operational purposes.

"The venomous campaign against the traditional rural credit institutions carried out in 1950s succeeded because of the gullibility of the farmers who thought that the replacement of moneylender by the more benevolent sounding cooperative primary societies would do them good. The political domination of cooperative societies has shown that the cooperative societies are even worse than some of the private moneylenders.

"While there have been a lot of arguments about the rates of interest charged by the moneylenders, economists agree that the ground rates charged by the moneylenders are consistent with the level of risk involved in the lending operation as also the extra facilities given by the private moneylender about making the credit readily available any time of the day, any time of the week, any time of the year. Further, the effective rates charged by the cooperative banks do not appear to be any more lenient than those of the private moneylenders.

"Recently the Reserve Bank of India (RBI), following upon a judgment of the Supreme Court, has issued orders that the farmers should be charged interest only at annual rates and that the interest should be compounded only in cases of default.

"While the commercial banks have been following this edict of the RBI, most of the cooperative banks do not follow the instructions of the RBI and even the RBI does not appear to be particularly enthusiastic about ensuring compliance with its own orders."

The group further felt that "the improvement in investment levels and financial credit to agriculture would require:

- Chastisement of cooperative societies,
- Ensuring that the moneylenders continue to operate under an appropriate regulatory mechanism, and
- Reviewing the entry restrictions and exit systems for agriculture."

I do not hold any brief for the private moneylender. It is undoubtedly true that private money lending became a flourishing business only after the British imposed revenue payment in cash.

Even the better-off farmers found it difficult to raise the money required for the payment of the revenue and had to resort to borrowing from private moneylenders.

It is also understandable that some of the moneylenders, given the caste structure of the society, used both illegal and immoral *modus operandi* for their recovery activities.

In 1950s, the private moneylender was driven out, and it has left the farmers in a lurch. The informal credit organisations continued to work and are still the source of the major part of credit available to the agriculture.

Do we need to stoke the fires of communal hatred and revive the old anti-moneylender tirade at the present juncture? Or do we need to find a rational and local solution in the interest of agriculture?

---

11 January 2006.

17 Give Private Credit Institutions a Chance

One solution to the credit crunch in the farm sector is to harness the moneylender's services but ensure that he operates under the discipline of a regulatory authority.

I expected sharp reactions to my article "Moneylender surfaces again" (*Business Line*, January 11). I expected objections from a handful of co-operative barons because it was the cooperative credit network which was my principal target. I was not prepared for the tide of protests from those unconnected with the cooperatives. "Is the farmers' organisation in Maharashtra turning into a moneylenders' organisation?," one person asked, rhetorically. I owe my readers some explanations.

For long years, any discussion on rural credit has begun by separating the roles of the formal and informal credit sectors. It is pointed out that while the role of the formal sector is widening and expanding, the informal sector continues to survive and often plays a significant role in many regions. The volume of credit made available by the cooperative banking system has been on the decline, amongst other things, on account of the increasing incidence of rural indebtedness and the inability of farmers to repay even crop loans. The farmers are being pushed towards the old moneylender.

The cooperative barons are obviously unhappy that the meek moneylender has survived while the State-sponsored powerful cooperative network is floundering. The main objective of my article was to suggest that, rather than being stuck with the dichotomy between the formal and informal sectors, attempt should be made to open the field of agricultural credit to the private moneylenders, albeit subject to the controls of an appropriate regulatory mechanism.

Agriculture is starved of funds and credit. Obviously, private individuals continue to have a certain financial capacity to provide the necessary support to the sector. However, they are unable to operate properly because of the unreasonable animus towards the private moneylender. The immediate provocation for the article was the fact that prominent political leaders as also a part of the Media were trying to pin the burden of responsibility for the large number of farmers' suicides in Maharashtra on the minuscule group of moneylenders. The facts show that neither the private moneylenders nor the commercial banks indulge in brutally coercive methods to recover loans. That heinous work, putting to shame the worst of the old world 'moneylenders', is done essentially by the officers of the cooperative organisations, who feel confident about the political support to cover up their brutality.

Attempts are being made to dig up cases where some farmers had sold a part of their holding to other villagers, most of whom were landless labourers and, consequently, in a better position of liquidity. The years-old transaction of sale was made to look like a transaction of loan against the mortgage of land. This permitted a massive attack on the moneylenders, which was certainly undeserved. The moneylender in the villages in Maharashtra was considered as one of the 12 humble village artisans (*balutedars*) before the British came in. The British drew up the land-maps and revenue records and established systems of cash and revenue. Even the better-off farmers found themselves in a cash crunch for payment of government dues.

As the date for revenue payment neared, they had to approach those with a greater degree of liquidity, thanks to the nature of their professions. These happened to be either the traders or the priests. Very soon, the moneylender developed into a power centre and was treated as one of the pillars of village society, unlike the poor village artisans.

During the freedom movement, abolition of the moneylender became a popular slogan. The Deccan riots in Pune district were targeted against the moneylenders. The British government, judging the situation correctly, introduced the system of *taqavi* loans. Dr. B. R. Ambedkar made a caste issue out of it and started a campaign against the Khots in the Konkan region of Bombay province. In the early enthusiasm of the post-

Independence era, both money lending and *zamindari* were sought to be abolished by tinkering with the basic structure of the Constitution. The cooperative village primary society and its hierarchy of district and state banks largely replaced the private moneylender. By 1955, it was obvious that the cooperatives had failed. But, concluded the Rural Credit Survey, the cooperation must succeed. This provided justification for massive influx of State funds into the cooperative structure. Fifty years have passed since then and there is no improvement in the availability of credit to the farmer through the cooperative network.

Once again, the Minister for Agriculture and even the Prime Minister are talking of restructuring and reinforcing the cooperative structures by pouring in thousands of crores of rupees into the pockets of the co-operative barons. Such a programme can only mean political reinforcement of the cooperative movement and the political party it supports.

It is at this juncture that I ventured to suggest that if the moneylender continues to survive, and even to progress, the institution must have some merits of its own which should not be lost sight of.

The urban sectors were inimical to the private moneylender in the countryside, not for the reason they stated—his tyranny. The moneylenders, at least a good number of them, were brutal, ruthless and cunning. But that was not the real reason why the urban sector wanted them removed. It had its eyes on the rural surplus, which remained in the countryside in the coffers of the *sahukars*, and wanted private moneylenders to be abolished and replaced by the formal credit institutions of urban links, so that the agricultural surplus may start flowing out of the countryside into the urban areas.

The penury of credit and finance, both public and private, in the agricultural sector are well known. All kinds of methods have been talked of to overcome the situation. One solution that has not even been mentioned is harnessing the moneylender to operate under the discipline of a regulatory authority.

---

25 January 2006.

18 Give Farmers a Real Way Out

On the eve of the Budget, the Finance Minister, Mr. P. Chidambaram, had indicated that this year's exercise would be pro-farmer. That was taken as a hint by the friendly Press, which promptly reported on March 1 that the Budget has gone the extra mile for the farmer.

The mainstream Press, however, found nothing in the proposals that would arrest the farmers' suicides. During the debate on the Budget in Parliament, the Finance Minister faced strong criticism for what was termed his lack of sensitivity to the farmer's plight.

The Finance Minister seems to have seen the writing on the wall. Speaking at a public meeting at Baramati, in Maharashtra, the backyard of the Minister for Agriculture, he stressed the need to transform agriculture into agribusiness and remove the mindset that the farmer is destined to a life of poverty.

He outlined a roadmap by which farming can be made profitable. The government, he said, is taking steps to improve the supply of water and credit and market facilities.

While reiterating several of the Budget provisions, he avoided talking about the retail sector, clearly unwilling to rake up any controversy on the subject with the Left. Loftily, he called for the end of the politics of poverty.

Politics of Poverty

If over 14,000 farmers have committed suicide during the last 3 years in different states, there is something far more amiss than the politics of poverty. It was hardly necessary for the Finance Minister and the Agriculture Minister to come together on one platform to tell the world that agriculture needs water and technology.

Since Independence, various governments have tried their hand at providing inputs and technology to the farm sector. All of them systematically overlooked the need for infrastructure and assured and profitable markets.

This was not oversight. Rather, it seemed to stem from an adherence to a philosophy in the erstwhile Soviet Union that held that cheap raw materials and wage goods for industry had to be provided by agriculture.

Experience shows that farmers, like all other entrepreneurs, are discerning people and make their business decisions after weighing the pros and cons and the economics.

In an environment in which the government used a whole armoury of instruments, such as banning export of agricultural produce and dumping of foreign agricultural produce in India, as also restricting the movement, storage, processing and marketing of farm produce within the domestic market, the farmer has lost hope of agriculture ever becoming profitable.

This, indeed, is the rampant politics of poverty. It has been played out over the last six decades by the party that raised slogans of eradicating poverty.

Mr. Sharad Pawar was evidently not too pleased that his guest should score a march over him in his citadel. On his return to New Delhi, he declared that the Centre would announce, in May, a special package including institutional credit, insurance and financial aid for farmers in four states where thousands of them have committed suicide in the last few years. The package is supposed to benefit 30 districts in Andhra Pradesh, Kerala, Karnataka and Maharashtra. The package is to be finalised in the coming month and a multidisciplinary team is to be constituted to ensure effective implementation.

On the Wrong Track

The announcements of the Agriculture Minister are, again, on the wrong track. Provision of credit without ensuring that agriculture becomes a profitable vocation is a recipe for further indebtedness and more suicides. The Minister intends reforming the crop insurance scheme by making the village *panchayat*, rather than the revenue block, the unit for insurance.

That could be a step forward. But the basic difficulty about any crop insurance scheme still remains unaddressed.

Even within a single village, the crop mortality experience is widely divergent. The level of management and inputs used are the prime factors governing the loss of crops, even in a situation where the weather conditions are more or less the same.

Has any serious study been undertaken to prepare a crop mortality database?

If the premiums charged are less than those indicated by the crop mortality table, any organisation responsible for the insurance of crops will be required to pay out, year after year, more by way of compensation than what it receives as premiums; such an insurance scheme would just not work.

Neither the Finance Minister nor the Agriculture Minister appears to be aware of the stark reality in the field today. Everyday, farmers are being forced to take poison, to hang or immolate themselves. This is a crisis situation. The experiment of providing a helpline to farmers on the brink of suicide only results in the kind of Kafkaesque experience that has been brought out so poignantly in the case of Boya Madhiletti of Mahbubnagar by P. Sainath (*The Hindu*, March 16, 2006).

Offer them an Alternative

Poverty in agriculture is a chronic disease and is unlikely to be cured by such prescriptions. Whether other solutions offer a way out or not, it is essential that the affected farmers are given an opportunity to quit the vocation that was forced on them by the simple accident of birth and to choose another profession. And they should be helped by being provided with a good amount of capital, to start with.

This is possible if the farmers are allowed to benefit from the booming real estate market.

Rather than provide a nominal helpline, the government should offer to take over their land on cash payment of a sum equal to the stamp value of the land, with the provision that, in the 12 months following, the government will make up the difference between the market value and the stamp value of the farmers' transferred holdings.

This would permit the exit of those who lack the training and the mindset to face the challenges of the second Green Revolution and would permit the entry of those who have the necessary technology, managerial and financial background to make agriculture a prosperous agribusiness.

The Chidambaram-Pawar prescription will only be valid once this transfusion operation is carried out. Otherwise, it is difficult to envisage an early end to the spate of suicides.

---

22 March 2006.

19

A Chance to do Justice by Vidarbha's Farmers

While farmers of the region are hoping for the best outcome from the Prime Minister's fact-finding visit to Maharashtra's Vidarbha district, it would be fitting and in the larger interests of the nation if agriculture is to occupy centrestage, at least in Act 2 of the reforms show.

The Prime Minister, Dr. Manmohan Singh, will be visiting the Vidarbha region of Maharashtra from June 30 to July 3 to find out by himself what the whole phenomenon of the suicides by farmers in Vidarbha is. The Chief Minister of Maharashtra had declared a package, particularly for the districts reporting the largest number of suicides. But after the package was announced the number of suicides actually went up sharply, rather than the reverse.

The Agriculture Minister, Mr. Sharad Pawar, held a meeting in Hyderabad of chief ministers of the states that were recording farmers' suicides in large numbers and decided to carry out an in-depth study to determine the main cause of the suicides, which continue despite the Finance Ministry's claims that increased credit had been made available to the farm sector.

While all farmers would wish the Prime Minister good luck in his fact-finding mission, there are certain things Dr. Singh must remember if he wishes to have even a modicum of success. One, Mr. Pawar's statement, based on the statistics of the Home Ministry, that there has been no major change in the phenomenon of farmer suicides is incorrect. The statistics on which it was based are themselves of questionable accuracy. The fact remains, however, that the suicides in Vidarbha are not caused by knee-jerk reactions by farmers to cataclysmic natural disasters or governmental measures. They are not linked to the droughts or the floods that the region suffered last year.

Exploited Region

It must also be remembered that this crisis does not go too far back in history. In the memory of the present generation, there was a time, not long ago, when Vidarbha was considered a richer region than Western Maharashtra. That was the time when people in Western Maharashtra prided themselves on marrying their daughters to grooms from the Vidarbha area. The tragedy in Vidarbha started somewhere around 1960s, when Vidarbha joined the state of Maharashtra as the result of a gimmick of the political party to which the Prime Minister belongs, to ensure the rule of the Congress in Maharashtra and, particularly, in Mumbai. After Vidarbha joined Maharashtra, the state government took a number of rapid measures that resulted in the exploitation of the raw materials produced in Vidarbha, which is, of course, famous for its oranges and well-known for white gold, that is cotton. The region is also rich in coal, uranium and iron. It is the major producer of thermal electricity.

All these features were exploited for the benefit of the industrially advanced Mumbai city and Western Maharashtra. The Maharashtra State Cotton Monopoly Procurement Scheme, for example, has been solely responsible for the loss of around Rs. 30,000 crore to the farmers of Vidarbha since its inception about 30 years back. Similarly, the power generated in the area, and the coal and uranium mined there are taken away on terms of trade that are patently disadvantageous to the region.

Cotton and Coercion

These are the chief causes of the misery but, more important, the farmers have been affected because they could not get a price for their cotton that was available in the open markets of the adjoining states of Madhya Pradesh, Andhra Pradesh or Gujarat. Cotton, the main produce of the farmers in Vidarbha, also happens to be one crop on which the government has imposed the maximum negative subsidy for several years by keeping prices deliberately depressed in comparison with the international markets.

The cotton farmers lost, year after year, and got further and further indebted. This is the chronic malady, manifesting itself several years later in the form of a spate of suicides.

The farmers can stand some level of indebtedness. What they have difficulty in withstanding is the public humiliation and social stigma heaped on them by certain types of creditors. Unlike what is popularly believed, the private moneylenders have little ability to enforce cruel coercive methods for recovery of their loans because they have to live in the villages and have to be aware of village sensibilities. The commercial banks are not prone to using harsh methods of recovery, either. In most cases, the farmers are driven to suicide mainly because of the coercive methods used by the cooperative bank recovery officials, who feel that they have the necessary political support.

Another interesting aspect is that almost all the suicides are of landholding farmers. There are very few, if any, landless labourers who have committed suicide. This proves that while the economy of cotton may have been hard hit, the brunt of it is borne by the landholding farmers, who bear the risk of both natural calamities and governmental tyranny. The landless labourers might get poor wages, but there are no deductions made subsequently on account of the failure of crops or fall in market price. That is why landholding farmers are much worse off than the landless labourers, in general. Enthusiastic announcements in favour of the *aam aadmi* might ignore this fact and do the landholder farmers an injustice.

The Remedies

Once the fact-finding mission comes to some sort of a conclusion on what is causing the suicides, the next important step is to prescribe a remedy for this catastrophe. Dr. M.S. Swaminathan, in his report, had made a list of immediate measures that should be taken for slowing down the tempo of suicides. The Prime Minister's efforts would be applauded by all if he takes some action that will put immediate brakes on the suicides and also provide for the long term.

One immediate measure that can be taken by the government is to develop a land market, where the farmers who find themselves incapable of coping with the situation in agriculture would have the option of offering their lands for sale and quitting agriculture. This will also enable those with the necessary financial, technological and managerial capacity to face the problems of the WTO epoch and deal with the biotechnology reality.

Also essential is the setting up of a comprehensive helpline, whereby farmers who feel desperate can immediately attract the attention of the authorities so that the latter can step in and curb the creditors using harsh coercive methods or, alternatively, offer the suffering family a package tailored to their needs to see them through the crisis situation.

The Maharashtra State Cotton Monopoly Procurement Scheme must go, and the government must declare categorically that it is ready to purchase the cotton at the minimum support price, but that there will be no restrictions on the traders entering the market and offering whatever prices they can to the farmers. The Agriculture Minister tried this experiment in the wheat market this year, with very promising results, and there is no reason why the same experiment should not be tried for cotton.

Restoring the Balance

Dr. Manmohan Singh may recall that in the days when he was the Finance Minister under the then Prime Minister, P.V. Narasimha Rao, and when he kickstarted the globalisation process, all the measures he initiated were related to investment, finance and industry, the economic reforms of the first generation did not touch the farm sector at all. Agriculture continues to be dominated by a number of measures that may prove cumbersome to any economic enterprise.

The Prime Minister will have to be really candid and just in analysing the situation if he wants to arrive at positive conclusions that will help save the situation. On the other hand, if he permits himself to be led by the political considerations of his party, that would indeed be a great tragedy for the people of Vidarbha and for agriculture, in general.

---

28 June 2006.

20 The Other Side of Microfinance

In banking and finance, India has long, well-rooted traditions and institutions. Whoever thought there would be the need to ape the newfangled institutions even in this field? Indians grow under the shadow of the Banyan tree of ancient history and have an innate tendency to refer to the past precedent than innovate. Alternatively, they tend to refer to what happens elsewhere on the globe and plagiarise it. This is generally admitted in science, technology, economics and even literature.

Even in social matters, Indians brush aside native institutions and prefer to replicate those developed elsewhere, without even trying to find out if they can be transplanted to our soil. For hundreds of years, the farmers have depended on the local moneylender to meet their needs of cash and credit. The local *sahukar* was always accessible 24×7 to meet their cash needs, no matter what the purpose and what the security offered were. Since most *sahukars* combined money lending with trade, more often than not, both the loans and the repayments were in kind rather than in cash.

Suppressing the Moneylender

Given the perishable nature of agricultural produce and the caprices of the weather, the rate of interest was often high. It was also complained that the *sahukars* used harsh methods for recovery. The evil features of local money lending became even more prominent during the British Raj, as agriculture came under heavy taxation. It became a common belief that the misery of the farmers was largely caused by the moneylenders rather than by the vagaries of monsoons and the tyrannies of the government.

Suppression of moneylenders became the popular demand of both the farmers and the politicians. The farmers wanted to drive away the moneylender because he was perceived as the tyrant, proximate cause of all his problems. The politicians capitalised on this popular demand to serve their own political agenda. Even during the British rule, there were instances of farmers' revolt against moneylenders. Abolition of the *sahukar* became an important agenda of the freedom movement. So on after Independence, the moneylender in the informal sector was sought to be abolished and replaced by the cooperative or commercial bank network in the formal sector. Given the rigidities of the formal banking sector, it could never really meet the needs of the agriculturists.

Networking with Banks

Post-Independence, agriculture became an even more losing proposition, most debts remained unrequited. Consequently, there could be no further extension of debts and the whole wheel of credit in the agricultural sector came to a screeching halt. Every 20 or 30 years, under one slogan or another, government money was pumped into the cooperative network to give it a further lease of life. If the money that the government poured into the cooperative network were used for loan waivers of the farmers, no farmer would have been driven to suicide, there would be no problem of agricultural indebtedness and there would be nothing like agricultural stagnation at 2 per cent growth. The formal sector, nevertheless, accounts for less than 40 per cent of the agriculture and rural credit.

A proposal was given that, rather than carrying out a hate campaign against the moneylenders, it might be a better idea to regulate the moneylenders by reviving the old Usurious Loans Act that set a limit of 4 per cent on the rate of interest and a ceiling of 2 times the principal on debt accumulation (*daam duppat*) and develop a regulatory mechanism for keeping a watch on the moneylenders' operations.

The proposal was briefly to formalise and regularise the moneylenders' network that had worked in spite of all odds without any governmental subvention for so many decades. But, that was not to be. For the populist politician, moneylender was a favourite hate-object. Even though the politicians recognised the need for a highly flexible mechanism for financing of the farmer and other weaker sections as also women, they were not yet prepared to recognise local structures. They went in for the more fashionable "microfinance".

Obsession with Microfinance

In the 1970s, the microfinance and the self-help groups (SHGs) in Bangladesh were claimed as a great success. Dr. Muhammud Yunus received accolades and numerous international awards for his accomplishment, so much so that many believe that microfinance as institutions began only in the 1970s and that too only in Bangladesh. In fact, there have been earlier claimed successes. Wilhelm Raiffeisen's Village Banking Movement, the Caisse Populaire of Alphonse Desjardins in France were amongst the notable instances where considerable improvement was brought about in the condition of the extremely disadvantaged people.

The world over, microfinance institutions are evaluated on the basis of five criteria:

- Has there been a significant improvement in the living standards of the people targeted?
- Has there been the development of a sustainable microfinance institution?
- How reasonable the rates of interest charged?
- Are any coercive methods used for recovery of loans?
- Is there an element of government subsidy involved?

In India, forming SHGs and microfinance organisations became a favourite hobbyhorse of the NGOs. Most of them fail on all the aforementioned criteria.

They are all beneficiaries of governmental subsidies, they charge rates of interest as high as 30 per cent and use coercive methods for recovery that had driven, in some cases, loanees to suicide. Further, the choice of the loanees is far from transparent and it is believed that in most of the cases, the loans given will become non-performing assets.

NABARD Initiative

The government and the bureaucracy are, however, bubbling with enthusiasm as regards the microfinance network as if that will be the panacea for all the problems of rural credit and poverty. The National Bank for Agriculture and Rural Development (NABARD) is planning to start a microfinance institution to take financing to the "poorest of the poor". The venture will be launched in partnership with commercial banks (49 per cent). NABARD (51 per cent) will also launch a Financial Advisory Unit to help bring down the high incidence of farmers' suicides. The government is also proposing legislation on microfinance. The expectation is that the Bill will regulate the microfinance institutions to ensure fair, equitable and ethical practices and democratic functioning. Under the Bill, NABARD, which is the regulator for the formal sector in rural areas, will also assume responsibilities as regulator for the microfinance institutions. Under the Bill, there will be a ceiling of Rs. 50,000 on loans by microfinance institutions (MFIs).

It is quite clear that the intention of the government is to hand over the MFIs to those who have already failed in ensuring successful operations of the formal sector in the rural areas.

5 September 2007.

21 Case for Total Farm Loan Waiver

> Though a number of political parties and NGOs have demanded some relief for farmers on the debt front, there is really a case for complete waiver of all farmers' debts. A total debt waiver is the only way the government can compensate farmers for its 'anti-farmer' policies.

The present battle for the farmers' *karj mukti* (freedom from debt) is reminiscent of the old practice of plunder indulged by conquering armies during medieval times. The last full Budget of the UPA government will be presented by the Finance Minister on February 28. The biggest blot on the record of the UPA government has been the large number of suicides committed by farmers under the burden of indebtedness. There is expectation in some quarters that the Finance Minister will try to seize this opportunity of declaring, if not a full *karj mafi* (loan waiver), at least some kind of a gesture for alleviating the burden of accumulated agricultural loans and the interest charges.

Suddenly, a large number of individuals, groups and even political parties have moved in to issue ultimatums, threatening dire consequences if the government fails to take concrete steps in that direction.

The Shiv Sena in Maharashtra was the first to start a campaign for *karj mafi* to farmers. It had earlier promised full *karj mafi* to farmers in its manifesto in 1994 but had failed to deliver after it won the election. In the 2004 elections, it tried to make a similar promise but failed to evoke any response from the farmers. It is trying its luck once again.

The Union Minister for Agriculture, Mr. Sharad Pawar, has publicly justified at least a partial loan waiver, stating categorically that only the poor and the deserving farmers should benefit from any such measure. But he refrained from specifying the criteria to be adopted for the selection.

The Secret Agenda

The Bharatiya Janata Party, in its recently-held conclave in New Delhi, also adopted a similar resolution, demanding a waiver of loans across the board with a limit of Rs. 50,000. A Pune district-based NGO of environmentalists has jumped into the arena. Its leader, a former Union Commerce Minister, stigmatised for having followed anti-farmer policies on prices of both onions and tobacco during his regime, had gone on fast demanding loan waiver last year on the eve of the Central Budget. But he later withdrew the fast when the Union government did not oblige him. He too is trying his luck again.

There is reason to believe that the intention of these people is not limited to claiming credit for the *karj mukti* in case it comes along. Their secret agenda is to sidetrack the mainstream farmers' movement that has been agitating for decades for a general and total waiver of all loans to all the farmers. Those who think that only the deserving farmers should get benefit of *karj mukti* or that the waiver should not be total but limited to a certain amount have not really understood the case for it.

The case for a total and general *karj mukti* is based on the premise that all agricultural loans are illegal and immoral. Illegal because in all contracts for agricultural loans, the government is party to depressing agricultural prices, making it impossible for the farmers to repay the loans. Any action by a party to the contract to frustrate performance of the contract on the part of the other makes the contract void under the Indian Contract Act.

Net Debtor

Do the farmers owe any money to the government at all? If one draws a balance sheet of the amount due from the farmers and the loss caused by the government to the farmers on account of its policies calculated to depress agricultural prices and impose "negative" subsidies, it will be obvious that the farmers' liability is only a fraction of what the government owes them. The government is the net debtor to the farmers, and not the other way round.

On the record of the government, the loss caused to the farmers due to its policies of negative subsidy, in 1996-97 alone is Rs. 1,13,748 crore.

The Task Force on Agriculture (2000-01) estimates the loss caused to the farmers on this account between 1980 and 2000 at Rs. 3,00,000 crore. Compared with this, the total loans extended to the farmers, by any estimate, do not exceed even a third of that.

The best estimates of non-performing agriculture loans are given at a mere 7 per cent. Clearly, there is nothing illegal or immoral about writing off all the loans of all the farmers. An across-the-board waiver of a fixed amount of loan has been misused in the past. The experience of the loan waiver in 1990 of Rs. 10,000 in the days of Mr. V.P. Singh shows that it is the banks that benefit more from such limited and across-the-board loan waivers than the farmers. In 1990, the banks adjusted the amount of waiver to the loans that had already been repaid and denied the benefit thereof to the farmers for whom it was meant.

Unfair?

Is there not something unfair about waiving of loans of farmers who have not repaid them when others in similar circumstances have somehow managed to do that? This point raised by some only reveals the innocence of the interlocutors. If details of farmers' loan accounts are scrutinised, it will show that the repayment has come mostly in cases where the farmers have a secondary source of income—a directorship of cooperative body or the salary of a primary teacher in the family.

It is near impossible to come across a case of a farmer's loan at more than 4 per cent rate of interest being repaid exclusively from agricultural income.

Two Courses

But if the government has some compunction about the consequences of a general and total write-off of farmers' loans, it can follow one of the two courses. One, it can treat all farmers with outstanding loans as having filed insolvency petitions and examine each application case-by-case by appointing an adjudicator.

Two, in the case of every farmer, whether loanee or not, it could prepare a statement showing the crops produced, the quantity of production thereof, the coefficient of negative AMS (aggregate measurement of support) as submitted to the World Trade Organization in 1986-1989 by the Ministry of Commerce and arrive at the quantum of AMS, positive or negative, to which the farmer has been subjected.

In cases where the final result is negative, if the amount is less than the amount of loans owed by him, the government should not only write off the entire amount of loans but also make up for the loss caused to the farmer on account of its own anti-farmer policies by reimbursing him the excess of AMS over the amount of outstanding loan.

Both the exercises are fairly complex and it would be much simpler to write-off all existing loans and make a formal commitment that never in future will the government follow policy measures that end up depressing domestic agricultural prices below the price level prevailing in a free market.

---

06 February 2008.

22 Debt Relief and Waiver Scheme

Effective only if it is Total

Every year, soon after the Budget, there is a debate about the relative merits of various indices of popular reaction to the proposals. The stock market has often been discounted as being susceptible to manipulation. Popular demonstrations can also be manipulated.

This year I was a witness to crowds of farmers being brought into the vicinity of 10 Janpath jointly by the Congress and the UNPA leaders. Whether the crowds were to hail Sonia or denounce her was to be decided at an appropriate time.

Finally, the crowd drove in on tractor-trolleys under the leadership of the young Deepender Hooda to felicitate the President of the Congress party.

Having slept two nights over the initial euphoria at the Debt Relief and Waiver Scheme (DRWS) of the Finance Minister, Mr. P. Chidambaram, farmers are waking up to the devious character of the whole mechanism, which will do more harm than good to the farm community.

Genesis of Indebtedness

There is a general agreement that the basic cause of the farmers' inability to repay loans is the uneconomic character of agriculture as a whole. There is little dispute that this is a consequence of the negative subsidies imposed by the government through market interventions. It is generally conceded that the loss inflicted on the farmers far exceeds the pittance of input subsidies the government feigns to give.

The most dependable estimates of the loss caused to the farmers from negative subsidies between 1981 and 2000 is Rs. 300,000 crore.

Against this, the estimate of indebtedness of the farmers, according to the Radhakrishna Committee, is only Rs. 1.3 lakh crore and the total quantum of input subsidies reaching the farm sector is barely Rs. 80,000 crore. If one draws up a tally sheet, it is clear that the farmers owe the government nothing.

The justification of the farmers' organisations demanding total waivers of all farm loans was that these loans are both illegal and immoral. Illegal because the government, which is itself a party to the contract of the loans, frustrated the honouring of the contract by the loanee farmer, which renders the contract a void. And immoral, because on the balance, the government owes much more to the farmers than the other way round.

The debt relief had to be total in order to be just and moral. There is no scope for making any differentiation between the givers of loans, such as private moneylenders, formal sector banks, and so on.

There is no basis for making any differentiation between the loanee farmers either. Differentiating between farmers who hold less than five acres is good politics but bad economics that could prove to be disastrous for agriculture in near future.

Meaningless Discrimination

The smallness of the holding has very little economic significance. If agriculture is a losing proposition, the small holder should logically be a smaller loser than the larger holder. There is abundant evidence to show that the cost of production in small holdings is less and the prices obtained slightly higher. It should not be forgotten that it is not the small and the marginal farmer who made the country self-sufficient in food grains.

The more crucial section of the farming community is the surplus producer. If Mr. Chidambaram's DRWS frees four crores of farmers from the burden of indebtedness and makes them eligible to receive fresh loans, this community can make very little contribution to the solution of the problem of food security, particularly in the epoch of climate change.

Similarly, there is no justification whatsoever for discriminating between loans taken from the formal and informal sectors; the indebtedness of a farmer is the integral entity.

He borrows from banks and then, to repay those loans, borrows from the moneylender. It follows that, at any given point of time, whether a farmer owes money to the moneylender or to the bank is entirely a matter of accident.

Three-Fold Division

Any differentiation between short-term crop loans and long-term development loans is equally invidious. The Finance Minister himself does not explicitly say that his scheme will cover all kinds of loans; however, the criteria for eligibility that he lays down effectively rule out long-term loans becoming eligible for the DRWS relief or waiver.

The Finance Minister has thus created a three-fold division amongst the farming community. It is rather remarkable that the UPA government, which does not accept the theory of 'creamy layer' for the backward classes, is trying to use the same doctrine for farmers who are, as it is, in such desperation that they prefer death to the ignominy of living.

Even the friends of the Finance Minister would not claim that the DRWS was motivated by any serious concern for the farmers. If that were so, the Finance Minister would have first tried to correct market imperfections so that the farmers are not driven to the trap of indebtedness once again. It is exactly the opposite.

Last year, the Finance Minister imposed a ban on futures marketing of wheat and paddy. That was rather cruel blow for a nascent marketing system. This year, he has delivered an even crueller blow. Not only did he not lift the ban, but he has also imposed a tax on commodity market transactions, which could be crippling for the development of the futures market.

He could not be unaware of the fact that a liquid and buoyant futures commodity market could resolve most problems of farm credit and investment. Whatever gesture has been made by the Finance Minister has been forced by the suicides by about 200,000 farmers that amounted to a near genocide.

The Finance Minister had to do something. He, evidently, prepared the package in a last-minute hurry without carefully examining even the basic statistics relating to farm loans. The veracity of the claimed figure of the Rs. 60,000 crore has been questioned in various circles. Even providing for the fact that some banks that may hope to use a part of the waiver money for face-lifting their balance sheets, the bloated figure appears to have an eye on the political advantage.

The Finance Minister has demonstrated that economists can be very astute politicians, exactly like his mentor, the Prime Minister. In one single stroke, he has managed to expose all the parties that jumped into the arena of debt relief and caused fissures in the hope of claiming the credit thereof. At the same time, he has neutralised the non-political farmers movement, which is threatening to be a potent political competitor because of the suicides of so many of farmers.

Budget 2008-09 aims at the approaching elections, not in the sense that it provides bonanzas, but because it attempts to expose the hypocrisy of all the opposition parties and tries to cause the divisions among the ranks of the farmers.

---

5 March 2008.

23 Who Benefits from the Waiver?

The last act in the drama surrounding the Agricultural Debt Waiver and Debt Relief Scheme (ADWDR) announced by the Finance Minister on the February 29, 2008 is unfolding in rural India. All the leading banks were instructed to put on their notice-boards the lists of farmers who actually benefited from the scheme.

The banks faced a Herculean task and certainly tried their best to acquit themselves creditably.

The details of the scheme in close print cover some two dozen pages. On June 18, the Ministry of Finance issued clarifications on some 32 points. To prepare detailed lists of the beneficiaries of the scheme mentioning the financial extent of the benefit derived by them 12 days after the issue of clarifications was no simple task. In addition to preparing the lists of beneficiaries, the lending banks were required to issue individual certificates to each farmer loanee.

Guidelines

The small and the marginal farmers were to be given certificates mentioning the amounts borrowed by them since March 31, 1997 till March 31, 2007 and which had remained unpaid till December 31, 2007. The calculation was further complicated by the fact that the loans that were rescheduled under the packages announced by the government in the years 2004 and 2006, and which had remained unpaid, were also required to be mentioned.

On June 18, the Government made a further amendment and ordered that all loans, even those taken before 1997, were to come under the purview of the scheme if they were covered under the rescheduling packages announced in 2004 and 2006. The certificates for the small and marginal farmers had to give the total amounts of crop loans, short-term loans and long-term loans that had become overdue and hence, eligible for debt relief.

Other Farmers

As regards 'other farmers', that is, those holding more than five acres of land, the certificate was even more complex. It had to mention all loans taken between 1997 and 2007, which had become overdue. The loans rescheduled under the 2004 and 2006 packages taken before 1997 had to be taken into account.

Three-fourths of the amount overdue was to be paid by the loanee farmer in three instalments on September 30, 2008, March 31, 2009 and June 30, 2009. These farmers had to sign affidavits committing themselves to this schedule of payment. The certificates in their favour do mention the amount overdue as also 25 per cent thereof, which becomes eligible for debt relief.

The lists were put on the notice-boards of the lending banks, much to the disappointment of most farmers—small and large—who did not find their names therein. The farmers, however, did not fail to notice that the biggest beneficiaries were large farmers who had managed to avail themselves of big loans, taking advantage of their positions on the boards of directors of the lending banks. In Satara district of Maharashtra, a single individual who happens to be the chairman of a cooperative bank has benefited to the extent of Rs. 35 lakh from the scheme.

Overdues are New Loans

I organised interaction sessions in two villages of Satara district—Chinchani Vandan and Patkhal. The feedback from the farmers brought out some astonishing facts. The ADWDR scheme covers crop loans, investment loans for increasing production in agriculture as also investment loans in activities auxiliary to agriculture, such as dairy, poultry, piggery, and so on.

As regards the crop loans that are taken by the farmers for meeting costs of input such as tillage, seeds, fertilisers, manures, pesticides, power and labour, and which are supposed to be returned within 18 months, the whole scheme has become ridiculously pointless because of the widely rampant practice of conversion of old loans into new loans every year, year after year. This system works on the following lines.

At the opening of the crop season, a farmer who has not been able to repay his previous loans finds himself ineligible to get a fresh loan for the coming year. The chairman/secretary, very condescendingly, offers him a way out. If the loanee farmer can manage to pay the chairman/secretary about 4-5 per cent of the outstanding loan, he agrees to juggle the books of accounts to show that the old overdue loan has been settled and a fresh loan is paid to the farmer. Under this system, crop loans never become overdue. Consequently, the provision in the scheme for the write-off of overdue crop loans is entirely redundant.

In the two villages where I interacted with the farmers, I came across only one case of overdue crop loan. The case of this farmer is very peculiar. He and his brothers live together and cultivate the land together. However, on paper they are all small farmers because the ancestral land has been subdivided between them in successive generations. It so happened that in the last two years, for some reason, he was not able to convert his old crop loan into a fresh one. As a result, he will benefit from the loan waiver scheme. The small as also the large farmers, thus, gain nothing from the waiver of the overdue crop loans.

Investment Loans

As regards the investment loans, the position is more bizarre. The certificates issued to the farmers mention the amounts of loans taken between 1997 and 2007 and then mention the amounts overdue without mentioning the amounts repaid by the loanee farmer time to time.

The certificates do not mention the rates at which the interest was calculated nor is there any way of knowing for sure if the lender bank has charged simple interest or compound interest. There is, thus, no way of knowing if the lending banks have observed or flouted the instructions of the Supreme Court against charging of compound interest.

As if this is not enough, there is an even curiouser stipulation. The 'other farmers', that is those holding more than five acres of land, in order to be eligible for the debt relief, are required to repay the first instalment of 25 per cent of the overdue amount on or before September 30, 2008.

Now, the farmers in Maharashtra are unlikely to get any new income this year before that date. They would, hence, not be able to respect the schedule of repayment and would, automatically, be disqualified not only from the debt relief but even from getting fresh loans. The only way they can save themselves is by taking recourse to borrowing from the private moneylender. The ADWDR scheme thus contains within itself the seeds of a new generation of farm indebtedness.

The UPA government, in order to avoid owning up its responsibility for the farmers' indebtedness and mass suicides, announced a highly legalistic scheme. Indications are that the scheme will itself prove a massive liability for it in the ensuing general elections.

---

16 July 2008.

24 Debt Relief and Loan Waiver

A Bad Cheque that will Bounce

Sour grapes...A surprising number of cheque fraud cases are pending in the affluent Nashik district.

Section 138 of the Negotiable Instruments Act in India relates to cases of bounced cheques that are issued by persons in settlement of any financial obligations without the necessary credit in the accounts on which the cheques are drawn, whether done innocently or intentionally.

Section 138 provides for punishment to individuals who issue such cheques that can go up to three years imprisonment, in addition to a fine equal to the amount of the bounced cheque.

Frauds of this type generally happen in the urban areas where persons, fairly often, give cheques with the intent to give an impression that they are making settlements of obligations even though they know that the cheques will be bounced by the banks on which they are drawn.

But sometimes, this may happen in an entirely innocent manner. The drawer may write the cheque with no evil intent, genuinely believing that the account has the necessary provision at the time of writing.

It happens that in the interval between the drawal of the cheque and its presentation at the bank, some amounts may be withdrawn from the account through cheques issued previously, bringing the credit available below the sum of the cheque in dispute.

Cases of bounced cheques used to be very rare in the rural areas. First, very few farmers have bank accounts at all. Banking habits are not highly developed in the rural areas and people prefer to settle deals through cash rather than cheques.

Cases in Nashik

Recently, I had the occasion to notice that in Nashik district of Maharashtra state, each *taluka's lok adalat* had around 200 cases pending under Section 138, involving fraudulent issue of cheques drawn on fairly non-decrepit rural banks. The total number of cases pending before different *lok adalats* of Nashik district is about 9,000.

It should be remembered that Nashik is a relatively affluent district in Maharashtra. It is a major producer of sugarcane, grapes, onions and a large variety of vegetables for markets not only in Mumbai but also in neighbouring Gujarat.

How come the more affluent farmers have suddenly got into the criminal malpractice of issuing cheques without provision?

There lies an interesting story behind this that is very illuminating on the working of the cooperative and the urban credit banks in rural areas. These banks have developed a new *modus operandi* for giving loans to farmers.

When a farmer approaches a bank for a loan, even before the farmer sees the colour of the money, he is required to mortgage his land, whether the loan is required for agricultural purpose or not, and confirm the same by getting his land revenue records marked as being mortgaged to the lender bank. As if the security of the land were not enough, the farmers are asked to go through a ridiculous routine.

He is advised to go to some other bank in the area and open an account there with the minimal deposit of Rs. 250.

When a bank account is opened, the farmers are issued, depending on the amount of initial deposit, 3-10 blank cheque forms for eventual use, if and when needed. The lender bank forces the applicant farmer to sign the cheque forms without mentioning any specific amount. In course of time, when the farmer is unable to repay the loan, the lender bank proceeds under Section 101 of the Criminal Procedure Code.

Ruthless Section

Under this Section, the land of a defaulting farmer can be seized and auctioned by the revenue authorities if a decree is passed to that effect by a court of law. Given the actual situation of the farmers, it so happens that in many cases the authorities are not able to seize and auction the land and handover the proceedings to the lender bank.

In such cases, the banks file cases in the court of law claiming that the cheques that bear the signature of the accused farmer, on which the amount of the debt and issuing date is now inserted by the lender bank, was issued without provision in the account.

Kafkaesque Experience

Section 138 of the Negotiable Instruments Act is far more ruthless to the farmers than any comparable provision in the Indian Penal Code or the Criminal Procedure Code. A farmer unable to repay the loan can be sent to the prison under a Section that is entirely unrelated to the agricultural vocation.

Recently, there were three cases in the grape-growing Niphad *taluka* of Nashik district, where farmers who were charged under Section 138 committed suicide. In the case, the farmer Shinde had taken a loan of Rs. 1,15,000. He required the amount for ensuring the education of his son.

He had earlier applied for an educational loan, which was refused by the bank. He, therefore, proceeded to ask for a loan that was granted by the lender bank as an agricultural loan, against the mortgage of his land and additional security in the form of blank signed cheques.

Desperate, and unable to face the ignominy of a jail sentence, Shinde threw himself in front of a passing train. The police maintained stoutly that this was an accident. His son insisted that his father was feverishly writing something the day prior to his death.

No writings were found back at home. There must be a suicide note on the body, he maintained. There was one, indeed, detailing the Kafkaesque experience of his dealings with the bank. The history of the two other cases is not very different. The Central government's Debt Relief and Loan Waiver Scheme (DRLW), 2008 failed to save Shinde's life.

Thousands of farmers in this single district of Nashik alone are awaiting imprisonment and being fined under the draconian and vicious applications of Section 138, and so many more have suffered confiscation of their meagre belongings. They are accused of having issued cheques that they never issued. DRLW was announced in the hope of rich electoral dividends. Chances are that it will prove to be a cheque without provision and hence, bounce in the face of its authors.

---

8 October 2008.

III

Environment

25 Agriculture and Environment

An Introduction

The subject of environment finds some strange bedfellows coming together. For long years, the protectionists the world over, particularly in the OECD countries, were fond of giving environmental protection as an excuse for the high level of subsidies that their countries paid to the farmers. There was considerable sympathy for this argument even amongst those who championed the cause of free trade.

The countries that had made rapid advances in industry faced two separate sets of problems—one, environmental and the other, social. The industry produced too much pollution and carbon dioxide and other greenhouse gases. It was necessary to grow vegetation/forests and greenery to make up for the oxygen imbalance. Socially, the backwardness of agriculture created a divide that was found to be politically undesirable. The officers in the European Economic Community (EEC) openly admitted that the city girls were reluctant to date the young farmers and that this was creating a new schism as pernicious as racism.

The subsidies to agriculture were, the protectionists-cum-environmentalists argued, necessary in order to ensure a better ecological balance, a more even society that ensures more acceptable standards of living for the farming community.

There is a lot of sound logic and truth in the basic environmental argument. Nobody can deny that the growing trees and allowing the forest to develop is good whatever it does to the global environment. In India, traditions testify that there will be over 10 successive years of drought and famine due to the failure of the monsoons. This happened periodically even in the days when the vast areas were covered with forests. Clearly, there is no irrefutable correlation between forests and rainfall and agricultural development.

If the environmentalists confined themselves to champion the green argument, they would possibly not have received the kind of attention, much less accolades, international recognition and awards that they habitually receive these days.

There is another less benign aspect of environmentalism. This argument, quite contrary to the green argument, actually tries to oppose the basic instincts in human beings. The argument accuses industrialisation and consumerism for the deterioration of the ecology and the environment.

Firstly, there is a deliberate attempt to cause large-scale scare amongst the good honest human beings. Now, they will frighten them with the forecast that the natural resources like copper, zinc and other metals as also fossil fuels are being fast depleted and will soon be completely exhausted. Briefly, if human enterprise continues at the historic pace that will bring the death of the planet earth. The more philosophical environmentalists preach pontifically, "There is enough in nature to satisfy everybody's needs but not anybody's greed".

Secondly, there is a deliberate argument which opposes the whole human enterprise based on the instinctive tendency to build ever expanding network of perceptions, sensations and the horizons of experiences.

Rapid industrialisation has certainly caused some damage to the world we live in. However, that is only one side of the story that is even more important. It is an equally irrefutable fact that science, technology and industrialisation have widened the field of human observation and experimentation that has added greatly to the comfort of the lifestyle with higher degrees of freedom. The earlier generations of environmentalists were present to cry of hoarse, "How Green was my Valley!" When men started exploring the bowels of the earth for the hidden wealth of minerals, the environmentalists of the epoch strongly resented; even the introduction of the railways they cried on the grounds that the railway tracks, steam engines and the smoke they emitted will cause irreversible environmental damage.

The environmentalists strongly opposed use of chemical fertilisers and pesticides that have made it possible for masses to have two or even three square meals a day. They rose in force when the Bt cotton seed appeared on the horizon. They mustered considerable forces to oppose the introduction of the genetic engineering and GM foods. Today, they are provoking mass hysteria against the GM brinjals. Briefly, environmentalists oppose the advancement of each and every frontier technology and industry at the threshold itself. This is a lucrative business that has brought good dividends in the past and holds promise for all times to come.

History shows that the environmentalists are wrong at each step. Minerals formed the basis of our present civilisations, railways started the transport revolution and the introduction of biotechnology is bringing in and expected to continue to help a great deal in meeting the threatened consequences of climate change. Not one as representative environmentalist ever expressed regrets about the position they adopted about the threat of the advancement of technology on the environment and employment.

The environmentalists are politically a very strong lobby. They even managed to hijack the United Nations apparatus and pass resolutions of questionable merit that had to be, per force, taken note of by all national governments.

Today, no government can afford to flout the dictates of the Kyoto conference resolution without running the serious risk of meeting their political Waterloo at the next political electoral hustings. The environmentalists have also painstakingly gathered a tremendous aura of pseudo-scholarship, pedantry and respectability that they have done little to merit.

Today's environmentalist lobby gathers a good part of its moral strength from eminent people like Tolstoy and Mahatma Gandhi. The people at large are conditioned to accept that there is an impeccable moral argument and even cosmological evidence that justify the measures advocated by these busy bodies if they wish to protect our globe and the species living there in.

Protection of the threatened species is a favourite hobbyhorse of the environmentalists. Notwithstanding years of steady campaigning, the threatened species actually continue to register decreasing numbers. The protectionists argue for anti-poaching laws in order to save the species like tigers, and understandably, crocodiles. These laws have been found to be counterproductive. The ban on poaching invariably creates a new more growing and lucrative market for the parts of the animals. This, in turn, encourages poaching. So the vicious cycle rolls on and the subject species continue to be depleted faster and faster. Tigers in India is a blatant example where the government, the bureaucracy and the animal lover environmentalists have been working at tandem for decades.

The only countries where some degree of success has been achieved in protecting the endangered species and actually increasing their numbers are those that deliberately encouraged development of markets for the animals and their body parts. The prosperous market actually encourages people not so much to do illicit poaching as to develop breeding farms of the threatened animal. There is a possibility that the animals from the breeding farm may not exactly have the same traits and attitudes as those born and brought up in nature. Nevertheless, the process of extinction is clearly reversed.

It must be recognised that no species including the human can be said to have the ultimate stage in evolution. Men and women of today are not the same as those in the epoch of Rama or Seeta. We are all evolving all the time. Mosquitoes of today are quite different from their pre-DDT ancestors. With increasing proportion of greenhouse gases, humans may develop a capacity to breath greenhouse mixture of air.

The environmentalism starts from certain implicit premises about the character of the cosmos and the mother planet. It takes for granted the cosmology of the Old Testament, according to which man was created on this earth, that he was given this earth as his abode and the earth was given to man for its enrichment.

That is not the only cosmological hypothesis that exists. There is greater reason to believe that all life is likely to have migrated to the earth from some place in the universe. The life could have begun on the earth itself. But that eventuality is statistically as probable as a man developing AIDS or venereal diseases without some kind of contagion. The universe is full of life and it is much more likely that life in its most primitive form migrated to this earth because earth was found to be a more congenial habitat for its development.

Darwin's theory of evolution describes only one channel through which the evolution of the human species could have happened. There is nothing in Darwin that specifically precludes the possibility of developed human migrating from other livable planets.

Statistically, it is more reasonable to believe that human beings at some stage in the evolution migrated to earth. The most probable scenario would include of scientifically advanced communities managing the interplanetary migration very similar to the enterprise of Noah and his ark. Humans are a species that have, in times, historically moved from planet to planet colonising each planet and giving full scope to their basic instincts of maximising their degrees of freedom through networking, innovation and industry. If the process makes the currently inhabited planet unlivable, he will try his best to continue living there. But if that looks like an improbable task, nothing stops him from contemplating another planetary migration. Human beings cannot help the fact that his lifestyle makes an abode inhabitable, given the basic instincts that are given to him by the nature itself. If our ecological fears come true, rational human societies will start exploring more habitable planets rather than the doomed task of saving the sick earth.

The diagnosis of the environmentalists' resolution is correct. The earth is rapidly degenerating. It has already declined to such an extent that even if the demographic rates of all societies actually become negative and every single child born is born an ascetic like Gandhi, the planet earth can still not be saved.

The campaigning of the environmentalists reminds mc of thc story of a young man who was an addictive smoker. Wiser men succeeded in persuading him and to give up smoking after strenuous efforts. Within a few days of his beginning of abstinence, he started feeling healthy and felt like going out for a walk. Just as he stepped out of his garden gate, a speeding truck knocked him out.

The earth certainly faces the threat of an ecological disaster, global warming, pollution and eventual death. However, that is not the only threat the mother earth faces. The chances that the globe will meet its end by an accidental collision in space, calculating it statistically, are much larger. If the environmentalists are honestly keen on avoiding/postponing the end of the earth not only by slow poisoning but also by collision, they would have to advocate the development of a large network of space stations capable of monitoring the movement of these spatial bodies and the techniques of diverting them. That kind of an enterprise will involve a massive dose of industrialisation work that would go against the grain of the environmentalist argument.

Environmentalists are certainly not any kind of philosophers or moralists that they feign to be. They are busybodies on the lookout for popular causes, provoking scare mania amongst the populations in order to make a lucrative business out of environmentalism.

24 November 2009.

26 Contradictions at Earth Summit

The Earth Summit 2002 has opened at Johannesburg. The focus of the electronic media and of various environment groups is now on the main conference centre at Sandton as also at the NGO meeting centres at Nasrec, in Soweto, at the end of the town.

The advance parties of all the contending groups arrived early in Johannesburg and local TV channels had a hectic time telecasting the statements and interviews of leaders of different schools of thought. On August 23, a full three days before the inauguration, 77 demonstrators were rounded up by the police. Those opposed to freedom and globalisation have meticulously planned massive demonstrations with a view to catching the global limelight, obstructing the proceedings of the conference and if possible, frustrating it.

Over the last two years, the rag-tag coalition of sundry groups of environmentalist, socialists, trade unionists and luddites joined by that sophisticated instrument of frontier technology—the Internet—have succeeded in making their presence felt. This time they will have to contend with the police in South Africa, who are known for their toughness; the highest number of custodial deaths occurs in South Africa.

What is the Summit about? The agenda relates to the most fashionable cliché of the present epoch—sustainable development. The Johannesburg conference is a sequel to the earlier 1993 Rio de Janeiro Summit, which gave birth to this now widely used term. The predecessor conference was a success and its resolutions certainly figured on the agenda of most governments. That little was accomplished in consequence is due more to the complexities of the issues, as also to the wide divergence of interests between poor and rich countries, than the lack of interest and political will.

The Earth Summit 2002 has certainly bitten off too big a slice to be done justice to in the short duration of the meet. The very concept of sustainable development is a limitless canvas.

Agriculture is only one chapter in any developmental programme. The heads of State/government who have converged to confabulate will, no doubt, be more interested in industrial growth, increase in employment, transfer of frontier technology and facilitation of finance. Agriculture does not figure at the top of their agenda.

The list of subtopics covered under the chapter of agriculture is spread out in alphabetical order from 'A' for agriculture to 'W' for water. Clearly, the Summit can do nothing more than make some kind of recommendations on action programmes that may barely scratch the surface of the issues involved under each topic.

One could perhaps start drafting the final resolutions straightaway. The Summit would decide to promote, encourage and support the national governments in implementing the standard prescriptions in each domain, no matter if some of them contradict each other.

Anybody who is a head of a State/government is unlikely to be enthusiastic about presiding over the liquidation of his own estate. The action programme would, understandably, highlight the active role of the State while paying lip service to the forces of liberalisation, globalisation and the market.

As regards agriculture, the fact is that it would benefit more if the governments refrained from intervening—either positively or negatively—than from any programme of action.

From a global point of view, sustainable development will be helped if the governments of rich countries scaled down the various subsidies they shower on their farmers and if the governments of poor countries ceased to persecute their peasantry.

No head of State/government is likely to take such a global long-term view. Each of them, rich or poor, will perorate to present and defend his/her own national interests and agenda.

Two events occurred on the eve of the Earth Summit 2002 that may cast their shadow on the proceedings.

Fishermen in Scotland are agitated that their highland rivers, which used to brim with fish, particularly salmon, have been emptied out due to reckless commercial mechanised fishing without adequate measures of replenishment. A discussion of their brief will bring out the intricacies of the 'man *versus* nature' conflict involved in all measures of contrived development.

The Earth Summit will certainly be seriously over-shadowed by something that is happening in its very backyard—Zambia. The Director-General of the World Food Programme (WFP), Mr. James Morris, has declared the inability of his organisation to provide food to the estimated two and a half million starving people in Zambia and another 13 million who will soon be affected, unless the Government of Zambia agrees to receive the genetically modified (GM) food supplies.

The genetically engineered seeds have proved their merit as regards production, yields and cost as also quality. There is, however, a strong lobby interested in the continued use of chemical fertilisers and pesticides, which are important elements of the Green Revolution package. The lobby has succeeded in creating a scare about, both probable and improbable, hazards for environment, plants, cattle and human population.

The Zambian government, as of today, appears determined not to allow the entry of GM foods, even at the risk of exposing millions of people to starvation. In the past, Africa has witnessed the curious spectacle of a national government preventing food supplies from abroad from reaching its own starving people. It need not shock anyone if the government of Zambia uses the anti-GM arguments rather than some tribal diatribe to justify its policies.

Eventually, people the world over will come to consume GM foods. If in the course, they notice any unsavoury effects, human ingenuity will produce the necessary antidotes. In any case, in another decade man will have no alternative but to adjust himself to GM foods.

In the meanwhile, the Zambian authorities' stance will provide a good backdrop for discussions on biotechnology, environment and sustainable development for the Earth Summit at Johannesburg.

---

28 August 2002.

27 The Economics of Tsunami Relief

Recently, I had occasion to attend a seminar organised by the Centre for Civil Society in New Delhi, especially for members of Parliament, on relief work for tsunami victims. Present at the seminar were representatives from numerous organisations that have been busy in the relief and rehabilitation work for the tsunami victims.

According to government sources, 105, 171 and 8,009 persons died in the three states of Andhra Pradesh, Kerala and Tamil Nadu, respectively. The number of deaths in Pondicherry was 593 while it was 1,395 in the Andaman and Nicobar Islands. The total number of deaths in India is estimated at 10,273. The overall losses in these five states and territories are estimated at Rs. 11,544.91 crore and the total assistance rendered Rs. 2,822.17 crore.

The Central assistance is being extended through the Calamity Relief Fund and the National Calamity Contingency Fund to the states and the union territories.

This is only the first phase of the assistance plan for the victims, which corresponds to the relief phase, the earlier rescue phase was taken care of mostly by the NGOs. And rehabilitation will be a much longer process for which blueprints are being drawn up to ensure that the new constructions will be able to withstand any recurrence of the tragedy.

From the advertisements in the print and electronic media, one saw a large number of organisations taking the initiative to collect funds for the relief and rehabilitation of tsunami victims. It was obvious that the public contributed generously and that large sums of money were available to those who intended to take part in the relief work.

The response of the people—both in India and abroad—was overwhelming. The more serious problem was to ensure efficient distribution so that the aid reached the needy. The work of the NGOs was commendable in general, though, in the occasional case, the approach did seem somewhat amateurish.

Many of the NGOs that came forward to help responded to the demands of the victims as swiftly as they could. For example, when several fishermen complained about the boats they had lost, the NGOs had them replaced immediately.

Many of these organisations were perhaps unaware that fishing is already a crowded sector and that, before the calamity struck, the shores were so crowded that fishermen sometimes ventured into the waters of the neighbouring states, even countries, often at risk of being taken prisoners.

The post-tsunami phase should have been used as an opportunity for helping a section of fishermen out of the sector into vocations with better prospects. In some areas, boats lost to the tsunami have been replaced to such an extent that, shortly, there is going to be a super-saturation of fishing capacity.

Poverty eradication has been 'good business' since the 1950s. The United Nations, its specialised institutions and various aid agencies as also many NGOs have over the years focused their efforts on providing technical assistance, organising seminars, training courses and expert missions and carrying out studies on how to eradicate poverty.

Social service and civil society activity has been an equally attractive business now for decades. Natural calamities such as droughts, floods and earthquakes cause widespread misery to the affected people.

The state governments hit by the tidal tragedy have made their own subjective assessment of the damage caused and have asked for special assistance.

If the demand is fully met, the Central funds would cover not only the damages but also, *inter alia*, some of the pending projects entirely unconnected with the calamity.

For some NGOs, it is a great opportunity to come to the limelight and at the same time, reinforce their economic situation. At the end of the present financial year, the Union Ministry of Home Affairs proposes to make a comprehensive audit of the assistance received and its utilisation. There is also an unseemly hurry to announce and pay compensations to the bereaved families. This is inevitable since the bodies decompose fast and can be produced as evidence of death only in the first few days after the calamity.

A number of false claims are made and there is little possibility of carrying out any objective verification.

Even in the horrendous situation following the calamity, the temptation for unscrupulous elements to lay hands on some extra money is strong.

Another aspect of the calamity is the issue of a disaster warning system. Among the survivors of the catastrophe, there is great resentment about the fact that they did not receive any advance warning of the disaster. The proposal to have an early warning system for natural calamities was mooted around the advent of El Nino.

It was also discussed at the time of the earthquake in Kutch. In 2004-2005 itself, erroneous meteorological forecasts resulted in considerable damage to agriculture.

It took a tsunami for the government to get ready to establish an early warning system. If that concern, awakened at the time of El Nino, had been concretised, the death toll in the tsunami might have been much less.

---

23 March 2005.

28 Weather Insurance

Taking on the Rain God

Recently, a photo in a business daily featured Mr. Suparas Bhandari, Chairman and Managing Director of the Agricultural Insurance Company (AIC), alongside the Finance Minister, Mr. P. Chidambaram. The Finance Minister, the accompanying report said, had launched the Weather Insurance Scheme 2005, Varsha Bima, for the benefit of two lakh farmers, and 13 crops in 10 states at a premium of just 4-8 per cent or of the crop value.

Ironically, a second report on the page, spoke of the 34 per cent deficit in the monsoons in June. The Bangalore-based CSIR Centre for Mathematical Modelling and Computer Simulation (C-MMACS) had revised its earlier estimate of 22 per cent excess rainfall for June.

From 22 per cent excess to 34 per cent deficit! And that too, for the crucial month of June when sowing for the *kharif* season is in full swing.

C-MMACS is categorical about its predictions of 12 per cent deficit for July and 13 per cent excess for August. This prediction for August has to be understood separately for each region.

North (+1 per cent), West (+30 per cent), East (+15 per cent), South (+22 per cent), North East (+3 per cent), Central (+28 per cent), South Central (+10 per cent), the Andamans (0) and Lakshadweep (+17 per cent).

It is on erratic predictions such as these that 50 per cent of the agricultural sector depends, a sector that continues to be the primary determinant of the rate of growth of GDP. Further, the success of the monsoons is to be assessed not by the total quantum of rainfall but by the effect it has on the overall agricultural produce. If the rains are abundant and cause water-logging and loss of crops, it will be a calamity.

All the sophistication of mathematical models is, as far as the farmer is concerned, pointless unless it can produce district- and month-wise predictions.

Now, what does the AIC mean by Varsha Bima? If the purpose is to provide insurance cover against deficit or excess rainfall, a number of questions arise. First, rainfall is of interest not only to farmers, but also to people at large. Why is it the AIC's domain to provide insurance against the vicissitudes of weather?

Second, why is it that the AIC proposes to collect insurance premium from farmers alone for something every person in the country has an insurable interest in? Further, when a business enterprise such as the AIC offers insurance coverage, should it not be on the basis of some recorded statistical experience of the contingent event? Are there dependable mortality tables for rainfall?

It is evident that even experts and institutes are unable to make informed forecasts about the onset or the overall quantum of rainfall as late as one week before the onset of monsoons.

It is a basic principle of insurance that risks caused by acts of God and enemy action cannot be insured. It may be said that rains are an act of God and therefore, insurance against weather is an *a priori* non-starter.

Insurance on weather can, at best, provide a measure of the efficiency of the meteorological department and other research institutions working in the field of weather forecasting.

Why does the AIC presume that the premium on weather insurance should be based on the value of the crops rather than on the quantum of physical production on the farm?

The value of the product is not even remotely related to the total quantum of rainfall. It depends more on the distribution of the rainfall over time.

Further, abundant production does not necessarily mean good income. The income will depend on market-determined prices and the policies of the government.

Varsha Bima as agricultural insurance makes no sense whatsoever. It is an insurance against an act of God, so to speak.

Even then, it is offering insurance without any statistical recorded experience, such as mortality tables. The quantum of rainfall does not determine that of production.

Linking the premium to the value of crops makes no sense because the income derived from crops depends on a number of factors, some of which are manmade and highly unpredictable.

Lastly, the institutions are predicting a plus or minus rainfall of 12-34 per cent this year. This is nowhere near the 4-8 per cent premium that the AIC is proposing.

One can understand Mr. Bhandari's enthusiasm about expanding activities of AIC.

But it is difficult to understand why Mr. Chidambaram is supporting this kind of a misadventure.

---

15 June 2005.

29 Is Saving Threatened Species Futile?

A Hindi daily carried a report on July 6 that the local residents around tiger reserves often stood with the hunters and poachers than with the reserve guards. The reason stated was that they were grieved about not being given a share of the additional income coming out of tourism around the reserves.

The Prime Minister, Dr. Manmohan Singh, reacted almost instantaneously to announce that the government would evolve a mechanism to offer the local residents jobs connected with the tourist services so as to dissuade them from lending a shoulder to hunters' guns.

The Prime Minister is reported to be taking the mission of saving the tigers very seriously. He recently assumed chairmanship of the Steering Committee of Project Tiger. Launched in April 1973 on the basis of the recommendations of a Special Task Force of the Indian Board for Wildlife, the objective of Project Tiger is to provide the big cats a sanctuary where they can multiply to keep the species away from extinction.

According to the Project Tiger website, nine tiger reserves were created initially; now 27 reserves extending over 37,761 sq km spread across 14 states have been brought under the ambit of the Project Tiger. Allocation for the Project in the Budget was increased from Rs. 8 crore per annum to Rs. 17 crore.

Unfortunately, these reserves do not seem to be providing sanctuary to the tigers. The reserves at Sariska and Ranthambore have proved to be highly inefficient in protecting the big cats. The Sariska Reserve has hardly any tigers. The situation in Ranthambore, Karnataka and Maharashtra, is no better.

A Task Force under Project Tiger recently recommended that the villagers around the reserves be relocated to ensure the security of the tigers. The cost of such resettlement is put at around Rs. 600 crore. Tigers tend to stray beyond the limits of the reserves. As a result, the terror-stricken farmers turn unfriendly. To provide security for the tigers, Project Tiger envisages displacing the farmers from their ancestral farms and habitat. The government and wildlife activists need to be congratulated for creating an awareness on the need to protect the Indian tiger. However, the important question is: Are the well-intentioned efforts well directed?

The African experience has shown that legislative restrictions on hunting are quite ineffective in protecting endangered species. For, these animals continue to be hunted with the poachers taking chances considering the handsome pay-off.

Also, such prohibitions only promote corruption. A more effective way is to legalise trading in animal skins and other parts. This is found to encourage commercial breeding of the threatened species.

Environmentalists generally clash with industrial and chemical polluters. When it comes to saving wildlife, their interests clash with those of the farmers and the tribals. Not that the farmers dislike tigers and other wildlife; they love them as long as they confine themselves to the jungles or the reserves.

If the animals stray into nearby villages and kill poultry or milch and draught animals, the farmer loses patience and seeks to devise ways to discourage the animals, either with the help of hunters or, as a final recourse, by poisoning the beasts. At a more philosophical level, is it not a futile effort to try and artificially save a species whose moment of extinction has come?

For, nature does not share the conservationists' view, but destroys ruthlessly hundreds of species even as it creates new ones through its own myriad processes. Any effort at artificial conservation of a species that has outlived its utility is doomed to failure.

Conservationists' efforts can perhaps be compared to state intervention in an economy for protecting incompetent factors of production and may actually prevent the evolution of new animal varieties.

---

10 August 2005.

30 Climate Change and the Ostrich Syndrome

When the wiser course would be to presume the worst effects of climate change and prepare for it, the country seems to be burying its head in the sand hoping that the storm will pass.

"Keep your faith in God, My son! and keep your powder dry," used to be the advice to youth facing an imminent danger. The dangers of climate change are very real. The Intergovernmental Panel on Climate Change (IPCC) warned the world as early as in 2001 of:

- Higher maximum temperatures; hotter days and heat waves over nearly all the landmass, that could increase heat-related deaths, particularly among older adults and urban poor; heat stress in livestock and wildlife; and damage threat to some crops;
- More intense precipitation over many areas resulting in increased floods, landslides, avalanches and mud slide damage, extensive soil erosion, flood run-off; and
- Increase in tropical cyclones, tornadoes, hurricanes over some areas raising the risk to human life, epidemics, coastal erosion; and damage to coastal buildings, and infrastructure and ecosystems.

The matter is serious enough to be taken on the agenda of the Security Council, which usually deals with more serious threats such as armed conflicts and warfare. This alone should be sufficient warning signal of a possible impending disaster.

Human knowledge is not advanced enough to spell out definitively what is coming over the long-term cycle, or the beginning of a linear trend that could only result in catastrophe. The wiser course in such cases would be to presume the worst and prepare for it rather than adopt an ostrich-like approach of burying the head in the sand hoping that the storm will pass.

Food or Fuel?

At the fifth Congress of the World Agricultural Forum held in St.Louis, US (May 8-10, 2007), the subject of climate change figured prominently. In the discussions at one panel discussion, attention centred on the back-to-the-wall firefighting with the objective of reducing the greenhouse gases by cutting down on the use of fossil fuels and replacing them by biofuels.

Yet another panel examined the consequences of the increased production of biofuel plants on the production of the food grains and pulses in a scenario where increase in the production of food grains by about 50 per cent is required to meet the food demands of a rising population.

Interestingly, a third panel went into the ethical and even cosmological aspects of the global warming. A question was raised if the damage to the global environment was at all reversible? A participant posed the question: If everybody stopped using automobiles and refrigerators as of today, can earth be restored to its pristine wholesomeness? A large number of the participants at the Congress appeared to feel that it was too late and that while the fight-back should not be given up, the other avenues of saving human civilisation should be contemplated as serious alternatives.

The hypothesis that earth is like an orange which has been eaten up by the human pests would suggest that there is some scope for beginning to plan an operation "Skywards Ho!" The reigning paradigm that man was made for the earth to lord over it will need to be given up and replaced by a worldview of a cosmic nomadic human race continuously in pursuit of greater freedom through networking. The only alternative course—reducing the population by about 90 per cent and inhabiting the world with ascetics—is far more improbable than the prospect of sci-fi migration to some other habitable planet.

Unconcerned in India?

Back in India, it is a different scenario altogether. Here, nothing unusual or astonishing is seen about the changes in the climate observed in recent times. They are seen as sufficiently explainable by local conditions quite unrelated to any global phenomenon. A senior meteorological department official has specifically denied any linkage with any global phenomenon. The annual general body meeting of the Indian Council of Agricultural

Research (ICAR), on May 11, 2007, hardly had any discussion on the matter apart from a casual reference in the inaugural speech of the Minister for Agriculture. One of the members did suggest the need:

- To develop crop varieties more resilient to extremes of temperature, salinity, acidity and humidity;
- To develop a comprehensive plan for the replacement of the cross-breed varieties of livestock such as Jersey and Holstein Friesian that are extremely vulnerable to higher temperatures, by upgraded varieties of buffaloes and sheep;
- To develop new technologies and systems of food processing that would not be dependent on the availability of cold storage and refrigeration which are likely to be frowned upon as major culprits for generation of greenhouse gases, by the global community in coming years.

Apart from an informal promise by the ICAR Director-General that his organisation was quite capable of developing programmes that would meet the threat of climate change, no concrete decision was made by the general body.

The Minister for Agriculture spoke of the substantial degradation of land in recent years. He, however, did not mention the possibility of further acceleration in the process because of the extremes of temperatures, frequent storms and skewed precipitation. He also mentioned with some concern the fall in the production of food grains and pulses. However, he did not spell out any measure, apart from massive imports, that he proposed to meet the food grains demand of a rising population in a situation where a tropical country like India could cease to be capable of producing any food grains at all.

Hopefully, the climate change we are experiencing may not be a part of an indefinitely continuing process. Maybe, this will all blow over and man can continue with this blithe ways, harming the environment. The fact remains that the ostrich will perish with the neck buried in the sand whether the climate change turns out to be a global linear phenomenon or a transient local one.

---

16 May 2007.

IV

Technology

31 Agriculture: More Technology than Land

An Introduction

Agriculture evokes images of land and farmers working thereon. Agriculture being the primary vocation of mankind, it is presumed that it involves almost entirely, application of labour to land. In fact, agriculture is much more than that.

The popular impression is that agriculture involves very little technology and whatever technology farmers use is very elementary in comparison to the sophisticated levels of technology used in most sectors of industry and services. A large number of people are, in fact, convinced that agriculture should remain away from the more sophisticated applications of technology and remain close to natural processes and organic methods.

The controversy about the application of technology in agriculture started with Dr. Malthus. Dr. Malthus questioned the optimism generated by Adam Smith's economics that any human society which has recourse to mechanisation, large-scale production, division of labour, technology and free trade would generate an economic growth that is limitless, at least in theory. Malthus questioned this optimism. He postulated, given the niggardly land resources and given the population galloping in geometric proportions, shortages of food that would inevitably bring in famines, pestilence, disease and wars for food is the inevitable destiny of mankind.

There is little dispute that history has proved Dr. Malthus a false prophet. Today, a population several times larger than that which lived in the days of Dr. Malthus enjoys reasonable food security, is free from pestilence and also eats more amply and enjoys a more varied and nutritious diet. The hoarse cries of the environmentalists notwithstanding, global warming or no global warming, the diversion of food grains for biofuels notwithstanding, governments and the farmers feel fairly confident of being able to feed the population dependent on them.

The total expanse of land available for cultivation has not much changed. However, man has invented ways of taking out much greater yields from the same land, its propensity to diminishing returns notwithstanding. This was made possible mainly through development of high yielding varieties of seeds, of methods of application of manures, fertilisers and pest and water management—a package known in India as Green Revolution Technology.

Land as given by God and nourished by nature itself without human artifices could not have produced even a fourth of the food as it is actually produced today. It can be deduced that productivity of technology is far more significant in today's agriculture than the productivity of the soil.

There was some truth in Malthus' contention. The size of human population at that epoch in the world over had reached a level beyond which God-given land could not feed it.

Agriculture in India at that stage was one of the most advanced in the world.

In the 18th and 19th centuries, it can be said on the testimony of most recognised experts of the time, that the Indian agriculture was one of the most advanced in the world. Most of the lands were then fertile as farmers brought them under plough by rotation or kept them fallow for long periods and systematically nourished them. Bulk of the nutrients came from the biomass, cattle manure and humus sustained by generations of earthworms. Widespread attacks of pests were not very common. The locust swarms that devastated the whole countryside were taken as of God's acts like the drought and the famine. With the exception of the caprices of the nature and the tyranny of the local satraps and the marauding invaders, agriculture was largely a sustainable vocation that required very few inputs from other sectors and was, in fact, able to meet the demands of food grains and raw materials of the rest of the population. The day to day attacks of insects were taken care of by plants nourished by organic nutrients and enriched soil. The organic technology was, however, incapable of forestalling periodical famines that visited almost every decade.

It was during the Second World War that India experienced food shortages at the national level. The colonial government followed the policy of shipping food grains on a large scale for the armed forces engaged in the world war in different countries. The famine in Bengal which killed millions was only the most extreme example of the famishing of the Indian population. The partition of the country saw most fertile provinces going to Pakistan. The traders continued their practices of maintaining large stocks of food grains and the bureaucracy continued the mentality it had developed during the Second World War and imposing all kinds of restrictions on the disposal of the agricultural produce. Right till 1960s, India lived from ship to mouth on the PL 480 shipments from the United States. The conflict with Pakistan came as a God-sent misfortune which forced the politicians in power to introduce the Green Revolution technology which they had resisted over decades. In less than five years, India changed into a food surplus country as against the basket case that it was before the introduction of the Green Revolution technology.

The introduction of the Green Revolution technology was fiercely resisted by the Left parties as also by the environmentalists. The politicians had their own apprehensions about the political consequences of the Green Revolution.

Once India had attained food sufficiency and started even exporting food grains, the opponents of Green Revolution rediscovered their voices and fears. They launched a fierce campaign against the use of chemical fertilisers as also pesticides as being detrimental to the environment and to the ecology. Many of them wanted the farmers to relapse into the obscurantist old world organic farming. The organic farming has the advantage of reducing the costs of inputs at the level of the farm and making the unit more sustainable. As against that, elementary calculations showed that the N, P and K requirements of the soil for feeding the rapidly increasing populations could not be marshalled from the resources of the land itself.

The World Trade Organization and globalisation changed the scenario a great deal. Organic produce had a limited domestic market because the consumers were not prepared to pay adequate higher price for the same. The globalisation, for the first time opened the possibility of a large-scale and profitable market in the OECD countries.

A major proportion of the pesticides used in India is for production of cotton. The appearance of the genetic engineering kicked up the controversy about the use of technology in agriculture once again. The little understood character of the genetic engineering technology permitted the obscurantists to carry out a vicious propaganda against the introduction of the Bt cotton seed. This introduction showed magic results and India became, in less than three years, the second largest producer of cotton in the world. The vicious campaign of the interested parties largely supported by manufacturers of pesticides, continue to oppose genetic engineering and, particularly, GM foods.

Every petty *jhola* carrying activist running an NGO can give himself the airs of being a latter day descendent of Tolstoy and Gandhi. The anti-technology plank has become extremely popular and paying in India.

Some of the important tenets that have been brought out by the mainstream farmers' movement are as follows:

- How do the meek inherit the earth? What helps them survive and improve their situation? In the course of history, no social institution, political organisation appeared to have really worked to improve the lot of the *aam aadmi*. Throughout history, the situation of the masses and the poor appears to have improved by advent of technology. Improvement of the meek appears to have happened in most cases, in spite of the social, political and religious institutions rather than because of them. The basket case India became a food surplus country not because of any governmental initiative and measures, the miracle happened because of the advent of the Green Revolution technology.
- The life expectancy of the Indian people, particularly of the poorer classes improved significantly after Independence. This had nothing to do with any of the measures taken by the political and social institutions to improve the medical services and access of people to health facilities. The longevity appears to be improved largely due to the invention of antibiotics which substantially reduced the threat of diseases like plague, cholera, smallpox, tuberculosis which used to take a very heavy toll on the Indians.

- The real improvement in the lifestyles of the masses happens not because of any political or social institutions but because of the appearance on the scene of new technologies.
- No technology is bad or good *per se*. Every technology has its benign aspects and vicious traits. A given technology becomes popular in an epoch when its benign traits are required by the society. The same technologies can become targets of vitriolic propaganda once they have crossed the line of optimum use.
- The remedy to the less benign effects of a technology is promoting a more advanced technology and not by going back into some kind of voodoo obscurantist rituals. For example, the malicious effects of a technology based on use of chemical fertilisers and pesticides will be remedied not by falling back into organic farming but by new technologies like the genetic engineering that permits reduction of the use of chemicals and provide the possibility of a further advancement.

Technology is coming to the aid of agriculture in order to improve the yields, ensure food security and improvement of the supply and quality of raw materials. This is not all a story of the past. New dangers lurking on the horizon today can be resolved by no methods presently known to the traditional human society. The global warming, the climate change might, even at this stage, reverse the advance in food security and make it difficult for farmers in traditional food grains regions to produce their crops due to the extreme vicissitudes of temperature and precipitation.

The fossil oils may run in short supply as it has already started doing. The energy crunch can be attenuated to a significant extent by production of biofuels. Productivity of agriculture can be further improved by dispensing with the land altogether and bringing in use contraptions that were used by the space astronauts to ensure the supply of fresh vegetables for them.

The frontier technologies like remote sensing technology, aeroponics, development of drought- and stress-resistant varieties can help agriculture overcome the challenges of global warming, food insecurity and energy crunch.

---

24 November 2009.

32 Power Needs a Pitroda

The Union Power Minister, Mr. Suresh Prabhu, is certainly one of the more aware ministers. A young successful politician with a brilliant academic background and experience of the finance portfolio in a state like Maharashtra, he holds fairly rational views on a number of subjects and therefore, stands out like a healthy thumb in the sore NDA Cabinet full of saffron mumbo-jumbo and supremacy of Indian systems, in general, and *Vedic* sciences, in particular.

India veered to the path of liberalisation abandoning the socialistic pattern mainly because of the miserable plight of the economic and the social infrastructure, particularly the area of electric power.

In the early days after the Bolshevik Revolution, Lenin had pronounced that social ownership of industry and electricity would produce socialism. The followers of the Soviet pattern in India failed more miserably than their Russian intellectual mentors, and the power sector has been in shambles for over two decades.

It is indeed lucky that we have somebody like Mr. Prabhu in charge of the power portfolio. Mr. Prabhu believes in putting his hands to the wheel and also keeps in touch with the knowledgeable and the common to keep them informed of what he is trying to do. In the very first week of the new year, Mr. Prabhu addressed a letter to thousands of people in the country to apprise them of the seriousness of the power situation, as what he proposes to do about it. In it, he also solicits advice and inputs from all who may care to give them.

Since Independence, the country's power generating capacity has grown by about 100,000 MW along with the associated transmission and distribution network. The consumer coverage has grown exponentially. Yet, underlines Mr. Prabhu, we have not been able to contain energy shortages, ensure quality power and make the sector self-sustainable. On the supply side, the generation capacity is inadequate, not fully utilised, high voltage transmission lines are limited and technological and commercial losses are sizeable. On the demand side, conservation of energy and efficiency in usage are the focus areas.

What is the minister going to do about it? Power is a concurrent subject: 60 per cent of the generating capacity, 70 per cent of the transmission network and the entire distribution system are controlled by the states. A pivotal role is required to be played by the state electricity boards that are unfortunately uniformly on the brink of financial collapse. The power minister has prepared an impeccable blueprint that envisages a six-level intervention strategy. Clearly, Mr. Prabhu is all set to clear the Augean stables of the power sector through governmental activism at the national, state, SEB, distribution circle, feeder and consumer levels. Lest one feels this is yet another governmental paper-tiger, Mr. Prabhu has set up a monitoring mechanism and assures us that considerable progress has been made in augmenting the generating capacity, encouraging private investment, distributional reforms through grid discipline and all.

Further, a Power Project Monitoring Committee has been set up to monitor and produce a report for the immediate attention of the Minister.

Discussions are on with the Planning Commission for allocation of funds. Sixty-three circles are to be developed as centres of excellence for distribution reform.

States have been asked to form district-level committees for distribution and generation resource planning and to prepare detailed project reports for the identified circles.

Mr. Prabhu's letter contains a tediously longish list of similar initiatives on the part of the young minister. I wish the Ministry of Power all success, but have a feeling that even by 2012, by which time Mr. Prabhu expects everything in the power sector to be hunky and dory, little would have changed and power will continue to be a stumbling block for the economy.

The failure will be largely because Mr. Prabhu expects governmental interventions to bring about reform, sanity and efficiency in the sector. Nothing in the past record justifies this simple faith. The power sector has suffered largely because of the rigid State control and is in need of de-statisation rather than incremental State intervention.

Mr. Prabhu is treading the path of the Minister of Agriculture who continues to pin faith in the effectiveness of the State as the prime mover of development. Mr. Prabhu would be better advised to follow the model of the communications sector. Power is supplied through cables, so are telecommunication services. Surprisingly, the situation of the two services is diametrically opposite. The telecommunication services in India were in shambles 20 years ago. New technology was blocked. It took years to get a telephone connection and hours to put through a trunk call.

All this has changed dramatically and rapidly. The whole nation is dotted with private STD and ISD booths, the waiting time for a phone connection is down to a few days. STD, ISD and Internet facilities have become remarkably good. Large number of customers are toting cell phones and a customer asking for one line is being offered two.

What accounts for the difference in the rapid progress of the telecommunications and the continued stalemate of power sector? The answer simply is 'openness'. The Department of Telecommunications (DoT) was split into private sector corporations and the field was opened up for the state-of-the-art technology and private investment.

In the power sector, on the other hand, doors are cautiously being opened for private investment under strict control of the very people who were responsible for the power imbroglio.

The authorities in the power sector recognised long back the need and superiority of the private enterprise but insisted on having the private initiative under the scrutiny of the public sector, the original sinner.

The power people persist in the doctrine of paramountcy of the State sector and, rather than opening it for private investment under free market conditions, are trying to canalise it through State monitoring. The power sector can yet be transformed almost overnight in a miraculous metamorphosis if only the Prime Minister could get somebody like Sam Pitroda, as Rajiv Gandhi did.

---

30 January 2002.

33 Why Farmers want GEAC Scrapped

Farm organisations have launched an attack on the much-hyped Genetic Engineering Approval Committee for its action of arbitrarily clearing three Mahyco varieties of Bt cotton seeds while ordering the uprooting of cotton plants grown from an unapproved Bt seed, despite the latter's superior yields and environmental advantages. The farmers are justified as the GEAC has clearly overstepped its mandate.

As far back as in 1984, the farmers' movement demanded that the Agricultural Prices Commission (APC), as it was then called, be scrapped. The farmers accused the APC of deliberately manipulating and vitiating the methodology relating to the calculation of production costs of agricultural commodities in a manner that resulted in fixation of low minimum support prices.

This also resulted in procurement prices being much lower than the prices prevailing in the open market and, in fact, served as a signal of the maximum ever prices that the farmer should be allowed to receive.

More recently, in October 2002, the farmers' movement struck at another major pillar of the State domination of agriculture and demanded scrapping of the Food Corporation of India (FCI).

The FCI colossus was chargesheeted by the farmers on various counts: establishing an expansive and expensive bureaucratic set-up that had a vested interest in continuing the syndrome of food scarcity and turning it to the advantage of its sprawling empire; failure to render any worthwhile service either to the farmers or to the consumers; frustrating the objectives of the PDS and failure to ensure development of infrastructure for post-harvest handling, especially for warehousing, grading, processing and export.

The farm leaders are clearly encouraged by the results obtained. The APC was not scrapped but supplanted by the CACP (the Commission for Agricultural Costs and Prices) with a modified composition and mandate.

The whole methodology of computation of costs was reviewed and modified substantially as regards inclusion of domiciliary labour and of wages at rates lower than the statutory minimum wages.

The FCI has not become extinct either; but proposals to promote emergence of private sector warehousing networks that give an advance of over 70 per cent of the going market price and warehousing receipts that are negotiable instruments under law are under active consideration in various ministries.

Now, the farm organisations have opened attack on yet another much hyped institution: The Genetic Engineering Approval Committee (GEAC) under the ministry of Environment and Forests.

The Kisan Coordination Committee (KCC), which brings together the pro-reforms farm organisations, targeted the APC and the FCI, while the Leftist organisations stood by them. The GEAC, by contrast, is under attack from both the Left and the Right.

The green brigade NGOs—which, like watermelons, are green outside but red inside—have rallied together sundry with splinter groups of erstwhile KCC organisations and are enraged that the GEAC cleared, in March 2002, three Mahyco varieties of Bt cotton seeds.

They have demanded that the Central Vigilance Commissioner carry out an investigation in the dealings of the GEAC. The more radical KCC has demanded straightforward scrapping of the said Committee and, further, exhorted farmers to disregard the injunctions of the GEAC if they find that the impugned seed variety is, in fact, good and advantageous.

The NGOs would not go as far as the KCC to demand scrapping of the GEAC. That is understandable. Some of their henchmen have impressive paper qualifications in biotechnology and entertain hopes to be appointed to the committee sometime in future. They would not torpedo their dreamboat by demanding the scrapping of the GEAC. It suits their plans better to target the present incumbents and help create vacancies.

The KCC farm leaders' ambitions lie elsewhere and they feel that the GEAC, as it is constituted and working now, can bring no good to the farmer and farm production. They would be happy to see it disappear from the scene altogether.

The GEAC, under the Ministry of Environment and Forests, is responsible for clearing specific applications of genetic engineering after taking into account the possible environmental and other hazards. It has been in the vortex of controversy for quite some time.

It took the GEAC seven long years from the date of first application of trials to final clearance for commercial production of Bt cotton. During this interval, using the same variety of cotton seed, other cotton-producing countries have gone ahead and increased the production, the yield and quality of lint and yarn, marginalising India in the international market.

When an accident put a variety with Bt properties into the hands of Gujarat farmers and produced a bountiful crop, the GEAC was peeved at the encroachment on its competence and ordered uprooting and burning of the unlawful bounty about a year back.

Three months later, it found it pointless to withhold the permission for commercial production and gave the green signal to three varieties of Mahyco seeds, with certain conditionalities that were patently unenforceable.

The KCC carried out a comprehensive exercise to assess the comparative results in the season that had far-from-normal monsoons and fairly unusual weather conditions.

The result would not do the GEAC proud. The weaknesses in the hybrids approved by the GEAC came to the fore, lending a clear advantage to the unapproved seed.

The KCC has questioned the decision of the GEAC to approve specific hybrids rather than limit itself to its legitimate mandate as indicated in its nomenclature and approve only the CRY-1 AC and leave it to the seed producers to engineer it in isolation or along with other approved genes to produce promising varieties.

All told, the GEAC has dealt a body-blow to gene technology in India.

Newspapers are full of stories of the disastrous results of GM cotton seeds when, in fact, it is the GEAC seed that failed, and the non-GEAC Bt seeds that yielded outstanding results: yields as high as 22 quintals per acre, drastic reduction in expenditure on pesticides and labour and clear environmental advantages for crops in adjoining plots as also for health of labour working in the fields.

The cost of production of the blacklisted cotton could be as low as Rs. 500 per quintal, against the going domestic market price of around Rs. 2,000.

India could shortly become world-competitive if only the GEAC could be quarantined.

In Hindi, *asarkari* means both private and effective. That sums up well the situation of the non-GEAC Bt seed and the KCC has done a patriotic deed in demanding the GEAC's scrapping and starting a civil disobedience agitation against its misdeeds.

---

20 November 2002.

34 Farmers want Freedom, not Panacea

Of course, biotechnology is no panacea for farm sector's ills. It does not take a learned scientist to say that (K.P. Prabhakaran Nair, *Business Line,* April 15, 2003); even the illiterate farmer knows that in this world there are no panacea, no utopia and no El Dorado.

Since I have written amply in this column about technology and, in particular biotechnology, I consider it necessary to clarify my position so that it is clear to all and sundry.

From various articles that have appeared during the course of the last fortnight in various journals, and the numerous e-mails I have received all harping on single theme—that the Bollgard seed has performed much below par—I suspect there is probably a conductor for this orchestra.

I learn that the champions of biotechnology are not sitting idle either. It is reported that a group of about 50 farmers, from Andhra Pradesh especially, tried to break an anti-gene technology meeting that was being held in Delhi.

The opponents of gene technology are, understandably, furious about it. They have probably forgotten that they used exactly the same tactics over the last three years from Seattle to Johannesburg, and that they have amongst their ranks the most notorious disrupter of meeting of them all from Uttar Pradesh.

It looks like both the champions and the opponents are determined to hijack the biotechnology debate and are trying to become unnecessarily vitriolic and polemical.

The facts of what happened since the Genetic Engineering Approval Committee (GEAC) allowed commercial trials of three varieties—Bt MECH 12, Bt MECH 162 and Bt MECH 184—developed by Mahyco are fairly clear. The performance of the Bollgard seeds—all the three varieties—certainly did not make even the Mahyco people proud.

There were many cases of wilting, of low production and even of incidence of bollworms. The scientific community has pronounced itself after careful investigation.

The three hybrids that were approved have certain traits that express themselves only in certain environment.

The large-scale failure of monsoons and the accompanying high temperatures could be factors that favoured expression of these traits. Nobody can be sure, not enough investigating work has been done.

The cultivating farmers, at the end of field visits covering both Bollgard and non-Bollgard varieties, came to objective conclusions:

- That the Bt seeds, approved by the GEAC or not, performed better than even the established hybrid varieties such as Shankar.
- That the GEAC-approved Bollgard ranked lower than the unapproved Nav Bharat variety.
- That the GEAC had erred in approving three specific hybrid Bt seeds rather than limiting itself to approving just the gene CRY1AC.

The applications regarding these hybrid seeds were filed by Mahyco seven-eight years back when they were certainly some of the better varieties. During the long time the GEAC took to make up its mind, a number of better and more popular varieties have been put on the market by Indian seed companies.

Had the GEAC remained faithful to its nomenclature, the Indian companies could have introduced the gene in other varieties and might have introduced some of other identified genes, for example, the drought-resistant variety. That would have given Indian farmers better Bt seeds and allowed a more competitive situation to develop rather than a virtual monopoly to a single combine. On the basis of these conclusions, the farmers' organisations demanded that the GEAC be scrapped and that the farmers use the seed they judge as the best whether it is formally approved by the GEAC or not.

It is remarkable that none of the opponents of biotechnology have even referred to the Nav Bharat phenomenon. Could be, because it puts a question mark on the merit and performance of the official biotechnology establishment!

When scientists become unscientific they err even on facts. The Chennai Declaration talks of the need for the public to accept biotechnology; the scientists are talking of acceptance by the GEAC. Of course, nobody is advocating any reckless plunges into biotechnology. It has, however, been said that shutting doors on it can possibly be as disastrous as some of the apprehended concomitant consequences of GM seeds.

Words like 'hysteria'and 'touting' have no place in a serious scientific debate. Comparison between the Green Revolution scientists and the Gene Revolution scientists is hardly relevant to the issue either. Mr. Prabhakaran Nair has completely missed the point by taking the debate to anti-Bollgard and pro-Bollgard levels ignoring the fact that there is, in fact, a Bt variety, albeit unapproved, that has performed remarkably well.

One cannot be for a technology or against it, much less against all technological development *per se*. Every technology has its positive and negative aspects. Some are noticed in a short run, some take longer time to manifest themselves. The real issue is of 'Freedom of trial' to the farmers. Scientists, both from the private companies and the government stables, would like investigation of every possible and impossible consequence to be thoroughly examined by their clan, however long it may take.

The real issue in the debate is whether farmers can be denied access to technologies for reasons that occur to only the extreme purists in the governmental technology establishment. It is not a mud-slinging match between the champions and opponents of Bollgard; it is a campaign for securing for farmers freedom of access to technologies that have had fair trials elsewhere in the world.

---

23 April 2003.

35 For Whom is the Research Anyway?

The British empire, it is said, was won on the football grounds of Cambridge and Oxford. The Soviet empire, it can be said, was lost in its research institutes. The US research, both in physical and social sciences, has been for over a century, more innovative, paradigm shifting, relevant to the felt needs and capable of direct field application.

Nothing succeeds like excess. Whether one measures in terms of number of persons engaged in or the quantum of investment, the OECD countries are far ahead of others in the field of research. In absolute terms, these inputs are not so relevant as their quantum relative to the population the research activity serves, the gross product of the sector the research caters to, the gross domestic product of the nation or the capital investment in research per scientific personnel engaged.

The OECD countries, particularly the former imperial powers, have enjoyed some inherent advantages. They were perpetually engaged in hostilities in regions of diverse climates and topographies against adversaries who deployed a wide range of armaments and means of navigation on land and water.

The plunder of the conquered territories and the colonies provided the resources required for research and the warfare provided both the justification and possibilities of immediate application. Wars are, as a general rule, bad for the humanity at large; but the periods of warfare have been historically the most fecund for advancement of science and technology. The Second World War brought forth technologies relating to radar, antibiotics and aviation. In peace times, the spin-off of such projects as the 'Man on the Moon' have opened up whole new areas including medical engineering that has revolutionised diagnostics.

Wars and peacetime giant projects that involve national pride have always been conducive to scientific innovation.

Economic development, poverty eradication and similar peacetime humanitarian endeavours, on the other hand, have produced very little paradigm-shifting innovative research.

Imperial powers had another advantage. Empires not only provided physical resources but also mobilised the cream of brainpower from the diverse regions of colonies to the metropolitan countries rich in research infrastructure.

Far more important than the advantages of the empire were the innate benefits of private enterprise and the systems of patents and rewards and the spirit of inquiry they engendered and nursed. Industry produced ever-higher incomes and lifestyles, and scientific innovation progressed more than commensurately.

Innovation not only helped meet the increasing needs but often created new ones that in their own turn created newer ones and so on. The virtuous cycle of innovation and needs rolled on to produce an era where technology became the prime mover of improving the lot of the masses and improving their standards of living.

This did not repeat itself in the socialist half of the world. The research activity there was handed over to giant State institutions that employed a whole army of duly qualified scientists and technicians that produced lots of papers but little substantive and worthwhile innovation.

Salaried scientist who is not protected by adequate systems of rewards and patents and promotions has no incentive to be inventive. Occasionally, diktats would come from above commanding a time-bound land-mass-shifting for formation of barrages in rivers or sputniks that spurted socialist pride and awe the world.

Advancement in the nuclear, aviation and armament sciences would come more through espionage and plagiarism than through genuine innovation. Equally likely, a Stalin's crazy whim would catapult a dubious geneticist like Lysenko to world notoriety or send a genius economist to death.

In India, the advent of independence and the ushering in of the socialist era witnessed the creation a large number of national, regional and specialised laboratories and research institutions to form an impressive network.

If the planners neglected agriculture as a sector, the research network that has been developed has been very impressive.

Each of these institutions has been bestowed with vast land for fieldwork and palatial buildings fully equipped to meet all needs of creature and intellectual comfort. They all employ munificently salaried technical personnel and armies of babus.

Their review and appraisal systems are well designed. Each of these institutions has produced an impressive array of reports. Their scientists have produced papers and articles that appear in learned journals of the field. Innumerable doctorates have been won as also a plethora of plaudits, fellowships, awards, visiting professorships and honours.

Their work alas shows great aptitude for areas of interest for European and American agriculture. There is precious little work on subjects of vital interest to drought-prone regions such as monsoon prediction, development of drought-resistant traits in Indian varieties, replenishment of groundwater and most important, the viability of farming as an economic activity.

The neglect of this last aspect of the agricultural problem has led to wrong State policies, heavy indebtedness of the peasantry and mass suicides.

We have, on one side, an imposing panoply of doctoral works, honours, prizes and other forms of academic recognition. On the other, there are mass suicides of farmers that signals gross system failure of which the grand empire of agricultural institutions cannot be entirely innocent.

Some years back, I visited a grand and reputed institute celebrated for its work in food technology. It had been active by then for more than a quarter century in half a dozen palatial buildings donated by a princely family surrounded by acres of sprawling lush green lawns.

The scientists there were keen on an interaction with me. At the end of the discussion, I asked the gathering a rather naive question: What do you consider has been the most outstanding invention of the institution? The unanimous view was: A process for making baby food from buffalo milk instead of from cow milk, as is done the world over. I was taken aback. But this is something every mother has known and has been practising for centuries. Why did it take all this paraphernalia a quarter century to discover it, I wondered.

---

13 October 2004.

36 Of Bt Cotton and the Criticism against it

India has recently replaced the US as the world's second largest producer of cotton. If only India had shed its reservations against Bt cotton earlier, and more farmers had started using the seed, it could have achieved this status some time ago.

The good news for the *rabi* season 2007-08 was that India has overtaken the US as the second largest producer of cotton in the world.

In the US, some of the areas under cotton were shifted to the production of food grains. The rise in production in India by everybody's account is due, among other things, to the increased use of Bt seeds. India's advancement in cotton production is not only quantitative but also qualitative.

The bulk of the Indian cotton production is now of longer staple and can be used for production of finer cotton textiles. In many areas, the yield has increased multi-fold, which is likely to have cut the cost of production substantially.

Opposition to Bt Cotton

This is a remarkable development. A recent advertisement in a well-known American weekly featuring a pretty young woman resenting competition from Indian cotton shows how drastically things have changed.

The genetically modified seed, particularly Bt cotton, had attracted severe opposition from various quarters, because a US-based multinational company sponsored it.

The environmentalists claimed that the Bt seeds might be disastrous for Indian farmers. It was even claimed that the cattle that had grazed in the cotton fields had died of poisoning.

Some self-proclaimed champions of the cotton farmers went to the extent of claiming that most of the suicides of cotton farmers were on account of the failure of the Bt seed.

How come the seed of disaster has turned out to be the seed of prosperity? How did the forecasters of doom prove to be so completely wrong?

Genetic engineering is a new technology and it is understandable if some of the even well-meaning people had apprehensions about it. But would it be too much to expect these people to retract their criticism now? Those who opposed biotechnology raised awareness of the threat from the use of such seeds, because of which a regulatory mechanism, the Genetic Engineering Approval Committee (GEAC) was created.

These bodies worked under pressure from domestic and European environmentalists. As a result, the first Bt seed became available for cultivation seven years after it was ready for trials.

The remarkable thing is that Indian farmers were already using the gene under scrutiny. It was well known that it had no pernicious effects, no economic disadvantages and no threat to plant, cattle or human life.

Stumbling Block

The environmentalists are as much to blame as the governmental machinery that is manned by people with little knowledge of the field.

Some of the organisations opposed to genetic engineering went to the extent of physically attacking the trial plots and destroying them, which resulted in further delays. India lost the incremental crop for seven years.

Even after the seed was officially released for planting, a vicious campaign was carried out that the germination was poor and that the incidence of crop failure was very high. It was propagated that many of the farmers' suicides were because of the use of Bt cotton seed.

This certainly affected the pace of adoption of the technology. Many farmers, ignorant about the Bt seed, bravely took to the seed only after being convinced by concrete evidence in the neighbourhood and by its beneficial effects.

Were it not for these delays, India may, by now, have been the largest cotton producing country. A study needs to be carried out on the monetary losses incurred by the country due to the delay in introducing Bt seeds and its impact on farmers.

The irony is that, throughout this period, those who opposed the technology have done well for themselves.

They have been honoured, received celebrity status and even 'parallel Nobel Prizes'. They produced mountains of glossy literature with multicoloured graphs and illustrations and photographs.

The NGOs that opposed biotechnology continue to frequent the prestigious seminars and mouth the well-worn phrases without regret.

What happened in the case of cotton was nothing new. In the past, obscurantist forces have opposed the advent of mines, industry, trains, computers, river valley projects, etc., on the ground that they will bring ecological or economic disaster. Their sister organisations have opposed the use of pesticides in agriculture, saying it is hazardous. In fact, some time ago, a well-known philanthropist announced a prize of Rs. 1 crore if the activists concerned could prove any of their claims.

Modern Technology

India is on the threshold of the modern era in agriculture. Nobody denies the fact that the old methods of agriculture had their own merit in an era where the population to be fed was relatively smaller. It is generally conceded that the old style of traditional farming will not be able to feed the country today.

Nobody denies that, in the long run, modern agricultural technology might have an adverse effect on the earth, as a whole. But it is equally true that nobody can accept policies that will result in food insecurity and starvation in the present and the near future.

---

28 November 2007.

37 Relying on Technology to Feed People

There is a lot of hue and cry about climate change and global warming, though nobody is very clear what it really means. Some experts say that the average surface temperature of the globe will start rising on account of greater industrialisation; glaciers will recede, sea levels will rise and temperatures might reach unbearable levels. They also say that the rise in the temperatures will not be linear. Temperatures might show extreme fluctuations between extremely cold and extremely hot. Similarly, rainfall might also become erratic, particularly in countries dependent on monsoons.

The precipitation expected over the entire rainy season might come down in single month causing large-scale inundations, loss of property and of life as witnessed these last few years in Mumbai. Some ecologists foresee earthquakes and volcanic eruptions that can cause tsunami-like tidal waves and massive inundations.

Since this year's Nobel Prize went to the leaders of the ecological movement, every *jholawala* with some sort of an NGO outfit to back him has added his voice to the outcry on how grievously erroneous the whole approach of mankind has been to economic development since the advent of industrialisation and how the human race will need a mid-course correction, if not an about-turn, that will be based on an arrest/reversal of demographic expansion and slowing down of economic growth.

A couple of decades earlier, there were similar tirades against "capitalist" growth by the Communists and fellow travellers, who argued that growth in a capitalist economy was bound to suffer from intermittent cyclical depressions and economic crises.

If we put the words 'global warming' in the place of cyclical depressions, we get the current picture. All citizens recognise the importance of the essential planks of environmentalism:

- avoid waste of non-renewable resources, water and power,
- avoid causing pollution and environmental damage,
- avoid cutting down trees, and grow more trees, to the extent possible,
- do not deprive project-affected communities of their natural environment, livelihood and lifestyle.

But the environmentalists of today do not limit themselves to that. They target the whole developmental process as mankind has known it. Our environmental saviour resembles a watermelon, green outside but red inside.

The Communists who, in their heyday, ridiculed Tolstoy and Mahatma Gandhi as obscurantist charlatans, have taken to professing environmentalism after the fall of the Soviet Union.

When Stalin lived and ruled, these very people championed the cause of establishing a Communist global hegemony as a legitimate revolutionary aspiration.

Now, they are opposed even to the establishment of a set of rules of international trade under the World Trade Organization.

There used to be a time when they defended Stalin's holding a brief for fraudulent biologist Lysenko; now they are opposed even to genetic engineering tried and tested over half the globe.

Once upon a time, they applauded the launch of the Sputnik; now they are opposed to all attempts at exploration of neighbouring planets as alternative locations for the settlement of humanity.

Environmentalism is good business as well. The leaders of the movement receive almost instantaneous recognition as 'visionaries' concerned about the long-term prospects of humanity rather than the short-term objectives of growth and consumerism.

Doomsdays did not Happen

Over the long history since industrialisation began, not one of the catastrophes the environmentalists forecast for the world and humanity have actually come to pass. Coal miners did not destroy the earth, nor did the railways destroy the countryside.

Despite the population multiplying, men eat better and live longer today. Pesticides have not brought about the large-scale disasters that the environmentalists foresaw and the introduction of biotechnology in cotton did result in affluence for some cotton growers.

The apprehensions of the environmentalists have often been found to be based on exaggeration and misinterpretation of facts. The temperature of the earth's surface, the melting of glaciers, precipitation and the availability of water, it has been established, follow a statistical pattern that is far from off-beat.

Even if the fears of the environmentalists of an impending doomsday look like materialising, human ingenuity is capable of coping with it. Already, plans are afoot to create an artificial sundial in space to soften the effect of solar radiation.

Neighbouring planets are being explored with a view to finding a congenial environment for the settlement of generations to come.

In fact, human ingenuity is such that, as Ayn Rand puts it, even if the sun itself were to collapse, human beings would be able to replace it with a sun of their own creation.

Malthus predicted widespread epidemics and famines in a situation where the supply of land was constant and the population increased in geometric proportion. He was proved false by technological innovations that permitted citizens of today to eat more and better than his forefathers did.

Farm Technology

The new agricultural technology presupposed industrial and transport revolutions with their inevitable consequences on the environment. Humanity has a better chance of surviving if there is a major shift to genetic engineering. There is nothing like 'evil technology'. Every technology has its beneficial aspects and its less beneficial ones. When the evil effects of technologies start manifesting, man has usually found a way to overcome them by innovating further towards a more advanced technology.

Global warming and climate change portend some serious consequences for Indian agriculture. Food grains production might be drastically cut down. The White Revolution might be checkmated by the adverse effect of the higher temperatures on hybrid cows.

The food processing industry may be hit hard by the greenhouse gas effect of the processing technology. There are many large demands on the limited cultivable land available for production of substitutes for hydrocarbon products. Humanity will take the problem in its stride and find ways of overcoming them.

Humanity lives by its more innovative and enterprising members. Human ingenuity is limitless. There is no doubt that each innovation may create some new problems. But those problems, one can be sure, will be overcome by man's ingenuity.

---

16 June 2008.

V

Marketing

38 Agricultural Marketing through the Ages

An Introduction

Food is the primary necessity of all life. Edible things that sustain life come out of the earth either as plants or comestible forms of life, which in their own turn, are sustained on plants.

The early man sustained himself by gathering food or hunting. The work involved was strenuous. Historical records do not show if there ever was any surplus left after meeting the needs of the man and his tribe. It can be surmised that the surplus was at best, reserved for future consumption. The parties primarily interested in this primitive food processing were most probably women, who found themselves at the short end of the stick where the gathering of food was concerned.

There is scriptural evidence to suggest that it was again the women who discovered that the grains, on some of the vegetation growing around had eminent "belly-filling" properties. They also noticed the fact that the uncollected grains that fell on the ground germinated and produced food grains in their own turn.

It follows, that the women were the first cultivators who used a part of the grains that they collected for sowing purposes. Scripture evidences again that the cultivation by women was carried out largely by the use of a simple scratching instrument, referred to as *sphya*.

It was possibly sometime later, when the collection and hunting started giving diminishing returns that menfolk were attracted to this cultivation activity of their womenfolk. Men would not be satisfied with the low yielding *sphya* agriculture. They brought in use the horse or the bullock that they had mastered during the hunting stage, along with appropriate equipment like ploughs and other land tilling gadgets. Women lost control of agriculture and the men took over. The changeover was not unwelcome since the new agriculture produced abundant crops from the virgin soil and the age-old grain seeds.

In India, in several regions, women observe something in the nature of a "protest day" by abstaining from all food produced with the help of the bullock.

The new surplus must have proved adequate for a long period for the entire tribe/village including those who did not take direct part in agriculture. Then the man looked for agricultural marketing and did not manifest itself because of the demand of the community artisans. It arose from an adversarial situation caused by a new community, which appeared on the scene as blunders of surplus agricultural produce.

No sooner the new agriculture produced food surplus, then appeared people who had reined in horses for less peaceful purposes and had developed gadgets not for cultivation but for killing and plunder. The tribe of the plunderers multiplied very fast since the vocation was highly remunerative. The leaders of sizeable hordes of the plunderers declared themselves variously as chieftains, kings, monarchs or emperors. Townships as distinct from habitations of food producers emerged out of the settlements of these plunderers.

The most primitive and crude form of trade in agricultural produce was outright plunder with no *quid pro quo* whatsoever. Even today, the essential character of the trade in agriculture remains that of plunder. The only difference is that, with civilisation, the element of coercion got increasingly attenuated. The armed plunder was replaced by the king's revenue, ransom, taxes and other more or less sophisticated forms of unequal exchange. The king's subjects, even the unarmed ones, realised soon the fundamental weakness in the bargaining position of the farmers. Undoubtedly with the active support of the monarch and benedictions from the priest, they managed to establish a thousand ways of unequal exchange.

Food Surplus

What would have happened had the plunder not appeared on the scene when the man succeeded in producing the first abundant surplus?

It can be argued that the food surplus would have been used for diversification into secondary and tertiary activities within the food producers' community itself without the need for the development of separate townships as the centres of political and eventually, commercial and industrial power.

The indigenous plunderer monarchs did not get much respite. Very soon hoards of invaders came from across the topographical/political frontiers. Some of them went back carrying the loot; some liked here enough to settle down and establish their own empires. Some others came from across the oceans and rather than establish the centres of the political power in the conquered territories annexed the same in the larger empire, leaving the administration to a viceroy.

It must be said in favour of these new imperialists that their pillage was not shortsighted; rather than slaughter the hen that lays the golden eggs, they found it more profitable to increase the yield and the production as also the infrastructure necessary for carrying the surplus food and raw materials back to the metropolitan countries and to their colonies.

The freedom movement in India was inspired by the Gandhian ideal of self-sufficient village as also of the nation. Gandhiji could not have been an obscurantist protectionist. He was a liberal to the point of being an anarchist. His economic programme could have been only a clever strategy ploy for cutting off the supply lines of the imperial structure. His candid statement that, "the British and the towns people in India will have to answer before God one-day for their inhuman exploitation of the peasantry" could not have interested his colleagues who came, preeminently, from the town and the West-influenced communities.

Soon after Independence, the reins of power were taken over by men who had little sympathy for the food producer communities. They had a predominant interest in rapid industrialisation that was urban-centred and run by, not the native practicing artisans, but by the pen pusher *babus* of the government services and public sector. Most people in the ruling classes were familiar with the colonial tools of keeping raw materials cheap and selling finished products dear. The Gandhian qualms about the plight of the peasantry were drowned in the Nehruvian panoply of "socialism" under which Stalin had provided the scientific (?) justification and the historical inevitability of treating farmers as class enemies. The situation of the agricultural markets in India today is the result of a long tradition of plunder by feudal kings and a variety of successive invaders.

Superficial Measures

The government of the newly independent India tried to appease the food producers by taking measures of a superficial character that would not change the hard core of the terms of trade between the agriculture and industrial sector. The *zamindar* and the local *sahukar* were abolished by legislative fiats. This was done mostly by tampering with the newly created Constitution itself. Stalin demolished *kulaks*. The newly independent India's government rendered the already enfeebled village community leaderless as also fundless.

Sir Chhotu Ram of the United Punjab had already instaured the agricultural *mandis* as an improvement over the age-old system under which the traders and the procurers moved from village to village and determined the terms of exchange separately for each producer. The agricultural produce marketing committees (APMC) were expected to provide a common meeting place for the producers as also the traders and where the weights and measures used were genuine, costs of porterage and "commission agents" minimal and where the farmers received prices determined in open auction in the minimum possible time.

To the farmers already relieved at their abolition of the landlord and the moneylender, the APMCs look like the realisation of a dream. The illusion was not to last long.

- Very soon, the farmers realised that they had some advantage in the old system of negotiating with the itinerant traders making rounds of the villages where their produce remained sheltered and protected. As against that, now in the APMC yard, he found himself away from home with no lodging/food arrangements for neither himself nor any protection for his produce. On the other hand, the traders arrived at the market yard were in their own territory, in the close proximity of their residential/business premises that was convenient to them and were in no hurry to fulfil their plans of purchase. The farmer, at the other end, got in trouble if the bargain was not struck within a day of the arrival in the markets. The farmer had no possibility of transporting back his perishable produce home.

Shortchanged on Prices

There was little chance of the price offered being enough to cover even his cost of cultivation. Firstly, the traders and the commission agents had a certain advantage in being able to decide amongst themselves the price range that should prevail that day.

Nominally, there was supposed to be a regime of MSPs that were fixed by the Central government on the basis of the recommendations of the Commission for Agricultural Costs and Prices (CACP). This commission appears to have given a reasonably creditable performance during the period 1965 to 1970. Strangely after that, the chairmanship of the CACP went to a succession of economists from the leftist stable. They did not even make an attempt to conceal their anti-farmer leanings and tried to use every possible argument and trek in the trade to deny the farmers the credit for expenses on account of domiciliary wages, risk of crop loss, informal processing and insurance for domestic contingencies. Very soon, the MSPs became indications not of the minimum level to which the prices should be allowed to fall but of the highest prices that the farmers need to be paid in the market.

There exists a study, which concludes that the MSPs recommended by the CACP, year by year, have been equal to the moving average of the last three years market prices; so much for the masquerade of the CACP in the name of ensuring fair prices to the farmers.

The government did much worse than that. It had recourse to a number of measures, like jumping into the domestic market, restrictions on exports, processing, storage and transport of agricultural produce under the Essential Commodities Act—the relic of a World War II legislation kept alive for the purpose of enforcing the "Low cost economy" policies.

The PDS Hobbyhorse

Apart from the MSP operations, the Central government fixes a procurement price at which it is prepared to purchase any quantity of agricultural produce offered on the market, subject to the requirements of the PDS.

The PDS is the successor to the wartime rationing system under which the government claims to ensure supply of essential commodities to indigent people at subsidised prices. The PDS has been revised from time to time to make it better targeted towards the "below poverty line" families. The purpose of the PDS is undoubtedly laudable. The question remains if it is fair to impose the burden of such a noble mission on the admittedly impoverished, indebted agricultural community, which has been lying on the brink of suicide for decades?

The PDS is a favourite hobbyhorse of the politicians as it permits them to put on airs of unbounded generosity at the cost of the farmers. Further, it offers vast possibilities of making money by patronising favoured applicants for PDS outlets as also from purchasers of supplies diverted from the PDS.

According to a recent study, the Planning Commission came to the conclusion that, on an average, 36 per cent of the PDS supplies get diverted. In some states like West Bengal, the proportion is as high as 90 per cent. It is not astonishing that the comrades from that state are the most vociferous advocates of the PDS.

Starting from outright plunder, the agricultural marketing has evolved into a scenario where the farmer finds himself surrounded by marauders on four sides: APMC, CACP, FCI and PDS. All this can be changed by a simple economic reform, if only the latest incarnations of the old primitive horse-riding plunderers are prepared to answer before God. The developments since March 2009, when the hullabaloo about inflation started, the UPA government is, once again showing the tendency to resume the old draconian character of the system of agricultural marketing.

---

9 August 2009.

39 Markets and Elections

The Delicate Balance

In 1978, Mohan Dharia, the Minister of Commerce in the Janata Party government under Prime Minister Morarji Desai, started the routine of imposing a ban on the export of onions immediately after the harvesting season, when the producers hold stocks and lifting the ban after 5-6 months, when the stocks pass into the hands of traders.

The objective was to keep the retail prices of onions depressed when the farmers were selling them. In 1980, the ban was imposed because the retail price of onions in the Delhi retail market touched a record high of Re 1 per kg. Consequently, the farmers' wholesale price collapsed to 13 paise a kg.

The farmers came out on the roads to protest, and the government had to set in motion a market support operation through National Agricultural Cooperative Marketing Federation of India (NAFED) at 60 paise a kg. Indira Gandhi termed the ensuing general elections of 1982 the Onion Elections.

A couple of months before the announcement of the Lok Sabha Elections 2004, the Ministry of Consumer Affairs again moved to ban the export of onions. The NDA government had to beat a hasty retreat to assuage the wrath of the onion farmers. India has seen several instances of the commodity market affecting voter preferences. Art Buchwald commented, at the height of the Watergate scandal, that the Americans would have taken more kindly to President Nixon's acts of profligacy had the beef prices not been shooting up at the time. The urban consumer's vote is particularly sensitive to the movement of prices, just as electricity is a key issue for the rural electorate.

The promise of free electric power by the Congress to the farmers of Andhra Pradesh was certainly a major cause for the debacle of Mr. Chandrababu Naidu's TDP in the Lok Sabha elections.

The recent elections also threw up a new phenomenon. Even as the exit polls forecast a hung Lok Sabha, the Bombay Stock Market Index (Sensex) crashed. The unexpected defeat of the NDA and the threat of dominance of the Left parties, which had 63 seats—the largest ever number they have won since Independence, including in the heyday of Nehruvian socialism—resulted in a crash of over 800 points on the NSE—a magnitude of decline never seen before.

The principal cause was the flight of FII funds nervous at the consequences of the strong position of the Left MPs in the United Progressive Alliance (UPA) led by the Congress. The stock market crash was certainly a factor that contributed to Ms. Sonia Gandhi's 'abdication'.

The damage to the stock market was contained only after Dr. Manmohan Singh gave assuaging assurances and stern warnings. Fortunately, the leaders of the Left front realised the gravity of the situation and made the right noises. That helped the market recover, at least for the time being.

But the question is: Can one segment of the economy—investors—be permitted to have a sort of veto on the will of the people at large? Throughout the feudal times and through most parts of democratic era, landlords have had an influence quite out of proportion to their number in the social set-up. For over two centuries, organised labour has sought to influence the character of elected governments through strikes and agitations.

Strikes have been often resorted to with express purpose of bringing down lawfully established governments and preventing governments considered hostile to the cause of the labour from getting into power.

However, any attempt by traders, industrialists and investors to influence the shape and character of a government has been frowned upon as illegitimate interference with the democratic process. Even the political parties that accept funds from the captains of finance and industry are sometimes constrained to attack the latter's policies, even if only in public posturing.

There exists too a serious flaw in the mechanism of democratic governments. They are elected through elections in which every citizen has one single vote. However, the governments elected hold power not only in areas such as law and order and defence, where all subjects are equal, but also in such fields as education and economy, where all citizens are not on par.

An ideal democratic system would have not one monolithic government wielding sovereign powers in all domains, including those where it has no mandate and limited competence, but a group of governmental and non-governmental institutions. Education and cultural affairs would then be the domain of institutions selected by scholars and savants.

Welfare, social justice and poverty eradication would be looked after by NGOs or charitable institutions rather than by politicians, many of whom make a lucrative business of it.

Thus, the sections of the economy that govern the lives of ordinary people and those from the weaker sections would be largely free of governmental intervention.

In sum, the electoral processes should have a weighted franchise. This might sound atrocious and many progressive people would perhaps rise to protest against such a concept. But the fact is that a system of weightage will, over time, introduce itself into the system, whether one likes it or not.

Investors make the economy function, and provide employment and higher standards of living. As citizens with equal rights, they will cast their individual votes for the least unacceptable candidate on the list. They will also vote with their feet by walking out of the market.

This holds true not only for domestic investors but also for those resident abroad and those of foreign origin. They have the right to indicate by their investment decisions what is good for them, and their opinions should count to the extent that the economy does depend considerably on their role in it.

---

26 May 2004.

40 Why Retail Sector Needs FDI

Some of the parties supporting the UPA government are opposed to foreign direct investment (FDI) in retail trade. One school of thought is that they are doing this as one never knows when they will have to take on the Congress in Assembly elections, and would like to have the use of the *aam aadmi*, or the common man card just as the Congress used it to telling effect in the 2004 elections.

While political opposition to disinvestment, opening up the economy and even the FDI are understandable, one wonders if this has not come to a point of opposing all measures that would diminish the size of the *aam aadmi* constituency by tackling the problem of poverty. The opposition to FDI in the retail trade appears to be of this genre.

The deficiencies of the agricultural marketing system in India are too well-known to be reiterated here. Post-harvest, there is no effective agency to take care of storing, processing, grading, trading and exporting farm products. This whole chain is left to the mercies of intermediaries who do little value addition.

The introduction of the agricultural produce marketing committees (APMCs) brought but little relief. In fact, this unwittingly added one more element to the long chain of intermediaries—the local political *neta*. With links to the ruling set-up at the state and the Centre, these *neta*s manage to stymie any effort to clip their wings or reform the marketing systems. On the threshold of the era of World Trade Organization and biotechnology, far more basic and structural reforms are required. The new system should provide an interface between the farm producer and the final consumer. It should be able to collect farm produce from across the country and after processing and storage make it available to the consumer who should be assured of a reasonable price and quality. It is necessary to minimise the post-harvest wastage and make the food items in the retail shops conform to health standards.

There are now no standards or facilities for farmers to even make a preliminary assessment of the quality of their produce. The Indian farmer is in no position to compete with his counterpart from other countries for space on the shelves of supermarkets the world over. In the last decade or so, a small number of super-shops have made their appearance. Some of them do undertake some sort of processing and storage. But there are no supermarket networks with nationwide coverage that collect farm products from all over the country and make them available after processing.

A nationwide retail network or, even better, a number of competing networks, will bring about an economic revolution and can deliver a body blow to the problem of poverty and unemployment. This has been proved by experience across the world. The creation of a national or even a regional supermarket network means large capital, sophisticated technology and management skills of a high calibre. In several countries, this whole chain is well established and working well. It would be pointless for India to reinvent the wheel. So the key is FDI, accompanied by technological and management know-how. The opponents of supermarkets sing the glory of the corner-shops that give a sense of personal touch and, of course, credit. Nowhere in the world has the corner-shop disappeared.

In fact, these shops score over the supermarkets by offering the consumer fresher products, a larger variety of foods and greater personal attention. But the supermarket has its own advantages, especially of scale. Also, it allows consumers to shop for everything, under one roof. So the supermarket and the corner-shop need to coexist for the greater good of the consumer.

Another common argument against opening up the retail sector to foreign investment is of job losses. *Per se*, this may be true. But if one also takes into account the jobs generated in a variety of connected and support activities—processing, construction, hardware, furnishing, packaging, data processing and management—supermarkets have a massive employment potential.

In Europe, 5-6 per cent of the labour force is engaged, one way or another, in the retail trade.

The Prime Minister, Dr. Manmohan Singh, must put his foot down and push for FDI in retail.

---

3 November 2005.

41 Some Hard Facts about Futures Trade

On February 27, at a meeting in Alwar, Rajasthan, the President of the Kisan Coordination Committee announced that the farmers of Punjab, Haryana and western Uttar Pradesh would sell their wheat in the ensuing season through one of the futures exchanges. The next day, making an extempore addition to his prepared Budget speech, the Finance Minister announced the government's decision to take wheat and paddy out of the futures market.

The government's decision so closely following upon that of the farmers' organisations could not have been a coincidence. The government has deliberately thrown the gauntlet at the farmers, who will respond in full measures.

Last year, the competition following the entry of private traders helped the farmers get about Rs. 100 above the procurement price per quintal. It was expected that the government would continue with the openness in the market this year too. The entry of private traders last year has not, in any manner, affected the overall stock position of wheat in the country. For some mysterious reasons in June 2006, traders in Chicago were already talking about the possibility of India importing around 10 lakh tonnes of wheat, while the Agriculture Minister held that there would be no need for wheat imports that year.

Finally, the government ended up importing about 30 lakh tonnes of wheat, at a price much higher than the domestic price. The government justified the dumping operation saying that the imports would be unloaded and used in south India, reducing the cost of transport and putting the imported wheat on par with the north Indian wheat. It would appear that this was an *ex-post, de facto* reasoning and that the decisions about imports had been made much earlier in the year.

The Fall Guys

The massive imports had nothing to do with the purchases by private traders. But the Left allies of the UPA mounted a campaign against the government on this score. By then, inflation had become a hot political issue. The Left and some of the NGOs said the inflation was caused by the futures traders. On the eve of the Budget, the Congress was routed in the Assembly polls in Punjab and Uttarakhand. Thus, it was that in a knee-jerk reaction, the government decided to take wheat and paddy out of the futures market.

Earlier, the government had sent a message to private companies not to enter the wheat market till the FCI had completed its quota. Instructions were also given to Railway authorities not to book railway wagons except for FCI. Thus cornered, the private traders found it wiser to refrain from entering the wheat market.

With the ban on both private trade and the futures market, wheat growers had no option but to accept the paltry procurement price offered by the FCI and sell their produce exclusively to it. In all probability, the farmers' organisations will retaliate by boycotting the FCI procurement. The ensuing wheat procurement season threatens to be a hot one.

Futures Plan

What was the farmers' plan for selling wheat in the futures market? Some of the futures market platforms offer operations through the Internet. Some of them also provide warehousing facilities.

Any farmer can take his produce to one of these warehouses and store it there after due verification of quality and grade. He can visually ascertain the prevailing spot price as also the futures prices in various languages on the monitor.

The farmer can decide to sell at the current price, in which case he gets the full amount in cash. Or, if he decides to sell at any convenient future date, he gets an advance of about 70-75 per cent of the current price as also a warehousing receipt, which is a negotiable instrument.

On expiry of the contract date, the holder of the warehousing receipt is assured of getting the contracted price. The farmers have no difficulty understanding the scenario and would rather transact through the futures market than face the bureaucratic hassles of the FCI.

Unfortunately, the mindset still persists among many that the futures market is purely speculative and leaves open the field to unscrupulous traders.

Matching the Bids

There indeed was a time when the farmer was not a participant in futures trade and the futures market could, therefore, be used for speculations. When the futures market is truly open to farmers, it takes on an entirely different aspect.

The farmer produces crops of different types; the existing socio-economic and political framework makes it difficult for him to change the form of his produce through value-addition/processing. It is also difficult for him to make his produce available in another location where the prices may be better.

He knows well that the immediate post-harvest prices are low and that prices will rise in three to four months. However, he cannot afford to wait to take advantage of this.

Concomitantly, there are traders and consumers who need the farmers produce, but at locations other than the point of production or at a specified time in the future. The objective is to avoid costs of transport and storage.

The futures market brings together these two elements and matches the offers to sell with the bids to purchase. For the first time, farmers can choose the price at which to sell their produce. The operations of "hedging" and "options" only facilitate price discovery and risk-cover. They can be misused, but to a very limited extent under the present regime in the Indian futures market, which provides for physical delivery in most cases.

---

7 March 2007.

42 Farm Sector

Hope Lies in Futures Markets

The futures market in farm products could bring in comprehensive systems of grading, certification, warehousing and warehousing receipts, which will benefit the farmers. Tinkering with the present system of agricultural marketing will be of little help.

On January 17, the Federation of Indian Chambers of Commerce and Industries (FICCI) convened a national seminar to discuss the model rules for agricultural produce marketing committees (APMC).

While the air was thick with expectation that the Union Minister for Agriculture who inaugurated the seminar would make some announcement about the resumption of the futures trading in wheat and paddy, the minister confined himself to making a statement on the government's Food Security Mission, the Krishi Vikas Yojana, Agricultural Development Programme, the Horticulture Mission, Bharat Nirman and the National Rural Employment Guarantee Scheme and the achievements on the agricultural credit front.

Supply-Demand

It is universally acknowledged that the prices of farm produce in India are not allowed to be decided by the forces of supply and demand. The policy of "low-cost economy" has resulted in a situation where the agricultural prices do not cover even the cost of the production, where there is no post harvest link between the farm and the kitchen and the markets are dominated by a long chain of intermediaries.

The system of APMCs has done nothing to remedy this situation. It has failed to ensure systems of standardisation, grading, weighment and timely payment.

These committees have funds at their disposal and have become the favourite playground of the second-generation politicians who are more interested in deriving benefit of the prime lands put at their disposal by the government, rather than provision of storage, processing and marketing services.

The failure of the marketing mechanism has been the cause of agricultural indebtedness and the farmers' suicides.

The situation in other countries is quite different. The consumer in the western world pays much higher unit prices, even for food grains, vegetables and fruits, even though food forms a relatively smaller proportion of his family budget.

The farmers there get a much higher share of the prices paid by the consumers. Still, the governments there consider it necessary to pay hefty subsidies to the farmers. What explains this contradiction?

The physiocratic truth is that agriculture is the spring of physical multiplication of wealth. A farmer sows a single seed and gets a thousand grains. Then where does the physiocratic surplus disappear in India?

By its very nature, agricultural production is relatively decision-inelastic. The farmer cannot respond promptly and adequately to the market situation. The decisions in the field take a long time to get reflected in the market.

Further, most of the agricultural produce are perishable in nature and need expensive processing and packaging to be able to stand in the market.

India-Bharat Divide

Lastly, social systems evolved over a period of time have made the town and country divide a universal phenomenon.

In India, caste system and the monsoons fossilised the town and country divide into a permanent feature through the feudal, the colonial (town and country) and the post-Independence (India and Bharat) periods.

The India-Bharat divide has also led to a degree of resentment. The consumers were required to pay prices that depended on urban incomes while the farmers had to submit to the prices that depended on Bharat incomes.

The policy of mopping up agricultural surplus for the benefit of the industrial development continued even after the 1991 reforms were initiated and also during the NDA and UPA regimes.

Futures Market

In spite of the new forms of agricultural marketing, involving such innovations as e-choupals' farm contracts, direct purchases by processing units are becoming increasingly common. The commodity exchanges and futures markets are multiplying real volumes of transaction.

It is futile for India to reinvent the wheel and tinker with a bygone marketing system. The futures markets offer the possibility of making up for the lost time and catching up with the rest of the world in one single stride.

Futures markets could lead to a paradigm shift in the Indian agriculture. It would permit scrapping of a lot of dead-wood, such as the CACP, the FCI as also the PDS and bring in comprehensive systems of grading, certification, warehousing and also negotiable warehousing receipts.

It would also promote consolidation of fragmented holdings. The FIIs and the FDIs can bring in the much needed investments in the agricultural sector.

Unfortunately, the UPA government, under political pressure from its Left allies, is unwilling to make agricultural markets really free and transparent.

Faced with suicides by thousands of farmers, it is putting on a show of bringing about major changes in agricultural marketing while, in fact, it is merely tinkering with the outdated system of APMCs and continues its age-old anti-farmer policies by resisting the installation of futures markets.

---

23 January 2008.

43 Futures Trading

Why the Panel may be Flummoxed

At the end of the discussion on the price situation in the Rajya Sabha on April 17, as the Minister for Agriculture, Mr. Sharad Pawar, came to the end of his reply, a question was raised from the Left benches about the government's position on the forward markets. In reply, Mr. Pawar mentioned that an expert committee appointed under the chairmanship of Prof. Abhijit Sen had been deliberating the issue for 14 months and was yet to submit its report, though it was to have done so in its report in the stipulated two-three months.

The Minister said that if the report was not submitted within the next 10 days, he would call for a meeting of experts on the subject and take a final decision on the future of futures trading, in the light of the severe opposition to these markets reflected during the discussions in the Rajya Sabha and in the recommendations of the Standing Committee on Agriculture on the subject. Coming from a politician and statesman of Mr. Pawar's vintage, this was an unusual statement.

Even presuming that Prof. Sen's panel had failed to show the necessary alacrity in respecting the time schedule, it would be unfair to decide the issue outside the Committee and punish the innocent market and the farmers for no fault of theirs.

Further, one wonders why the Minister took the trouble of appointing a Committee if he knew knowledgeable people who could be called for consultation.

Little Innovation

Throughout the discussion in the Rajya Sabha, the Minister dealt at length on the efforts the government was making to ensure food security, by restricting exports and facilitating imports, and the mechanisms of CACP

(MSPs), FCI and the PDS. This, by itself, suggested that the government was thinking more of the traditional means of ensuring food security rather than experimenting with innovative and little understood mechanisms.

The statement by the Minister of Agriculture seems to have made Prof. Sen's position even more difficult. Last year, at about the same time, the matter of the utility, or otherwise, of the futures markets was brought to him for examination. Even though the terms of reference of the Committee did not so suggest, it was obvious that the government was apprehensive about what the futures market could bring in.

It was quite clear that the futures market was an unwanted baby—of a different gender from the licence-permits-quota type of market systems that the government had carefully nourished till then. Prof. Sen's problem was that the baby was indeed of a different gender but, despite the crude attempts at getting rid of it, was alive and kicking and threatened the basic structure of the traditional agricultural marketing policies based on CACP-FCI-PDS.

Terms of Reference

The terms of reference of the Abhijit Sen Committee, as distinct from the unwritten agenda of the government, were benign. The Committee was appointed in March 2007 to:

i) study the impact of the operation of futures markets on commodity prices;
ii) suggest methods to minimise such impact; and
iii) recommend ways in which the farmer's participation in the futures markets can be increased.

It was not the case that the futures market possibly had an inflationary effect. The problem was that forward trading and the futures markets resurrected by the NDA government go against the Central government's policies since Independence in respect of commodity markets based on MSPs, procurement from FCI and the PDS in the name of the weaker sections.

The opposition of the Left parties to the futures markets came essentially from the conviction that it belonged to the wrong—liberal—

gender. It was hoped that the Sen Committee would give them the authority to abort it.

The mandate of the Sen Committee is simple enough. It is intriguing why the Committee is taking such a long time to submit a report which, it had been thought, could be submitted in just 90 days. The problem seems to be as follows. The Committee found little evidence to suggest any links between market price hike and volatility that could be directly linked to the operations of the futures markets.

Under these circumstances, all that the Committee had to do was to make recommendations about how the performance of the futures markets could be further improved by sanitising the spot markets, improving finance to the commodity markets and promoting farmers' response by facilitating it.

Uncomfortable Facts?

It is not that the panel was to study the desirability or otherwise of lifting/ continuing the ban on the futures trade. The futures trade was resurrected in 1993 and at least, three multi-commodity exchanges are doing pretty well with geometrical expansion of the volume of transactions.

Further, it shook up established notions that the commodity market should be eternally based on three pillars of CACP, FCI and PDS.

- CACP that would help determine the MSPs; Statutory minimum prices are also, by corollary, the procurement prices;
- FCI that manages procurement of food grains and their conduit to different states; and
- PDS that would ensure retail distribution according to decisions taken by the government.

If the Committee submitted its honest findings the government would be forced to permit the normal delivery of the futures market infant. The problem for the Committee, probably, is that it would raise a number of very inconvenient questions that would make the candid recommendations unpalatable to the government.

What purpose would the CACP serve in a situation where the futures market platforms offered not only a firm and timely indication of the prices to expect at the harvest but also provided an ironclad assurance, as also insurance, that farmers would be able to collect the prices? Further, since the commodity markets in India provide warehousing facilities, banking and finance, insurance as also negotiable warehousing receipts, what function would be left to justify the existence of FCI, which had become notoriously unpopular with the farmers, most of whom see it as both inefficient and expensive? Lastly, with the procurement of the food grains decentralised, was it really necessary to create a separate PDS network for the benefit of the weaker sections of the population? Would that purpose not be better served by simply mailing the targeted people food stamps or smart cards, which would also obviate the substantial diversion of food grains from the PDS system?

---

23 April 2008.

44 Ban on Futures Trading

Anti-Farmer, not Anti-Inflation

The recent ban on futures trading in four agricultural commodities is against the interests of the farmers. The ban is a result of the compulsions of coalition politics and is unlikely to bring down inflation.

On May 4, Mr. P. Chidambaram, the Union Finance Minister, announced in Madrid (Spain) that the Indian government might impose a ban on the futures trading in agricultural commodities, if there is a public perception, true or not, that futures trading led to inflation. A motion for breach of the privilege was moved in the Rajya Sabha against the Finance Minister for making a policy statement outside the House while Parliament is in session.

On April 30, responding to the debate on the Finance Bill 2008-09 in the Rajya Sabha, the Finance Minister had made a statement to the effect that the securities transaction tax (STT) is on all fours with the commodity transaction tax (CTT). It became quite clear that Mr. Chidambaram has rather woolly ideas about the working of the futures markets. He also seems to nurse a grudge towards the futures markets and also towards the farming community, its main beneficiaries.

Any doubts were soon dispelled when the Forward Markets Commission, evidently on signals from the Finance Ministry, banned futures trading in four agricultural commodities—refined soya oil, rubber, grams (*channa*) and potatoes—after business hours of Parliament on May 7. The objective of the ban was to curb the spiralling inflation over which the government had lost all control. The Left parties, allies of the UPA that have the critical number of votes required to sustain or bring down the government, have been vociferously demanding a ban on all trading in the agricultural commodities on the futures markets, if not the futures markets themselves.

An expert committee appointed under the chairmanship of Prof. Abhijit Sen, a member of the Planning Commission, had submitted its report only recently. Clearly, the majority view was that futures markets had no built-in inflationary tendencies. It is to be noted that the May 7 decision had brushed aside the recommendations of the Sen Committee.

What are Futures Markets?

In order to understand what the whole controversy is about, let us try to understand what commodity futures markets are and how they function.

Farmers, according to a schedule dictated by the monsoons, produce agricultural commodities. Most of the agricultural produce arrives in the market at about the same time. As a consequence, commodity prices sink during the harvest time to their lowest level and start rising after that till the next harvest.

Unfortunately, farmers do not have the ability to store their produce and wait for prices to become more favourable. Similarly, during the harvest, prices are relatively higher at places farther away from the fields. However, the farmer does not have the capacity to transport his produce to such locations and take advantage of the higher prices.

As the counterpart of the farmer, who would like to take advantage of higher prices in future or at a different place, there are consumers, traders, processors who would like to take delivery of the produce at a future date or at another place rather than on the spot and at the time of the harvest.

Their objective is to avoid the expenditure of storage, preservation, and also the interest charges for storing the produce till such time. The futures market essentially performs the role of bringing these two parties together. Further, it offers a transparent system of matching offers and demands to discover the right price. Thirdly, it offers the contracting buyer or seller the assurance of receiving the contracted price.

Farmers Benefit

The farmers are the main beneficiaries of the futures markets. Firstly, these markets give information at the time of sowing, the price that can be expected at the time of the harvest.

This helps the farmers to make an informed decision about what crop to sow. In the traditional system, this role was performed by the CACP, which announced the minimum support price before sowing started. Unfortunately, for decades the Commission has failed to satisfy even farmers' minimal aspirations.

If the producers and consumers were the only parties interested in business, the volume of transactions would be very thin; the entire business transaction would be limited to a few months around the harvest time. In order to ensure greater volumes of transactions, greater depth and greater liquidity in the market, the organisers of the futures markets permit the entry of speculators.

Speculators are essentially traders who buy at low prices and sell when the prices start rising. They essentially lend stability to the agricultural prices and eliminate erratic volatility of prices. The mechanism of the futures markets can also provide an insurance against price risks through hedging operations. Most of the members of the Sen Committee had given the futures market a clean chit and strongly supported its working, particularly from the point of view of the farmers.

The Government was expected to start taking measures, based on the Sen Committee report, that would foster the participation of the farmers and improve the working of the existing futures markets to make it more farmer-friendly.

Unfortunately, the ignorance of the working of the futures markets is too rampant, not only amongst the communists but also amongst the socialists of the local variety. The May 7 decision, where a ban was imposed on the four commodities, came out of the compulsions of the politics of coalition and the unwillingness of the UPA to do anything that would displease its Left allies.

No Effect on Prices

Let us examine the claim that the ban was motivated by the desire to curb prices. The facts do not bear this.

Right now, the prospects of an abundant potato crop look good and the farmers, particularly in Bihar and Uttar Pradesh, have begun to destroy their potato crop. Banning any kind of trade in potato at this point of time clearly goes against the interests of the farmers.

Banning of trade in refined soya oil follows a similar pattern. India imports edible oils in large quantities. Recently, the UPA government had reduced the customs duty on edible oils to encourage imports to bring down domestic prices. In this situation, futures trading provides traders the possibility of hedging in order to cover the price risks.

Futures trading in rubber has been working very well with farmers' participation increasing continuously. The ban on futures trading in rubber will be a setback for the rubber industry and producers. It is true that the *channa* (gram) prices have been going up in recent weeks. Since *channa* is a major *rabi* crop, there is nothing unusual in this trend.

The ban on futures trading in the four commodities is unreasonable, ignorant of the realities of the futures markets and possibly, disastrous for the futures trade. It is unlikely to have any impact on inflation. It is more political, as it is calculated to give the public an impression that the government is not sparing any efforts to come to grips with the problems of scarcity and inflation.

Last, but not the least, the order issued by the Forward Markets Commission (FMC) raises a very important question about the capacity of a regulatory body, subordinate to the government, to take autonomous decisions that would be in the interests of the market. If the members of the FMC were genuinely interested in the welfare of the farmers, they should have offered to resign rather than meekly endorse the ban order.

---

21 May 2008.

45 War on the Commodities Markets

About six months ago, the cries over rising prices started getting shrill. The UPA government found itself in a spot. It was difficult for the knowledgeable Members of Parliament from the Congress party to explain the high tide of inflation. The euphoria caused by claims of high rates of GDP growth started diminishing rapidly.

Even the Left allies mounted an attack on the treasury benches that was clearly embarrassing on the eve of the discussion on the Indo-US nuclear treaty. The Manmohan Singh government did exactly what every government since Independence has done when faced with a situation of shortages and rising prices. Are the prices of edible oil going up? Import it; if necessary, reduce the import tariff on it. If the farmers get discouraged and react by actually reducing production, so much the worse for the farmers and the future government that might be called upon to face the music. Are food prices going up? Ban the export of rice, corn, milk powder and what not. If depressed domestic prices make farmers unhappy, that is a problem for the day after; the important thing is to save the situation now.

Is the rise in prices significant in commodities that are traded on the futures market? Ban the futures markets. The markets are bad *per se* and futures markets are the dens of gamblers. That is a good slogan to appease the *aam aadmi* who is looking for a scapegoat for the rising inflation.

No Real Link

What does it matter that a committee appointed by the UPA government itself had come to the conclusion that there was no causal link between the working of the futures markets and the rise in prices or even the volatility of prices?

The government had earlier banned the futures trading in pulses, wheat and rice. It now proceeded to ban the trading of potato, rubber, refined soya oil and *channa*. The remarkable thing is that the ban on trading in potato and rubber came at a time when potato producers and rubber planters were desperate and even on warpath because of the depressed market conditions. The government further made its intentions clear by imposing a terrible commodity transaction tax (CTT) on the futures market of Rs. 17 per Rs. 1 lakh.

Understandably, the trading in the commodity exchanges started declining. It became quite clear that the government was determined to suppress all futures trading in agricultural commodities. The UPA government was never happy about the fact that futures marketing was resuscitated by the NDA government from the state of coma that the earlier regime had succeeded in reducing it to.

What does it matter if experts gave the futures market a clean chit? In politics, a handful of experts don't count, what counts is the swell of mass opinion.

The Finance Minister, Mr. P. Chidambaram, found it convenient to make a statement on May 4, 2008 that if popular opinion was against the futures market, the government could not be oblivious to that fact.

No CTT Anywhere Else

The Finance Minister made this policy statement in Madrid, when both Houses of Parliament were in session. The statement clearly constituted a statement of policy made outside Parliament. It was, clearly, a breach of privilege. The Finance Minister succeeded in getting a motion for breach of privilege scuttled.

Further, on May 30, 2008, while replying to a debate on the Finance Bill 2008-09, he brushed aside the criticism on the CTT, claiming that the CTT existed in many countries in the world and that the CTT was very much like the securities transaction tax (STT) on stock market transactions.

The leaders of the farmers in Parliament would not take this lying down. They went to the trouble of contacting all the commodity exchanges across the world and obtaining replies in writing if anything like the commodity transaction tax or any levy of that character existed there.

The conclusion was that the only case where something like a commodity transaction tax existed was in tiny Taiwan.

Even there, CTT exists only in respect of gold traded on TAIFEX, a stocks and derivatives exchange platform. And the rate of CTT there is only about 25ps per Rs. 1 lakh, against Rs. 17 per Rs. 1 lakh that the Finance Minister was defending.

It should be noted here that there is no transaction tax in India on gold exchange traded funds (ETFs), which are traded on the stock exchange platform.

Surprisingly, the situation in India is that the transactions in gold traded on the futures market will be subject to CTT, though the CTFs would be free of all taxes.

The world's top 25 commodity derivatives exchanges that record 99.99 per cent of the total volume of all commodity exchanges do not levy a CTT. The taxes imposed in some of the European countries are in the nature of a value added tax (VAT) on services rendered by the markets.

Soon after being sworn in as a Prime Minister, Dr. Manmohan Singh had articulated his vision of "creation of a single market across the country for both manufactured and agricultural produce".

How does that go with a Finance Minister who tries to snuffle out the futures markets, defies Parliament by making a policy statement in far away Madrid when the House was in session and gives Parliament incorrect information on the situation of futures markets worldwide?

The Prime Minister does not have even the pretext of the 'coalition *dharma*' to justify the departure from his vision statement. The anti-market parties are off his back now. It is time he listened to his inner voice.

---

10 September 2008.

VI

Exit Policy for Agriculture

46 Property Rights and Exit Policy for Agriculture

An Introduction

A widespread misconception about agriculture in India is that it is in the private sector. Agriculture is more in the public sector than in the private sector. It would be more appropriate to say that agriculture is in the captive sector.

The farmer in India is not a landowner. He is only a leaseholder. India has picked up the British concept of *"eminence juris"* which means that all land belongs to the monarch. All land in India belongs to the State. All private citizens are, at best, leaseholders. The transactions of purchase and sale take place, in fact, in lease property. The State continues to have the right to acquire any land for any purpose of the State.

Agriculture requires a large number of inputs. Most of the agriculture is dependent on monsoons and rainfall. It is only a small proportion of the agricultural land which is irrigated through the governmental schemes. An overwhelming majority of farmers irrigate their lands through open or bore wells and lift irrigation schemes.

All other inputs like fertilisers and pesticides are very strictly controlled by the governmental decisions. Until recently, even the seeds were a quasi-monopoly of the State. It is only recently that the private sector is figuring in the supply of seeds, particularly those generated by frontier technologies.

Even though the labour is hired locally by the farmers, the wage rates as also the perks for the farm labour are determined by the State. Much worse, the State enters the labour market by offering work under the employment guarantee schemes where little work is done, few assets created. The labour shows a marked preference for the work on EGS-like schemes irrespective of the relative wage levels since, more often than not, wages are paid for signature on the muster rather than for a day's work.

As regards the agricultural produce, the government has, over decades, followed a policy of deliberately depressing agricultural prices and imposing on the farmers a negative subsidy. Under popular pressure, the government was induced to introduce a system of procurements and minimum support prices. However, the system is so operated that the minimum support price announced by the State actually functions as a signal for the maximum price that need be paid to the farmer in the market.

The enterprises in the public sector are sheltered by the State in diverse ways. Agriculture is not in the private sector. It is a sector which is exploited by the government and according to its current policies.

The Indian Constitution, at its inception in 1951, guaranteed people the right to property including the right to acquire, maintain and dispose it off. In the first flush of anti-moneylender and anti-landlord enthusiasm, Nehru's government passed land reform bills that were declared by the judiciary as void. The government then proceeded to amend the Constitution itself, not to provide loopholes for land reforms but for abolition of the right to property altogether.

Under various laws passed successively, the government has the right to take over the land held on lease by any farmer given the pretext of some kind of a public purpose. In most cases, the courts even refused to entertain any applications against the government assertion of the land being acquired for a public purpose. More recently, the courts entertained applications about the adequacy of compensation.

Till recently, the right to dispose off agricultural lands was not felt as an important matter. The land prices were very modest, if not low. The acquisition order of the State was considered as a bolt from the blue and taken as one of the misfortunes coming through divine curse.

In the case of normal transactions of sale, there was a tendency to understate the price in order to reduce the stamp duty payable thereon. In order to remedy the situation, the government introduced a system of fixing the "stamp value" of land, which, amongst other things, was based on the prices recorded in sales deeds in recent times. Inevitably, the stamp value of any piece of land used to be much less than the going market price.

The post-1998 shift in paradigms of economic growth, the quantum jump in the rate of growth to over 9 per cent changed the scenario completely.

The appearance of the special economic zones made the prevailing stamp values as also the market prices largely irrelevant. The government sought to make available lands to the prospective industrialists at very low prices and acquire lands of the farmers at prices that were lower still.

There was considerable resentment and even resistance to these moves. The busybody NGOs found this a good occasion for opposing the industrial houses and the multinationals. While arguing the case for the farmers, they are unnecessarily opposing the concept of the special economic zones themselves, rather than confining themselves to defending the property rights of the farmers. One of the arguments they made was that good agricultural lands, particularly those that produce two or more crops in a year should not be used for the development of special economic zones.

By this time, the fact that agriculture is a losing proposition was universally accepted and recognised. Thousands of farmers had committed suicide to avoid humiliation at the hands of recovery officials. According to a survey conducted by the Planning Commission, almost half the farming community was inclined to leave agriculture as a vocation.

The industrial houses themselves found that getting lands through State acquisition was not a very attractive proposition. It generated resistance amongst the farmers which could, in the long run, be harmful to the peaceful operations of the industry. The industrialists as also the real estate builders started having a preference for approaching the farmers directly and paying them the price that would keep them contented. This resulted in an unforeseen skyrocketing of land prices.

The farmer who had suffered agricultural losses for generations found the new prices fairly attractive. At about the same time, the threats of global warming and climate change started looming on the horizon. The farmers realised that "under the sky" agriculture was not viable any more and that continuation in agriculture would demand recourse to a large number of fairly complex technologies. The prevailing high prices of agricultural lands were even seen as a good opportunity for a golden shake hand to agriculture.

The question of agricultural lands has never been viewed as a matter involving the fundamental right to property. Agreed that, agriculture is a thankless vocation that has driven thousands to suicide; but there are some people who like to pursue agriculture for the love of it, for the pleasure they get out of seeing plants growing under their own eyes and tending to them. Such people have the right to continue pursuing agriculture whether it is economically worthwhile or not.

The decisions about what kind of land to acquire is not a function of the fertility or the productivity of the land. As long as a farmer wishes to continue agriculture, no government should have the right to acquire it through legal fiats. On the other hand, if a farmer does not wish to pursue agriculture for whatever reasons, he should have the full possibility and freedom of disposing off his land in any manner, to any person, at any time at a compensation that would be acceptable to him.

For some time now, the industrial managers have sought to deal with the problem of low productivity, of labour and over-recruitment through offers of golden shake hand.

Most farmers in India pursue the vocation because their forefathers have bequeathed the land on them. They grew as young children in surroundings conducive to their adoption to the vocation. However, if a possibility offers itself they tend to leave agriculture and go into some other vocation. Farmers, on par with all the citizens have a right to pursue any vocation under the Constitution.

There has been an invisible wall between agricultural sector and other sectors. The immobility of labour has caused serious problems for agriculture. It is desirable to have inter-sectoral flushing of populations.

The post-Independence waves of abolishing of moneylenders, landlords and the advent of the Green Revolution technology forced many old farmers to accept whatever compensation was given by the acquiring authority and go and settle in some other vocation. None of them has regretted it, except for some kind of nostalgic rememberance of the old world life.

Agriculture needs an exit policy that permits unwilling farmers to leave agriculture and non-agriculturists endowed with the necessary managerial, technological and financial abilities to enter agriculture.

---

24 November 2009.

47 Picking up the Resettlement Gauntlet

By planning to bring before Parliament a Bill on the resettlement of people displaced by land acquisitions for various projects, Mr. Raghuvansh Prasad Singh is taking on a big challenge that could bring about a revolution in rural development.

The Union Minister for Rural Development, Mr. Raghuvansh Prasad Singh, emulates his Rashtriya Janata Dal leader in many ways. He is as effective a speaker as the Railways Minister, Mr. Lalu Prasad—minus the latter's inimitable humour—enjoys his rustic image and the company of people. This is common knowledge.

Daunting Task

What is not appreciated is that Mr. Raghuvansh Prasad Singh is bringing about a revolution in rural development on the lines of Mr. Lalu Prasad's in the Railways.

On June 9, speaking at a convention at Vigyan Bhavan, Mr. Raghuvansh Prasad announced his intention of undertaking a task so daunting which no predecessor in the Ministry had dared even mention—to bring before Parliament a Bill on the resettlement of people displaced by land acquisitions for various projects.

One can understand what provoked him to do this: The recent demand by Narmada Bachao Andolan (NBA) activists that work on the dam be stopped till the resettlement process is complete.

Right to Property

What is the claim of the project-affected people to resettlement? Some time back, the Judiciary struck down the idea of the government promising project-affected people priority in governmental jobs.

"If those who had property at some stage can claim privileges because they lose that, what about those who never had any property?", questioned the court.

The claim of the project-displaced people cannot be based on the tenuous humanitarian argument. It must have a sound legal basis. Unfortunately, none exists.

Those who drafted the Constitution had provided for a right to property. It was specifically laid down that no property could be taken over by the State except through legal processes and that too, on payment of adequate compensation.

This provision by itself was a rider to the Principle of Eminent Domain that India borrowed from the British.

Vesting of all property in the State is a part of political sovereignty.

The State allows its citizens enjoyment of land, subject to such conditions as it may impose, including payment of rent. Under Eminent Domain, the government merely takes away what it had given.

Under such a situation, there is no justification for the demand for compensation by the people whose land is acquired for what the State considers is a public purpose.

If the citizens had a right to property, one can imagine a system where they would have recourse to the judiciary to question the justification as also the compensation for the deprivation of the rights.

The fact is that successive pseudo-socialist governments have had a whack at the Article that confers right to property and Mr. Raghuvansh Prasad Singh will have to undo the effect of a slew of Constitutional amendments to restore the property right as was enshrined in the Constitution (in its unamended form).

Unless there is a right to property, there is no question of its claim, either for compensation or for resettlement.

The NBA leaders simply failed to grasp the legal situation in the Narmada issue and organised a campaign for the restoration of the property rights. This was not an innocent omission.

The leaders were obviously put off by the idea that the demand for restoration of property right would invite the charge of being pro-capitalism.

There was yet another complication in the Narmada issue. The land threatened by inundation belonged to the tribals, on paper. However, richer tenants, mostly from Gujarat, cultivated them. Any scheme of compensation or settlement would benefit only the tribal owners and not the moneyed tenants. It is this class that is trying to safeguard the land by opposing the construction of the dam itself and pushing the NBA leaders to an environmental agenda *vis-à-vis* the less glorious peasant agenda of resettlement/compensation.

When the government offered cash compensation, the leaders asked for compensation in kind.

The demand came from the urban elitist leadership that was ignorant of the fact that agriculture is a losing proposition and that anyone who had the opportunity to quit agriculture would benefit. The bureaucracy readily accepted this.

Then, the government offered for each acre of affected land, an acre of irrigated land; a minimum of five acres of irrigated land to those who had less than five acres; cash endowment for construction of houses; assistance for bringing the land under cultivation; and resettlement of integral communities in colonies with water, power and schooling facilities. This was, obviously, the most munificent compensation ever given in the world to project-affected people.

So much so, in many cases, the people in the resettlement colonies became the subject of jealousy for those in the neighbouring villagers, leading to frequent clashes.

The NBA, by opting for the environmental agenda, appears to have forsaken the resettlement question, although on the face of it, the activists continue to argue for resettlement.

Draft Resettlement Bill

Mr. Raghuvansh Prasad Singh was moved by the Narmada case that represents the cause of the project-affected people. But he will need to be wary in drafting the Bill on the issue of resettlement of project-affected people.

The Bill would probably propose a resettlement authority, with a chairman and a high-power panel that will be entrusted with all powers on compensation and resettlement. That will only be an addition to the slew of recent legislation.

One supposes Mr. Raghuvansh Prasad Singh would restore the Constitution to its original form by reinstating the right to property and scrapping all the amendments made by the pseudo-socialist governments to defeat judicial pronouncements. Further, the compensation for the acquisition should be equal to the market price of the property.

The state governments carry out this exercise of normative market prices by fixing stamp values, depending on the circumstances. As a consequence, in general, the compensation received by the aggrieved party is only a fraction of the market price.

To provide transparency, the government will have to develop a ready land market that will facilitate 'the exit and the entry' in agriculture. This kind of a solution will not be limited only to the problem of the resettlement of the project-affected people but will be a major step in the direction of agricultural take-off and 'Bharat Nirman'.

It is hoped Mr. Raghuvansh Prasad Singh will do a 'Railways' in the Ministry of Rural Development.

---

14 June 2006.

48 Let the Tribals Speak for Themselves

The National Tribal Policy should be based on opening up tribal societies and giving their members the freedom to choose the lifestyle they would like to lead. It is time tribals were allowed to take charge of their development rather than non-tribals with romantic notions of tribal life being empowered to decide their fate.

India's tribal communities rarely attract public attention. They become news only when they are displaced from their traditional environment.

NGOs are usually the first to take up cudgels on behalf of such displaced communities, demanding that tribal lifestyles and culture should not be disturbed and that their rights to the forest products should be protected. Otherwise, these 85 million people, constituting 8.2 per cent of the population, live isolated and unnoticed in 15 per cent of India's territory.

Now the Ministry for Tribal Affairs has started work on framing a National Tribal Policy, a draft of which has been circulated for comment.

The basic problem in drafting a policy for tribal communities is summarised in the Preamble: "The dilemma in preparing a new policy for the Scheduled Tribes in India is how to strike the right balance between preservation of tribal identity and ensuring their access to mainstream society." The preservation of the tribal lifestyle and culture appears to be a pet hobbyhorse of the urban gentry and of civil society organisations formed exclusively from the non-tribal segment of society. Centuries back, the tribals beat back the aggression of the non-tribal society and, since then, a sort of uneasy ceasefire prevailed till the commencement of British rule. The British, in general, respected the sanctity of tribal customs and territory.

With the advent of the British, tribal societies started getting the benefit of health services and educational facilities. Those few tribe members who qualified in the education system and ultimately joined the outside society never regretted the fact, nor ever seriously considered coming back to the tribal fold. And those of them who went back did not do so to resume the lifestyle of the tribals but as outsiders trying to bring home the values of another society.

The British clearly wished for a deepening alienation of the tribal society from the rest of the country. Thus, the missionaries, with an eye on conversions, and anthropologists with respectable academic credentials joined hands to uphold and justify the distinct identity of tribal communities. The political leadership that came to power after Independence shared the attitude of the colonial regime, except that relating to conversion to Christianity and providing a vast field for anthropological studies. Nehru had a fetish for artificially preserving islands of culture as pieces of archaic curiosity. He was keen on preserving Pondicherry as an island of French culture, and Goa as a piece of Portuguese history and mores.

Constitutional Provisions

The Constitution contains several provisions for ensuring a better quality of life for the weaker sections, including the Scheduled Tribes, based on a policy of positive discrimination and affirmative action. The Constitution contains several Articles exclusively devoted to the Scheduled Tribes; these include Articles 244, 244(AA), 275(1), 342, 338(AA) and 339. Schedule V of the Constitution provides for Administration and Control of Scheduled Areas and Scheduled Tribes under the governors.

None of these provisions has done much of good to tribal communities, which continue to be afflicted by poverty, disease and ignorance. Only the Christian missionaries appear to be bringing some substantive good, at whatever price. The situation of the tribals has become a favourite ground of the NGOs.

The colonial attitude of looking at tribals as an archaic curio, a tourist attraction, was inherited by civil society activists from the non-tribal society, which tries to politicise and romanticise the tribal identity and lifestyle. These enthusiasts, rosy-eyed about "living close to nature" and the "divine quality of rustic life", come from urban society, perhaps in the full confidence that they will never be required actually to suffer the hardships of the tribal lifestyle. Not many have cared to ask if the tribals themselves wish to continue with their old culture and values. If asked, the tribals would, of course, defend their lifestyle.

But the fact remains that every tribal who gets an opportunity to walk out of the quagmire of tribal life votes with his feet and leaves. In any case, they all do better by the Human Resource Development (HRD) standards; no matter where they figure in the anachronistic Tribal Values Index (TVI).

Real Freedom

The efforts to raise the HRD level of tribals have been seriously thwarted by the fact that we are in two minds whether the HRD standards are applicable to tribal societies at all.

We try, in vain, and ride the twin horses of preservation of tribal culture and of HRD, with the result that tribal societies have remained as backward as they were at the dawn of Independence.

A National Tribal Policy should be based not on the concept of striking a balance between these opposites but on the principle of freedom for each member of every tribal society to opt for either the old lifestyle or to go for the modern life, or choose access to both lifestyles. Tribal societies should have the freedom to march towards the future in accordance with their real wishes without being influenced by romanticists from the outside world.

The question of protection of tribal communities and their lifestyles becomes topical and makes glaring headlines in cases where the land of the tribal communities is sought to be acquired by the government for some development project or the other.

Unimaginative Policy

The market value of tribal land is very high and there is a good market for such areas. Unfortunately, the legislative restrictions on the transfer of tribal lands have made it impossible for tribal people to enter the market, cash in their assets and make a beginning in modern society. The legal protection of their land has thus actually been counterproductive.

The problem of the tribal communities can be compared with that of endangered species of animals. Attempts to protect such species as the tiger, the crocodile and the elephant have failed all over the world. The creation of reserved parks has not effectively stopped poaching and the market in their body parts continues to flourish. Actual experience in Australia, South Africa and China has shown that, rather than have closed reserves, it is more beneficial to open up and promote markets in the body parts of the endangered animals.

The National Tribal Policy should be based more on opening up tribal societies and giving their members the option to choose. All measures of governmental intervention that would tend to influence the choice of the tribals should be strictly eschewed.

The policies hitherto have given the right of deciding what kind of life the tribals will live to the outside society. The result has not only been the widening gap between the HRD levels of the two societies but also the actual shrinking of tribal populations. It is regrettable that the National Tribal Policy draft pays scant attention to these considerations and pursues the policy line that has proved disastrous for over 50 years.

---

2 November 2006.

49 Making Farmers Security-Savvy

The farmer is faced with a dilemma and is required to make decisions that neither he nor his forefathers were called upon to make. Traditionally, one was born a farmer, lived a farmer and died as one, all in grave indebtedness. The same was the case with the artisans living in the villages—the ironsmith, the cobbler, the barber and the weaver. All these artisans required few instruments and had a large degree of freedom across vocations.

This was not the case with the farmer. The farmer inherited land from his ancestors and bequeathed it to his descendants. Land represented substantial capital. Further, the pursuit of agriculture required capital and livestock, which needed a sizeable investment and represented social prestige. Farmers had a far greater reason to carry on their vocation by family tradition. It was a noble vocation, highly respected and therefore its members had little inclination to switch to other professions.

The farming community, grounded in the land, was disinclined to move, except in times of such natural calamities as droughts and floods. Under colonial rule, the non-farming artisans faced competition from higher-quality, cheaper goods from industry and often had to abandon their professions and shift to cities as, in most cases, simple manual labour.

Historically Vulnerable

Under the British, the doctrine of the *eminence juris*—the land belongs to the monarch—was established. The lands of the farmers were acquired for public works, such as railways, roads, dams and canals. The displaced farmers usually accepted whatever was paid by way of compensation and moved to the cities. After a few teething troubles, they found themselves more comfortably settled than they were as farmers.

After Independence, the doctrine of *eminence juris* continued to prevail. The new Nehruvian socialism proceeded with enthusiasm to impose ceilings on agricultural landholdings and to pass a series of anti-*zamindari* and anti-moneylender legislation. The landlords and the moneylenders found the whole rural environment too hostile to permit comfortable stay and shifted to the cities.

As massive projects of national importance came up, millions of farmers came under submergence or were displaced. By this time, resettlement in the cities had already become a tough proposition. There was a powerful "push" provided by uneconomic agriculture, but also a "push-back" by the unemployment and the filthiness of the urban slums. The balance tipped in favour of inertia, and farmers started resisting the government's efforts to displace them on payment of a meagre compensation.

Seeking "land for land and more" has become the popular plank of the activist NGOs, in spite of the fact that agriculture has been reduced to a state where farmers are committing suicide by the thousands.

Knowledgeable people are asking if it would not be better to give the farmers an alternative to suicide. If the farmer had the possibility of selling his land at the prevailing prices in a buoyant real estate market, could not at least some of them be prevented from killing themselves?

By way of compensation, the bereaved families come into sums of money that they are not used to handling, and it is often spent in a manner that could not be termed prudent in the long run.

Unfair Deal

The ushering in of the era of special economic zones (SEZ) has widened the dimensions of the problem. Every state has entered the race, sanctioning as many SEZs as possible. The industries that will set up shop in the zones are to get special concessions in taxes, tariffs, labour laws and even credit. This will certainly give the upcoming industrialist a breath of fresh air and prepare him for facing competition in a globalised world.

It is difficult to understand why the farmers, whose land is to be acquired for the benefit of the industrialists, alone should suffer from the old-world doctrine of *eminence juris* and lose their lands. Some wise thinkers and some politicians too have proposed that the farmers be given equity in the industry by way of compensation for the lands that they will lose.

The farmers, however, are not in favour of the idea, for two reasons. One, the quantum of the compensation has to be as free as the working environment for the industrialist. The farmer should not get anything less than the current market price as compensation for his land. If the compensation is inadequate, it does not matter whether it is in the form of hard cash or equity.

Two, there is no reason why the farmer should be forced to accept the equity in companies that just happen to come up there. They must have the full right to choose the equity that they consider safe and profitable. They demand that they be paid hard cash and given the freedom to choose the form of investment, according to their own rights.

Apart from the question of exit from agriculture, there is a question very similar that would arise even in case of practising farmers. The government is determined to move to create a network of warehousing companies to solve the problem. The companies will advance to the farmer, on delivery of the produce, 70 per cent of the value at the prevailing market price and will issue warehousing receipts that will be negotiable instruments in law.

What will the farmer do with these receipts? Is he required to keep them indefinitely? Can he transfer them when the market is favourable? Will he benefit from the information available on the futures markets? The introduction of the new scheme will presuppose the development of a market for these negotiable instruments.

Regulatory Role

In the near future, the farmer is likely to face the problem of being flushed with the kind of funds that he is not used to handling. If he makes wrong investment decisions we might have destitute farmers committing suicide instead of landholding farmers taking their lives, as is now the case.

The markets for securities, bonds, debt, etc., are highly complex. Even the educated urban middle-class is far from being finance-savvy about these areas. The farmer, caught as he is in the morass of indebtedness, and on losing his lands, will easily be tempted to shift into a sector that seems buoyant and profitable.

Various sectors of industry, and particularly information technology and services, can use the funds in the hands of farmers to their mutual advantage. The question is: Can the farmer navigate between the two?

These are areas that lie within the legal mandate of the Securities and Exchange Bureau of India (SEBI). The latter has the reputation of being perhaps the country's most effective regulatory body.

The manner in which the regulator handles this problem might well determine the economic future, not only of the farming community but of the economy as a whole.

---

18 November 2006.

50 Trampling Farmers' Right to Property

The judiciary does not take *suo motu* notice of any situation, howsoever in violation of the Constitution that may be. It can pronounce its position only when a specific case comes before it. On January 11, the Supreme Court, while pronouncing itself in a case relating to 69 per cent reservation by the Tamil Nadu government, held that enacting a law in the Schedule IX of the Constitution does not necessarily put it beyond judicial scrutiny.

Schedule IX was introduced in the first and the fourth amendments to the Constitution at the height of the anti-*zamindari* fervour. The legislation to take over land from the big landlords was struck down by courts as being *ultra vires* the Constitution and in breach of the fundamental right to property. The government tried a subterfuge—of amending the Constitution rather than the legislation. Initially, this contraption of Schedule IX was used mainly to regularise land reform legislation. It soon became an omnibus inventory of legislation the government was unwilling to defend. Farmers' organisations opposing land acquisition for public purposes have demanded for the last 25 years the abrogation of Schedule IX and the restoration of the fundamental right to property.

No Recourse to Law

The Supreme Court's January decision is a major victory for farmers and a setback for environmentalists demanding resettlement of displaced farmers without wishing to challenge Schedule IX. The Supreme Court has held that only laws placed in Schedule IX after April 24, 1973 will be open to scrutiny.

In the ruling in Keshavanand Bharati *vs.* State of Kerala on April 24, 1973, the Apex Court held that Parliament had the power to amend any or all the provisions of the Constitution except those that alter its basic structure. That the wording of the preamble to Schedule IX itself went against a major fundamental right and was, hence, *ultra vires* the Constitution, was not spelt out because the court was not called upon to pronounce itself on the matter.

The Centre has announced its intention to formulate, in the near future, a new resettlement policy. It is unlikely that it will wipe out the principle of *eminence juris* that justifies takeover of land by the government. The farmers might find some relief in the fact that the Essential Commodities Act, 1955, though enacted much earlier, was put in Schedule IX only in 1976 and is, therefore, subject to judicial review. Whether the farmers can commandeer enough resources to get it referred to the Supreme Court is another matter.

The 'Food Crops' Case

It is interesting that there is at least one governmental measure concerning agricultural land (also in Kerala) that has been taken under the provisions of the Essential Commodities Act, 1955. The Kerala government had issued the Land Utilisation Order, 1967 under Notification No: (p) 225/67/ Agri., dated 17-6-1967. By 1967, the Green Revolution had set in and the worst phase of food scarcity was over. It had become quite clear that the best way of ensuring food security was increasing production, productivity and yields with superior technology. Punjab and Haryana had launched the Green Revolution in wheat without forcing the farmers to continue growing wheat or any other food crop.

The provisions and wording of the Kerala government's order brings to mind the Stalinist campaign against farmers. The order provides: "If the State government are satisfied that it is necessary and expedient to increase the production of food crops in any area...direct that every holder of land in that area shall grow food crops as may be specified in the order. If any farmer was found to be wanting, the collector was to issue him a notice. If the landholder did not respond positively within 10 days, the collector could auction the use of his land for a period of 3 years in order to ensure that the land was used for production of food crops."

In the Kerala lexicon, 'food crops' include paddy, fish, sugarcane, vegetables, tapioca, yam, coffee, cardamom, pepper, groundnut, banana and plantain. The farmers were prohibited from changing from one food crop to another and the collector could order them to grow the food crop(s) he so desired. If the purchaser in the auction failed to grow food crops as directed by the collector, his tenure could be terminated and he could be evicted.

Unfortunately, in most cases, it was the Kerala State Karshaka Thozhilali Union (KSKTU) that intervened. There were a number of cases where small farmers holding less than half a hectare wanted to discontinue paddy cultivation because the government had artificially hiked the wage rates to prohibitive levels and the prices of paddy were unremunerative. When the farmers planted, in small patches, rubber or arecanut saplings, they were uprooted or destroyed. In no case did the district collector initiate action against the unlawful forces nor was any compensation paid to the victims. The Communist governments in Kerala increased the wage rates of the paddy workers without caring to examine if the cultivation could support it. In the last 20 years, the daily wage rates of paddy field workers have been hiked by 11.95 per cent every year. They have risen from Rs. 8.83 (female) and Rs. 12.74 (male) in 1981-82 to Rs. 101.64 (female) and Rs. 148.72 (male) in 2003-04. However, during the same period, the paddy prices increased at an overall rate of 7.36 per cent—from Rs. 178.78 per quintal in 1981-82 to Rs. 694.69 per quintal in 2003-04.

The Issue of Acreage

Did the government succeed in increasing or, at least, maintaining the acreage on the food crops? In several cases, sizeable paddy land was taken over by the government itself for the declared purpose of cultivation. Many such land are lying fallow and being eyed by politicians and the real estate industry. In 1980-81, Kerala had 8,01,691 hectares under paddy and produced 13,64,867 tonnes of paddy. By 2003-04, the acreage had come down to less that one-third (2,87,340 hectares) and the production to less than a half (5,70,045 tonnes).

Government interventions of this type have always failed in agriculture. It would be acceptable if the government simply scrapped all legislation, at least those included in Schedule IX after 1973 and if necessary, replaced them with laws consistent with the present times.

---

24 January 2007.

51 Reaping the Whirlwind

The angry reactions of West Bengal's peasantry to the attempts to take away their land for SEZs are founded.

I visited Nandigram and Sonachura villages in Eastern Midnapore district of West Bengal, and managed to have fairly extensive interactions with the villagers as also with those injured in the police action, still in hospital. The West Bengal Governor, Mr. Gopalkrishna Gandhi, himself admitted that it was filled with "cold horror". The Governor earned a lot of sympathy from the people at large and quite some admiration from the Opposition parties. Yet, "cold horror" is rather a mild expression used for what has happened in that region since March 14.

A posse of over 5,000 policemen attacked a gathering of farmers protesting against the acquisition of their land for a special economic zone to house a chemical complex to be constructed by Salem Corporation of Indonesia.

Travelling from Kolkata to Nandigram and further to Sonachura, even to a casual observer it is obvious that the area is essentially an agricultural zone. Small *badis* (houses) surrounded by coconut palms, fishponds and lush green fields, swaying gently to the breeze, nature seems bountiful to the agriculturists here. But lying dangerously close to the refineries of Haldia make these lands the target for downstream chemical companies, and now, West Bengal's government and politicians.

Unexpected Resistance

In most villages on the Nandigram-Sonachura road, red flags flutter with the 'hammer and sickle', 'sickle and corn', or the 'white star' emblazoned on them. Some villages also have the tricolour with 'TMC' printed on them. Clearly, this is a stronghold of the Communists who never thought that their plans to acquire the land would meet with such stiff resistance.

The villagers in the 'red' habitats were said to be quite enraged that 'the counter-revolutionaries' of Nandigram should be evoking so much sympathy from outside West Bengal and from the Governor himself.

By all accounts, the Communists have used all possible techniques to hijack elections in West Bengal, and particularly in this region. The police and the home guards are apparently packed with young comrades. That by itself ensures victory in elections. Under the banner of land reforms, land has been distributed to small tenants and landless families; but the title documents are all said to be with the party apparatchiks. That ensures that the peasantry will march to the polling booths and vote appropriately. Had the Left parties won the last Assembly elections with a less thumping majority, Nandigram and Sonachura would never have happened, is a refrain.

According to official statistics, 12 protesters were killed by the attacking forces, which it is alleged contained, in large number, the party cadres. For, the policemen are said to have developed a fairly amicable relationship with the villagers over the period of the protests. The comrades-in-uniform were said to have been unhappy with this development. According to a report, the Chief Minister himself had addressed the cadres and asked a rhetorical question, "Enough of barking, when are the dogs starting to use their teeth?"

The villagers strongly repudiate the estimate of 12 dead. They put it all above a hundred. Some claim to have seen three large trucks loaded with dead bodies taking off from the site of the shooting. Hopefully, the CBI, which has been charged with the investigation by the Kolkata High Court itself, will set the matter at rest. In one hospital, I saw a number of patients, mainly women with blue and black marks on the body; the effects of the lathi charge. I got an impression that the agitators had deliberately put the women and children in the vanguard in the hope that that would take the edge off the police attack. But these hopes appear belied.

The Governor cannot be entirely unfamiliar with the kind of terror the Left parties are said to have let loose in the West Bengal countryside. He could not be unaware of the manner in which these parties have reportedly marshalled refugees from Bangladesh. He should have felt "cold horror" at what was happening during the elections that have given the Leftists a clear mandate.

Love for Land

One very remarkable thing in the happenings in Nandigram area is the peasantry's fierce love and pride for the land. They all talk of giving up life rather than their land. This is not quite the case in some other states with the farmers driven to suicide willing to hand over the land provided the price is right. What makes the Bengal farmers different?

The Left parties are apparently reaping what they sowed. For decades, they have trumpeted the virtues of land reforms and how important it was to possess land. The people have obviously learnt the lesson well and are now ready to lay down their lives for their land—the icon of social prestige. Once again the Communists are coming to know the wrath of the peasantry that is now going around tearing down the red flags and turning against their commissar tormentors of three decades.

---

21 March 2007.

52 Time the Indian Farmer got his Due

To lift Indian agriculture from its present moribund state, the agricultural marketing and extension systems must be reformed immediately. Also needed are a policy to prevent fragmentation of landholdings and a farmer-friendly exit policy.

There has been, as early as 1929, only one real issue in Indian agriculture. It has been a non-paying vocation. The American Civil War sucked Indian cotton into the world market. Since then, Indian agriculture has become marginalised.

After the Great Depression, the Second World War ensured low agricultural prices coexisting with food scarcity. The British followed the policy of "procuring cheap raw materials in India and importing expensive manufactured goods into India". Indian industries were also beneficiaries of this policy. Independence came with the Partition. Some of the agricultural surplus provinces went to Pakistan and the flood of refugees worsened the problem of scarcity. The dependence of the government on the bureaucracy and the incipient mindset of socialism ensured the emergence of the licence-permit-control-quota-inspector *raj*, euphemistically called "low-cost economy".

This policy had a built-in bias against the farmer. The socialistic pattern of society only made things worse because the emphasis on industrialisation required a regime of cheap raw materials and wage goods.

Green Revolution

The Green Revolution in the 1960s marked the end of food scarcity but also introduced expensive agricultural inputs like fertilisers, pesticides and electricity. The weaknesses in the marketing system and infrastructure made agriculture a losing proposition.

The establishment of the Agricultural Prices Commission (APC) and the system of minimum support prices (MSP) did bring about a brief respite of about five years, from 1965 to 1970. After that, a change in the character of the APC and its successor, the Commission for Agricultural Costs and Prices (CACP), saw a period where the MSPs recommended by the Commission were deliberately depressed and, as a consequence, the MSP came to be the highest prices that needed to be paid to the farmer.

Restrictions on export and trade, inadequate storage, processing, transport has kept Indian agriculture mired in poverty.

Economic Reforms

The economic reforms of 1990s were limited to the domain of industry and finance and left agriculture totally untouched. The period of the National Democratic Alliance (NDA) saw some reform in the marketing front. The second phase of reforms under the UPA has again left agriculture a closed and State-dominated sector. There is also talk of a second Green Revolution. There is a general awareness of the need to reform the present system of agricultural marketing. Suicides by over 1,50,000 farmers in the last decade has brought in a sense of urgency to reforms.

Unfortunately, while the mindset in the Congress party has undergone a major change, it is the voice of its Left allies that continues to dominate. As a result, the UPA government appears to be bringing in changes that are irrelevant and inappropriate.

The rate of the growth of GDP is entering an era of double digits while that of agriculture is yet to cross 3 per cent. The policymakers are putting great emphasis on ensuring a rate of growth of 4 per cent in agriculture. Of course, a higher rate of growth in agriculture is welcome. But it should not be forgotten that the target of 4 per cent was fixed without any study of the correlation between the rates of growth of GDP and that of agricultural product.

Experts were talking of a target rate of 4 per cent when the GDP rate was just around 6 per cent and they continue to do the same even though the rate of GDP has gone above 9 per cent.

The preoccupation with the cooperative form of business organisation for everything that is rural and agricultural will need a second look.

Cooperatives, as a general rule, have failed except in cases where there was inspired leadership or a situation of monopoly advantage.

Food scarcity was a problem in the pre-Green Revolution days and it continues to be so even today despite India becoming a major producer of a number of commodities.

In order to justify the talk of food security, the definition of "food security" is being enlarged. Food security no longer means mere physical availability of food. It is supposed to include the purchasing power to acquire it, availability of water, fuel, adequate levels of literacy and even women's empowerment.

The NGOs obviously have a vested interest in expanding the scope of the term "food security". The government has succumbed to popular pressure in creating a Food Security Mission. This mission is pursuing the "grow more food" strategy, similar to the one that failed in the pre-1960s period, reinforcing infrastructure and technology with little or no attention to the economic incentive for the farmer.

Small, Marginal Farmer

The influence of the Left economists has also dominated the agricultural debate by emphasising the condition of the marginal and small farmer. The fact is that the size of the holding of an individual farmer depends more on the cohesion of his family than its economic situation.

The small holders generally come from families where the land gets divided between the siblings in each generation. Remarkably, these economists do not suggest any way of operational consolidation but recommend further land reforms and fragmentation. This has to stop.

There is a similar prejudice against the moneylenders in the rural scenario. The fact is that despite insistence on enforcing formal credit organisations, the informal moneylender continues to provide a major part of the agricultural credit, and that too at no cost to the government. The rates of interest that they charge and the methods of recovery they adopt are not worse than those used by the microfinance organisations.

Rather than ape the Bangladesh model, it would be a much better idea to recognise the moneylenders as a formal credit institution and revive the

"Usurious Loans Act" in order to eliminate unsavoury practices in rural credit.

The "dig and fill" schemes, such as the National Rural Employment Guarantee Scheme (NREGS), that have become hotbeds of corruption, do not produce any tangible assets.

On the contrary, these schemes jeopardise the agricultural labour market to the detriment of the farmer.

The Issues

Having made a sufficiently long list of issues that have ceased to have relevance since Independence, it may be useful to shortlist some of the major issues that will confront Indian agriculture in the decades to come.

Most Indian farmers are trapped in agriculture because their parents left them the land. According to surveys, a majority of the farmers would, given the choice, leave agriculture. On the other hand, there are others better endowed with finances, managerial skills and technological know-how that appear to be anxious to enter agriculture.

Agricultural land is becoming increasingly scarce and there is a ready market at attractive prices for it. It would be inappropriate, under these conditions, to enforce on the farmer compulsory acquisition for schemes such as the special economic zones (SEZ).

It would be more appropriate to draw up a farmer-friendly exit policy under which the farmer will have the right, if he so wishes, to pursue agriculture and also have the sole authority to dispose of the land if he wishes. The process of globalisation would have little meaning unless there is some scope for inter-sectoral transfer of factors of production.

Global Warming

A new calamity for which India is largely unprepared is that of global warming. Most of the good work that has been done since the 1960s may be totally nullified by climate change. The high yielding variety seeds that paid rich dividends during Green Revolution might cease to play the same role in times when temperatures and precipitations become profoundly skewed.

As admitted by the Finance Minister during last year's Budget speech, the systems of agricultural extension and input subsidies have collapsed. The extension system must be reformed from one based on the salaried adviser to one involving commission-earning consultants.

The mockery of terming subsidies, such as those on food and fertilisers, as subsidies to farmers must stop. It is not difficult to ensure that the advantage of subsidies reaches the farmers directly, but only if there is the political will to do so.

---

20 February 2008.

VII

Economic Reforms

53 Freedom is the Thing

An Introduction

I have been one of the more steadfast defenders of economic reforms in India. In fact, I have been an opponent of all forms of State interventions in the economy in general and market mechanisms in particular since as early as 1978 as an activist of the farmers' movement. My position I owe largely to the experience I have had as a farmer facing the tyranny of governmental policies calculated not only to depress agricultural prices and appreciate the terms of trade but to keep the prices of farm produce below their cost of production and actually drive the farmers to the point of suicide.

In agriculture I have stood for nothing but freedom of access to markets and to technology.

In arriving at this position, I have been greatly helped by the positions taken by Chakravarti Rajagopalachari, the founder of the Swatantra party and Dr. B.R. Shenoy also.

There is nothing new about the classical free trade argument. Lest it be taken as a blind faith in Adam Smith, I would rush to add that my intellectual conviction of the economics of Adam Smith was greatly supported by my personal experience as a farmer. This also led me to a more philosophical or metaphysical realisation of the unique character of faculties endowed by nature on an individual—thought, perception and decision. It is the privilege of an individual to have an apparatus that permits him to register, store varied experiences, satisfactions as also deprivations and pain in units that can be subjected to Boole's Algebra without obliterating their individual identity markers. It is this special ability of an individual that allows him to come to decisions that are entirely rational for themselves at a given point of time.

It follows logically that groups of individuals, communities and nations cannot arrive at any rational decisions as they do not possess collectively any comparable apparatus. And, the group decisions are invariably arrived at best by surrendering the individual sovereignty to an outsider who has no claims to superior vision, understanding or decision-making. This again is just a restatement of Arrow's theorem.

There is really little realisation amongst economists as also politicians that the fall of Soviet Union is fully explicable only through the Arrow's theorem—sheer impossibility of rational collective decisions.

The articles on the agricultural situation as also those by way of case studies are clear illustrations of the superiority of decisions arrived at by untrammeled interplay of individual desires and plans.

Markets are far from perfect. The fact remains that human societies have not invented anything better. In free market systems, there will be ups and downs; the growth and recessions. This is an indication of a living organism. My experience as a farmer taught me that periodical shedding of leaves is a healthy sign in plant life—a process of midstream correction and elimination of the unviable and the inefficient. Socialist economy in India moved all along like snails. Economic reforms brought in free markets that made a "take off" about which Socialist planners wistfully dreamt. The post-reforms economy took flight. The consequence was a shift from the Hindu rate of growth to near double-digit rate of growth of GDP. Even an eagle has to come down and rest on a perched branch of a tree. That does not make the eagle inferior to an earthworm crawling its weary way life long.

The tenets of my thought (See Annexure) are well summarised in a statement that is included in the constitution of the political party Swatantra Bharat Paksha of which I have the honour of being the national President.

In the current situation of global financial crisis and large-scale retrenchment, it is necessary that the discerning people stand for encouragement of the entrepreneur rather than going in for some kind of *aam aadmi* welfarism that has all the vices of the socialist regime minus the political discipline involved.

Annexure

Swatantra Bharat Paksha

Self-evident Values, Tenets and Principles

- that, all men are created unique though not unequal;
- that, they all pursue the fulfilment of their unique personality in their own singular way, through maximising options and freedom of choice, learning through deduction and induction as often as through trial and error;
- that, there are no 'Masters'—neither spiritual nor economic; that the dictates of the self-proclaimed prophets of time and space bring disaster; that, despite all shortcomings, there is no better guide than the lights of the aggregate of individuals striving to excel through competition and mutually rewarding cooperation;
- that, power corrupts and absolute power corrupts absolutely;
- that, the remedy for corruption lies not in a mystical moral elevation of mankind—through saints, socialists, trustees—but in pluralism and competition;
- that, help and protection given to those that need it not, harm the giver and maim the receiver;
- that, competition is the best training ground for competition—one learns to compete by competing;
- that, the weak and invalid are an integral part of any population and have a rightful claim on the community for the pursuit of happiness and fulfilment without being subjected to uneven competition; that, growth and development are in nature and suffer only when deliberately thwarted; that, all the help the poor need is that the world get off their backs;
- that, any interference in the work-ethics, freedom of exchange and competition can only be harmful;
- that, the business of the government is government and not business; that, the government is not an instrument of change but an unfortunate necessity; that the government can solve no problem because it is **the** problem.

---

24 July 2009.

54 Soft is Cruel in Reforms

According to knowledgeable people, China is slated to be the world's economic power in the near future. Indians fear the Chinese; this is because Indians find the Chinese inscrutable and enigmatic. As Communists under Mao Zedong, the Chinese took 'long leaps' to State socialism at the price of millions of lives. Now that they have turned liberal, they are being equally ferocious about it.

The inaugural speech of the Chinese Prime Minister on March 6, 2002 was markedly forthright. Compared with it, even the front-ranking reformists in India sound soft and suave.

Indians pride themselves on their softness and confuse it with moderation.

This softness and the secularism of the Indian Constitution have been two points of pride for India. But the events of the last fortnight have put a question mark on both these. "The riots in Gujarat have unmasked India's secular pretences", goes the Pakistan Television propaganda line.

In the Aesop's fables, there is a tale about a fox that was born without a tail and is gleeful every time another fox loses its tail in an accident or a combat. If India can no more claim to be a secular nation with the same kind of haughty air as before, Pakistan never was one. It was born a denominational Islamic State and does not consider it necessary to shroud, even for the sake of appearance, its fundamentalist character.

The Indian people, on the other hand, never claimed to be secular. They reflect the largest possible religious plurality. Every Indian, including the agnostic and the atheist, has a basic religiosity that is predominantly conditioned by faith and by the caste-culture to which he belongs by the accident of birth. These diverse people deliberately came together to constitute a State that is secular in Constitutional provisions. It is certainly not sceptical of all religious dogma in the dictionary sense of the word 'secular'.

No one can dispute that the Indian State is multi-denominational. In public matters, it certainly does not deliberately and consistently side with one community against another. The people are religious but the State is as secular as they come.

The Gujarat riots proved that, contrary to folklore, Indians are not a soft people; they are as hard as the Israelis. The masses reacted to the Godhra incident as harshly as the Israeli army does to Palestinian provocation.

The State machinery, after the initial hesitation, responded. In less than a week, life returned to normal, even in Ahmedabad—the epicentre of the riots. The security forces had orders to 'shoot at sight'. They shot down more than a hundred miscreants. The vigorous action by the security forces testifies to two things. One, the State continues to be secular, even under the NDA government in New Delhi and the Narendra Modi regime in Gandhinagar. Two, India is not a soft State in dealing with domestic disorders or insurgency. It is soft *vis-à-vis* Pakistan; it is yellow in the face of China, but quite brutal at home.

The Indian people are religious, the Indian State is secular. Indian people can be harsh. The Indian State, by its very nature, is unharsh. The State is not uniformly harsh in domestic matters.

It is harsh only against the unempowered masses. It is pusillanimous against criminals who inflict massive losses on the community through economic manipulation.

Jawaharlal Nehru, in his characteristic rhetoric, talked of hanging the corrupt on the branch of the next tree. Not one person has been hanged or shot in spite of the fact that corruption is all-pervading and rampant. The Indian State and the Indian people are soft on economic crimes because few feel righteously indignant enough to cast the first stone. This woolly-woolliness is patent in the liberalisation process.

Over a hundred corrupt Chinese officials were shot on the eve of the inaugural session of the Chinese Parliament on March 6.

The Chinese Premier denounced the inefficiency of the public sector, the corruption among the bureaucrats, and the laziness and inefficiency of the workers. He announced a five-point programme that puts enhancement of agricultural income at the top of the agenda and includes massive reallocation of employees—a Chinese euphemism for the 'pink slip'.

The day an Indian Prime Minister puts that kind of vehemence and conviction in speeches on economic matters will be the 'D'-day for economic reforms.

It is widely recognised that India needs to bring down further its fiscal deficit without increasing the tax burden.

This can be done only through ruthless slashing of unproductive expenditure.

Indian politicians dither where the self-professed Chinese communists turn tough on labour. Vituperative harangues against the 'haves' is good electoral politics. So is softness on numerically stronger communities.

Populism and the politics of bribing the electorate at the expense of the exchequer was good politics for some time and we had single-party rule for nearly half a century, with all its pros and cons.

Populism is a game that many can play, and cannot remain the exclusive privilege of one political party. Everyone would like to play with subsidies, 'free lunches', reservations, regional identities and 'temples and mosques' and everyone does. We have, in consequence, the coalition culture, fractured assemblies and horse-trading.

The gunman who shot down Manzoor Ahmed, the socialist party member elect of the Uttar Pradesh Assembly warns us of a new political era. If a party cannot purchase voters and legislators, it can certainly eliminate them. Gandhiji's non-violence and communal amity brought us the horrendous Partition conflagration. Our softness on the economic front might purchase peace for some time; in the long run, it will bring bloodshed, of the Lucknow kind.

We are a selectively soft people. Our priorities are topsy-turvy. Dithering on liberalisation might ultimately bring in far more violence than harsh measures to discipline the corrupt and inefficient. A stitch in time might be kinder than major surgery later.

---

13 March 2002.

55 Measuring Poverty, Welfare and Freedom

Swaminathan Anklesaria Iyer's article "Starvation diet may, in fact, be good for health" (*The Sunday Times*, June 16) was brought to my notice by a doctor in a nature clinic, who is himself a fanatic about fasting and its virtues. The doctor was thrilled to find support coming from such a celebrity liberal on the virtues and merits of abstinence in diet.

Swaminathan Iyer's basic contention, keeping aside the rhetoric, is: Less-than-a-belly-full diet is good for one's health. No one would dispute that. As early as in 1980, a prison warder told me this while I was in Nashik jail in the sugarcane agitation. He was undergoing a life sentence and explained to me the secret of his blithe spirits in spite of the long sentence, "*Kam khana, gam khana, tab katata hai jail-khana*" (Eat frugally, master regrets and the time of the sentence does not sit on you). That is the germ of Swaminathan Iyer's article and I wish he had stopped just there. Like my jail-mate did, at extolling the merits of abstinence and moderation in food as a personal virtue. He goes on to make it a national objective.

To this end, Swaminathan Iyer presents unauthenticated data about the calorie content of a typical American's day's fare (1500) and claims that the latter is, by the standards of our nutritionists, on a starvation diet, and that Americans, by our poverty-line definition, are far poorer than Indians. He cites also experiments with monkeys and other species to claim that lower calorie intake gives better health and longevity. He admits, however, that it might lower testosterone levels and libido.

The facts that Swaminathan Iyer marshals are quite impeccable: Even in a poor country such as India, it is not the well-fed rich who enjoy better standards of health. True. There are a number of studies, which show that till recently the incidence of heart ailments, blood pressure, diabetes was remarkably lower in Indian rural countryside. There is, clearly, something wrong in defining the poverty line in such a manner that it comes out that the poor are better off.

International comparison between levels of calorie intake also does not establish conclusively that the richer consume more calories than the poor ones. Also true. It is a known fact that the proportion of income spent on food diminishes with rise in income and that the better off consume more proteins and fats than carbohydrates-diversified diet.

The indicator of poverty line in India is based on calories alone to the exclusion of proteins. It is clearly a gaff. But there is a story behind it.

The Sukhatme-Dandekar debate on the definition of poverty line resulted in a consensus that the human body is capable of ensuring availability of diverse components if the general level of food intake is sufficiently high. The intake of proteins and fat was kept out of the definition of poverty line. And now Swaminathan Iyer is complaining about a calorie-centred index. He does not pitch for a more polyvalent indicator but appears to propose an index of development that may be inversely correlated to the quantum of calorie intake. Swaminathan Iyer goes even further. If monkeys and their descendents do better on low-calorie diet, so must the human beings and their communities. Lower food intake means greater well-being and hence, national poverty should not be defined in terms of food intake.

Wrong. Individual virtue can be public vice. Spartan habits may be good for individuals; but Spartan nations may perish because there, as Churchill's dictum goes, "Nothing succeeds like excess".

Lord Keynes observed about frugality, "Individual virtue can be public vice". There is often an inversion during the shift from the micro to the macro.

The matter cannot be resolved by equating lower consumption with higher development. That would be even more absurd. Creating a more composite and comprehensive indicator might be an improvement but not an ideal one.

Any single indicator of poverty—even a composite one—would be equally faulty. The UNDP's development indicators are by now familiar all over, but no one takes them very seriously. There prevails a large sense of dissatisfaction about all indicators of development—simple or composite—based on physical criteria.

Dr. Kurien, the architect of "Operation Flood", argued that milk proteins being highly expensive, the farmers and the poor should renounce them in favour of the cheaper vegetable proteins (pulses and lentils) and let the milk go to the richer urban consumer. The ideal indicator will not distinguish between the rich man's and the poor man's proteins.

Marie Antoinette said, "Let the poor eat cake if they do not get bread". Swaminathan Iyer, Dr. Kurien, Dr. Sukhatme and their like are, in fact, arguing that the poor are actually eating cake because their starvation ensures them better standards of health. Blessed are the undernourished, for they shall enjoy better health and longer life! The front-ranking liberal is joining the ranks of ascetics that extol the glory of poverty.

Swaminathan Iyer, an eminent liberal, has allowed himself to fall into pitfall of conceiving development and well-being as a function, direct or inverse, of quantity of physical entities. Socialist planners do it for their subjects; so do the broiler farmers for their chicken. Both think they know what is good for their domain. Subjects should become loyal citizens and hard workers; the chicks should show a weight of 1,200 grams in about six weeks. The minimum agricultural wages in Maharashtra have been computed for decades, not so as to ensure adequate supply of personnel with requisite abilities and qualifications and a satisfying life-long career for the entrants but so that they may purchase for the family of the labourer food, that is, evaluation of human life intake of about 2800 calories per day.

What are the expectations from human beings?

If the supreme goal of human life is to remain free of hypertension, heart ailment and diabetes and live long, naturopathy, probably, spells out the best regimes and diets. There are any number of ascetics who lead long Spartan lives. They have not discovered new continents; nor ravelled any new frontiers of knowledge, science or technology. They do not bring to use their physical excellence for climbing the Himalayas or even winning gold medals in Olympics.

As long as the aim of human lives remains undefined, it would be impossible to spell out what is the best or optimal diet, habitat or ware to achieve the same. It is degrading to human dignity at attempt to do so.

The fundamental error in the present indicators of development is that they correlate well-being with acquisition and consumption. Swaminathan does not address himself to this fundamental error. In fact, there is no such co-relation. Men do not live by bread alone or by Marie Antoinette's cake or by the biblical word of god.

In his attempt towards upward mobility, human being does not seek higher level of consumption or even well-being. He seeks ever higher degrees of affluence and plenty not in a spirit of gluttony or voracity. The search is to be free from want in the normal times, of course.

They also search to provide for the rainy day against the risks of natural calamities and acts of god and of enemy. They lay aside surplus as a cushion against such contingencies.

Human beings as also nations, in all income brackets, consume more or less the same quantity of food though of widely different types and value. The difference between a poor and a rich man lies in the fact that the latter is in a better position to face contingent risks.

And that, in all departments of life and at diverse stages, he is in a position to choose from amongst various options. Individuals, as also their nations, can be compared on the basis of:

- Number of occasions they exercise choice over a given period of time;
- Number of options from which they can choose;
- The range of options available; and
- The number of virgin options available.

The test of affluence lies in the degree of risk-bearing capacity and the extent of choice enjoyed. Swaminathan Iyer has effectively marshalled a case not for abolition of indicators of poverty that emphasise more-than-optimal consumption.

What is required is not a lowering of consumption-based indicators but a breakthrough for evolving a new indicator based on capacity for risk-bearing and degrees of freedom of choice.

---

3 July 2002.

56 Economic Reforms at the Crossroads

The next Budget is still a full month away. The pre-Budget consultative meetings are on. So have rumblings in different quarters.

A spokesman of the Left bloc has made clear his wishlist. He has demanded vociferously that everyone who has the capacity to pay should be taxed so that all the poor and the needy can benefit. In particular, he wants industrialists, traders, landlords, professionals of all kinds and exporters taxed. That is not all. Even the Reserve Bank of India Governor, Dr. Y. V. Reddy, suggested having the option of imposing a ceiling on foreign institutional investments or even taxing them.

What will happen by end of February 2005 is difficult to say. But it looks more or less certain that the advance of economic reforms will slow down if not halted and reversed.

The economic reforms and the liberalisation started under the Prime Ministership of P. V. Narasimha Rao when the present Prime Minister, Dr. Manmohan Singh was Finance Minister. The whole concept of liberalisation was so new then that not only the parties in the opposition but even a considerable number of leaders in the ruling Congress were unhappy about it. The first stage of economic reforms was limited to minor alterations in the licence-permit-quota regime and the investments from abroad. Even these measures came not out of any conviction but because of the conditions of general bankruptcy and the severe depletion of foreign exchange reserves. It was largely believed that the reform measures were being taken under pressure from the World Bank and the International Monetary Fund.

Fortunately, the initial reform moves paid off and the foreign exchange and the fiscal deficit position improved dramatically within a very short time. But the immediate fiscal and exchange pressure for reforms having lost the steam, the reformers of the first age did not even bother to extend the liberalisation process to the largest sector in the economy—agriculture. In fact, agriculture was in a far better position to seize the opportunities created by the forces of liberalisation and globalisation by making a stand in the world market to compete with all and mighty.

The economic reforms received a major push under the BJP-led National Democratic Alliance regime. Unfortunately, the communal elements of the alliance reduced even the modest success that India had achieved—the unprecedented high rate of growth—to suspicion and ridicule. Liberalisation essentially means a challenge and an opportunity.

Those better endowed appeared to be moving ahead faster than the rest. Consequently, those with limited initiative and enterprise developed a grouse and a grievance. That defeated the NDA in the hustings and the Congress-led United Progressive Alliance came to power with the empty-pragmatic idiom of economic reforms with human face.

The presence of the Leftist parties and the caste-based alliances made unthinkable the continuation of economic reforms at anything like the NDA tempo. Now the question is: How much of a roll-back will there be on economic reforms notwithstanding assertions to the contrary by the senior government leaders?

The political opposition to economic reforms is not a new thing for the Prime Minister. He has always been conscious of the fact that the reforms are not vote-catchers and have to be brought in at an optimal tempo.

So several questions rise at this 'do or die' stage for economic reforms. Are economic reforms divisible within an economy? Can reforms be implemented in the industrial sector without encompassing agriculture? In the implementation of economic reforms, are there various alternative paces from which the politician chooses an optimal or ideal one?

Given the historic cultural and physical characters, can there be one ideal pace and strategy for reforms? Is there anything like a middle path in economic reforms? Whether the expression economic reforms with human face make any sense?

The answers are simple and brief. Liberalisation should not have any compartments. In any country, where the polity is integrated and there is no neo-colonial relationship between various sectors/communities, economic reforms will have to be all-pervading. However, the schedules and strategies for their implementation in different sectors can be divergent. Implementing economic reforms in a number of steps is like trying to cross the river in multiple steps. To say that economic reforms that aim at creating market forces that determine the allocation of sources and distribution of the wealth is doomed to disaster reveals a bias. There can be nothing fairer, more just and more humane than the market.

In fact, it can be said that all interventions in the market are essentially aimed at bringing in inhuman injustice against a section of society, which is not preferred by the ruling powers.

Economic reform in a licence-permit-quota society is like the de-addiction of a drug addict. The doctors would be unkind to the addict if they listened to his entreaties to let him have the 'dope' just once. The doctors have to be a little unkind in the larger interest of the patient and offer him some other kind of relief.

Or economic reforms can be compared to making a non-swimmer swim. The beginner is essentially hesitant to enter the water. He knows that once he gets into the water he will enjoy swimming; but there is the strong initial inhibition. It can be overcome occasionally by gentle persuasion. More often, somebody pushing him in achieves the desired effect. After the initial discomfort and fear, he starts floating.

India stands at the threshold of prosperity but its political leaders and the people must have the courage to take the plunge, breaking away from the medieval, licence-permit-quota mindset. They must prepare for a new epoch, not of capitalism nor of socialism but of entrepreneurism. Markets arc good for cradication of poverty. Markets are good for expanding employment except of course those who are unemployable in any case.

One of the initiators of economic reforms is at the country's helm now. He can take the nation forward and need not feel restrained as the last time round. But it is unfortunate that his own partymen and political allies have little interest in bringing to a happy conclusion the great endeavour that he began in the early 1990s.

Perhaps, the Prime Minister, Dr. Manmohan Singh, is caught between his 'inner voice' that calls him to make India a great nation by giving its people the opportunity to display their talent and ability, and the political pressures that curb his reform initiatives so as to pay lip service to the 'human face'.

---

19 January 2005.

57 Right Medicine for Inflation

What is happening under the banner of "war on inflation" launched on June 25, 2008, the 33rd anniversary of the declaration of the infamous 'Emergency', reminded me of a delightful Gujarati folk tale regarding a "camel-riding apothecary".

Once upon a time, there lived a celebrity apothecary who sat all the time on the back of a camel and refused to come down or to let the camel sit down. He was the disciple of a renowned guru and had no peer in the art of medication and surgery. It so happened that there was some kind of an epidemic that had affected the entire population of the walled village.

People rushed to the great apothecary (*vaid*) and prevailed upon him to treat the afflicted villagers. The sapient doctor came to the village but got stuck at the entry gate. It was too low to allow both the camel and the apothecary riding on its back to enter at the same time. If only the great doctor had agreed to take down the sizeable bundle of medical volumes that he carried all along, he might have succeeded in getting through the village gate.

Since he could not be prevailed upon to separate himself, even temporarily, from his books nor get down from the camel, the entry into the village became practically impossible.

The wise man gave suggestions one by one, advising the villagers to pull down the gate, or cut the camel's neck. His advice was promptly acted upon but to no avail. Finally, he entered the village, but only after the entry gate was broken, the camel's neck cut and the burden of his learned books removed.

Present-Day Counterpart

On his part, the learned doctor who is in charge of the 'War on Inflation 2008' finally started treating the nation afflicted by soaring prices on June 25, putting all his prejudices and points of honour aside.

When inflation was in the incipient stage of 7-9 per cent, the Finance Minister concentrated all his attention on the most superficial symptoms of the disease and tried to treat the rise in prices of vegetables, fruit, pulses and edible oil, in the manner of Attila the Hun. He ordered reduction in the customs duties on edible oil, opening the floodgates of the commodity. He was not deterred even when the countries exporting edible oils clamped a massive export duty on edible oil, wiping out all the advantage of production and customs duty in India.

He banned the export of non-*basmati* rice, though it was quite clear that it was difficult to distinguish between the non-*basmati* varieties and some others that pass for *basmati*. He imposed a ban on the storage of food grains and let loose a spate of police raids on warehouses. The traders' stocks went even deeper underground and the prices went even higher.

Finally, to deny all freedom of marketing to primary producers, he banned futures trading on four agricultural commodities in addition to the four already banned in 2007, taking the total number of banned commodities to eight. As if all this was not sufficient, he imposed a commodity transaction tax (CTT) so hefty that it threatens the very existence of the commodity futures markets.

Too Little, Too Late

Just as, even before entering the afflicted village, the learned apothecary had caused general devastation all around, the producers of the commodities whose prices increased were in utter despair. In spite of the fact that the monsoons arrived on time, they had little enthusiasm for increasing either the yields or the production. It was quite clear that the *vaid* had little interest in improving the lot of the ailing people.

Then suddenly, inflation rose to 11 per cent. Remarkably, at this point in time, rise in the commodity prices was actually negative and the learned doctor could, by no stretch of imagination, pass on the blame to the minister in charge of agriculture. The situation became so serious that it looked as if the Queen might order, "off with the apothecary's head" for fear that the people might otherwise clamour for hers.

Now the *vaid* had to give up all his pride and prejudices. The learned pharmacist knew all along that the affliction of inflation was caused not by the high prices of primary commodities but by the enormous purchasing power that had been pumped into the hands of urban consumer under the "inclusive growth" doctrine of the UPA. He had, deliberately, avoided attacking the real source of the affliction, lest that line of treatment invoke the Queen's wrath.

Classic Measures

The learned doctor finally started the classical deflationary measures. The Reserve Bank of India had been controlling both the cash reserve ratio as also the repo rate that would signal an all-round increase in interest rates and make loans more expensive. The decision to start the new line of treatment would affect only the purchasing power of the urban consumer that is obtained through bank credit. No improvement is expected in the near future—not, at least, till the arrival of the new *kharif* crops. Only then can the prices be expected to ease.

The Governor of the Reserve Bank of India has already hinted that the monetary policy moved only by signals from the Ministry of Finance which may not be sufficient to meet the current crisis. 'The Working Class Family Income and Expenditure Survey' recently released by the Ministry of Labour brings out clearly that the monthly incomes of the salaried and wage-earning classes have been increasing substantially. It also brings out that the family expenditure on food items is declining.

This clearly points to the need to curb not only the credit available to the urban consumer but restrain their incomes as well. Further, it confirms statistically that all policies aimed at depressing the prices of agricultural commodities are misplaced. The policy calculated to curb the incomes of the fixed income groups will not be palatable to the UPA since it will burst the balloon of its "inclusive growth" theory.

The village may still be saved. But the mystery is: Why did the learned doctor not start treating the known cause of the disease straightaway rather than causing the general devastation at the entry gate to the village?

---

2 July 2008.

58 Wanted: A New Global Currency

> The global financial crisis can be blamed on the world's dependence on the US dollar as global tender. It is time to discard the dollar and look for a more credible alternative to prevent such crises in future.

It is over a month since Lehman Brothers caved in, and more than three weeks since Iceland's Prime Minister warned that his country was close to national bankruptcy. Over the last few weeks, there have been a number of high-level meetings, as global decision-makers slowly begin to understand that this is no ordinary crisis.

The 43 nations' Asia-Europe Meeting ended with a bland declaration that there was a consensus for a reform of the system. Only the UK Prime Minister, Mr. Gordon Brown, came out with the suggestion of devising a regulatory framework for international monetary institutions that work with little or no regulation at national or international level.

Mr. Brown could not have meant the Bretton Woods institutions as the World Bank and the IMF have their multinational governing bodies and boards of directors as also a plethora of advisers of diverse nationalities.

The Fed's Role

The one institution that is strictly an American icon but has a vast international footprint is the US Federal Reserve, which, as the US central bank, controls not only the total quantity of dollars but also the price for its supply and is clearly the one that needs watching.

The former Russian President, Mr. Vladimir Putin, has been saying for some time that the world should abandon the US dollar as a global reserve currency since its fluctuations tend to harm everyone who uses it for trade or as store of value. OPEC calls the US dollar a worthless piece of paper. Argentina, Cuba, Iran, Iraq and Venezuela have already said "no" to the dollar.

The fact that the Keynesian system held up the US dollar as virtually the global currency put an enormous responsibility on essentially a national institution. What was the role of the US Federal Reserve (Fed) in the train of events that resulted in the current crisis? What was the responsibility of the Fed in causing the consumer boom that resulted in the subprime lending in the US?

At present, the US government is primarily interested in rescuing Wall Street and the banking institutions by throwing hundreds of billions of dollars in the pit without knowing its precise dimensions.

The American tax payer, already deeply concerned about unprecedented deficits, huge expenses required for the restoration of infrastructure and the two wars, may not be fully sympathetic to the efforts of the government to save the banks without any attempt to save the economy.

Housing prices are falling all around and will possibly fall further. There will be more foreclosures on the mortgages. Mere pep talks by policymakers, no matter how influential and reputed, are unlikely to rebuild the confidence of the people in the financial institutions unless such talk is based on a deep analysis of the causes of the crisis.

The assets in which the big players such as Citibank, Merrill Lynch and Bear Stearns invested, have suddenly ceased to have any market, as the other banks are not keen on financing such insecure assets. The rest of the world is also fast losing confidence in the US-centred financial system. What started as a subprime crisis in the US is fast developing into a global crisis.

The rest of the world faces problems that are far more serious than those faced by the US. The essential functions of the central bank of any country are to raise money within the national boundaries and fix its price i.e., the rates of interest.

Central Bank for the World

It is well-known that the Federal Reserve is not only the central bank of the US but also the *de facto* central bank of all the national central banks in the free world whose reserves comprise predominantly dollars.

Furthermore, the Fed, as the central bank of all the nations, decides at what rate it will lend dollars to national central banks.

After the first Gulf War, dollar printing became the most profitable business for the US. The dollars, as global tender, was in perpetual demand by other nations as the Bretton Woods system was based on US dollars and gold.

In the post-Cold War years, in a situation of virtual US political and economic hegemony, the Fed appears to have followed a deliberate policy of large recourse to the printing press. The Fed cut interest rates repeatedly and the US households gradually stopped saving.

End of Thrift

Thrift, the much-prized virtue in the *laissez faire* system, became, in the Keynesian ethos, an object of mirth and ridicule. Its place was taken by the Federal Reserve that prints and supplies more dollars to enable the consumer to spend on imports.

The malls import goods from China and elsewhere and sell them to American households, thanks to the easy money created by the Fed. The flight of the dollars to countries exporting commodities to the US is compensated by borrowing them from foreign governments to bridge the current account deficit. The foreign governments are also happy with this system.

The Fed has thus promoted and supported a global financial architecture in which it has the means of forcing central banks of other nations to hold the reserves in the US securities, very much like the SLRs.

The US dollars could function as store of value only to the extent that they are strictly limited in supply and the US government does not have the possibility of uncontrolled printing that allows it to print as many dollars as it wishes, at essentially no cost.

By increasing the volume of dollars in circulation, the US government can also reduce the value of a dollar in terms of goods and services. This has swollen the Fed's reserves outside the US to approximately $3.8 trillion.

The Great Depression of the 1930s was blamed on deficiency of effective demand caused, *inter alia*, by savings and thrift. Thrift ceased to be a virtue. The antidote to the 1930s Depression corrupted the work ethic and mores of the society at large, creating an impression that one could spend one's way to prosperity.

Easy Liquidity

It must be admitted that it was not US's consumers alone who benefited from this. It also created an environment of easy liquidity, which helped many countries in the developing world to escape poverty. Unfortunately, all good things must end.

When people start prospering by spending rather than by the sweat of the brow, it was only a matter of time before sharks appear on the scene. Bankers themselves ceased to be genuine bankers and thought nothing wrong about financing questionable investments that could make their balance sheets look good.

Finally, the reality of the supply-demand situation had to assert itself and the morality that was engendered by the Keynesian anti-thrift preaching, combined with the short-sightedness of the Bretton Woods agreements and the cupidity of those responsible for the monetary management in the US, was bound to bring about a crisis and not only in the financial systems of the US but also that of the world.

To overcome the present crisis, it would be necessary to introduce a global tender that would be managed more responsibly. The obvious solution is to make the euro the global tender. It has the advantage of representing some sort of a basket of currencies and is controlled by the entire European Economic Community.

Some of the developing countries that appear to be, for the time being, immune to the present crisis might start feeling the pinch when the global tender is more prudently managed. The governments will then face the problem of ensuring higher rates of growth that are based on hard work and thrift rather than growth based on stock market booms.

5 November 2008.

59 No! Not Back to Socialism!

Two events that occurred in the last month may influence the future of Indian polity and economics far more than one can imagine. Mr. Ratan Tata wrote an open letter to the people of West Bengal, particularly to the youth there, appealing to them to think whether they wished to support the progressive economic policies of the state's CPM government or lend support to the obstructive agitation politics of the likes of Ms. Mamata Banerjee that would cause a repetition of the exodus of industry from West Bengal, as happened 30 years back.

Mr. Tata, obviously, has forgotten that it was the agitation tactics of the present Chief Minister's party that had resulted in the exodus of industry from West Bengal three decades ago. Despite this, the head of one of the most respected industrial groups in the country has tried to influence public opinion in favour of one party and against the other.

In a second event, it was a political party that influenced the decisions of a private aviation company. The Jet Airways Chairman, Mr. Naresh Goyal, capitulated meekly and reversed the decision to lay off some 1,900 of the airline's staff, taken barely 24 hours earlier.

The reversal came so soon after the issuance of a threat by Raj Thackeray that it left no doubt in anybody's mind that Naresh Goyal had succumbed to the blackmail of the Maharashtra Navnirman Sena (MNS).

In the Singur case, the Tatas were seriously concerned about the safety of their staff facing the agitation that had clearly gone beyond the control of the state government. In the case of Jet Airways, Naresh Goyal's assertion that "the staff of Jet Airways were like members of his family" seemed exaggerated. If Mr. Goyal had entertained this lofty sentiment 24 hours earlier, when he decided on retrenchment, the crisis would not have arisen at all. Something had obviously made him change his mind.

In a rather amusing comical scenario, various parties including MNS's parent Shiv Sena as also the Civil Aviation Minister himself vied with each other to claim credit for Naresh Goyal's *volte-face* "Chi Chi".

Retrenchment

It cannot be ruled out that Mr. Goyal created a political situation that would corner the Finance Minister and the Civil Aviation Minister by creating a labour imbroglio with a view to securing a reduction in taxes on aviation fuel. If that was Mr. Goyal's strategy, it certainly worked. The major beneficiary was, of course, Marathi parochialism. The event underlined the sensitive character of the issue of labour retrenchment. Retrenchment and unemployment hurt those directly affected, of course, but even more so the politicians with populist planks.

Already, a number of columnists have started expressing their doubts whether Nehruvian socialism was not a better option than Dr. Manmohan Singh's liberalisation and globalisation. It is funny how so many economists who spent a lifetime building socialist theories and institutions switched over to economic reforms soon after 1991.

We will possibly witness a reverse flow towards socialism in the days to come. Systems based on the predominance of public sector institutions that generally have an employment orientation, are once again finding their defenders and champions.

Politicians, as a species, view retrenchment as a certain vote-snatcher. At the very first signs of economic recession and retrenchment, politicians and economists appear flabbergasted enough to beat a hasty retreat towards the illusion of a safer and more comfortable welfare/socialist regime. These neo-socialists appear to lose sight of the fact that India faced large-scale secular unemployment during the epoch of socialism.

The governments of the era concealed the massive unemployment by giving figures of employment created in the public sector rather than publishing the figures of those who remained unemployed.

Politicians and economists appear to prefer secular massive unemployment to temporary retrenchment here and there, now and then.

Markets are live organisms and not mechanical contraptions. They work like birds. The birds have to move their wings up and down in order to gain height. Even the strongest of the birds has to come down and take rest on a branch from time to time. That does not make the birds inferior to insects and reptiles.

Retrenchment is, of course, painful and undesirable and should be, in principle, the last option to be exercised by the employers. Mr. Naresh Goyal of Jet Airways rendered his fraternity a signal disservice by rushing into an ill thought-out mass retrenchment and reversing the decision with even less thought.

The economic plight of the company could have been easily explained to the representatives of the staff. They could have been convinced that temporary retrenchment was in the interest of the staff as also of the company.

The only alternative would be acceptance by the unions of reduction in salaries and perks that would, more or less, keep the total company wage bill constant. After all, trade unions work on the principle of collective bargaining. Collective bargaining does not mean only negotiating for hikes in wages and perks in days of prosperity, when the things are going well for the company. It also means collectively finding ways out of economic difficulties. The staff could have been easily persuaded to accept a pro-rata reduction in the salaries and perks to avoid a certain number of them being sent home.

Market-oriented System

Let no one forget that the socialist welfare State spelt secular stagnation for all the years since Independence. A market-oriented system might have its ups and downs. That is inevitable in any free moving body—economic, social or aerodynamic.

The social problems created by the recession should be taken care of by social safety nets, unemployment insurance and acceptance of uniform reduction in salaries and perks. It would be most unfortunate if the economists tried to frighten the people back to the days of the licence-permit-quota-inspector *raj*, where no one was allowed to do anything; but nothing was disallowed to those with the necessary political pull.

India lost over four decades experimenting with a system that has lost all credibility. Let us hope we have avoided a second bout of the same disease. Surprisingly, I found it easier to explain this phenomenon to an audience of semi-literate and illiterate farmers. The audience understood that leaf shedding is a part of the growth of any tree. All living organisms have their ups and downs. A mother would not exchange her baby for a doll simply because the doll does not fall ill.

The last 20 years have given the people a taste of near double-digit rates of growth. They would not settle for the old Hindu rate of 3 per cent for another 50 years, merely because the markets have their swings.

---

19 November 2008.

60 Clearing the Forest of Zeros

The half-page multicolour advertisement stood out in the regional print media even in the cacophony of the electoral campaign of Assembly elections in five states.

The advertisement was issued by the Government of India and flashed a claim that the Debt Relief and Loan Waiver (DRLW) scheme announced in February 2008 had given relief to over 4 crore farmers and that the total amount of debt relief was of the order of Rs. 71,000 billion (*abjas*).

Obviously, someone had blundered. The original DRLW scheme, including the modification thereof, did not claim to provide relief beyond Rs. 71,000 crore. It is possible that this was an innocent error on the part of the authorities concerned in counting the number of zeros after the basic figure of 71.

It is more likely that some political campaign planner had deliberately decided to take advantage of the confusion created in the minds of the public as also the experts by the co-existence of the two systems of numerals.

Decimal System

India switched over to the decimal system of currency and measurements about 50 years back. In the western decimal system, the numerals are counted in units of thousand. A thousand thousand make a million, a thousand million make a billion and a thousand billion make a trillion, and so on. But in adopting the decimal system, we indigenised it. For us, a hundred thousand make a lakh, a hundred lakh make a crore and a hundred crore make an *abja*. It is common to see even knowledgeable people wondering how many zeros need to be added to make a million.

The figures in the Central/state budgets are generally given in crores or thousands of crores. So is the case in most reports, governmental and non-governmental, on socioeconomic subjects. The confusion may not be limited only to this advertisement. The government may have issued several other advertisements making untenable claims using the combined confusion caused by the current system of numerals. Some authority should go in to this matter.

The confusion is compounded by the rupee shrinking in value to less than a hundredth of its pre-Independence value. In fact, it is no more a 'rupee' (silver); it is more a 'nickel' or a 'tinsel'. In fact, a rupee would not purchase even its weight worth of nickel. The combined confusion can produce serious errors.

The DRLW advertisement only brings out the confusion caused by the plethora of zeros. It would have been astonishing if an opportunistic politician had not thought of using it to his or his party's benefit.

It is remarkable that these advertisements were issued only in vernacular and not English language, newspapers. The intention is quite clear. It would have been ridiculous to mix up the 'crores' and the '*abjas*' (billions). Whatever be the intention behind the advertisement, it has served, at least, one purpose: bring out the confusion that is plaguing the Indian system of counting.

Lest this confusion be capitalised on again and again for mischievous purposes, it is time we chose definitively between the Indian system of counting, on the one hand, and the international decimal system, on the other.

The present financial crisis has added a dimension of urgency to this. The media often reports of relief packages of several hundred billion or trillion dollars. Those who attempt to convert these amounts into rupees find the exercise bewildering.

Disciplining the system of numerals alone will not suffice to clear the forest of zeros that plagues Indian socioeconomic literature.

New Unit of Currency

Another reform that is crying for attention is that of the 'rupee'. It is time to introduce a new unit of currency which will be equal to rupees thousand of today. It may be a good idea to call it '*sonya*' rather than '*rupiya*'.

Introduction of a heavier unit of currency and abolition of Indian units and numerals is a reform whose time has come.

It is difficult to say to what extent the DRLW advertisement has misled the farmers into swinging their vote to the party that authored it.

The Election Commission should take *suo motu* notice of this electoral 'malpractice' and take appropriate punitive measures that lie within its powers.

---

31 December 2008.

VIII

Farmers' Allies and NGOs

61 NGOs in Agriculture

An Introduction

Not so long ago, there used to be times when social service used to be undertaken in a spirit of mission by dedicated individuals, occasionally assisted by some of their close friends and relatives. These missionaries in *mufti* were moved by compassion and empathy. The projects included opening of schools, dispensaries, and shelters for orphans, supportless women and old men. Their campaigns were financed mainly out of their own personal resources. Such other funds as they required were collected by them by personal appeals to benevolence. The founders took personal responsibility for any of the legal consequences of the actions of their institutions.

Those times are changing rapidly. Smart people saw the business potential in enterprises of this type. The Economic and Social Council (ECOSOC) of the United Nations and similar international bodies that lacked the ground support found it a good idea to engage some of these bodies, initially, in a consultative status and later on as operational collaborators.

With the fall of socialism and the State apparatus, the NGOs started surfacing in all the countries of the world. The commanding heights of the State were taken by "the Regulatory Authorities" established by the government itself and NGOs. The regulatory authorities are manned by superannuated bureaucrats who had generally failed to deliver during their active service life. An NGO can be launched by any person who can claim some specialised knowledge and mass contact in a given field. It is quite common to see NGO bosses shifting the fields of operation depending upon the relative availability of funds from both the State and private foundations. The founders of NGOs are found to be coming from those who failed to get into administrative services or politics. NGOs permit them to maintain a standard of living for themselves and ability to employ others much higher than those enjoyed by the *babus* and the *netas*. It is remarkable that many a bureaucrat on the threshold of superannuation start sweetening the NGO contacts to wangle a 'quango'.

There must be some NGOs that do serious and honest work. One doesn't come across them every now and then, not in the agricultural sector in any case. The NGOs in the agricultural sector have played a particularly pernicious role largely to the detriment of the poor peasantry.

By 1980s, it was clear to all discerning people, that farmers continued to be poor and debt ridden largely because of the deliberate policies pursued by the government to depress agricultural prices. Before the fact of negative subsidy to agriculture was established by the WTO documentation, a large number of well-meaning people launched an alarming number of schemes and projects in isolated spots. They promoted dispensaries, schools; they launched campaigns for popularising *gobar* gas plants, soak pits, smokeless *chulhas* and water harvesting schemes. Most of these projects were benign and caused no actual harm to the rural community except that their projects wilted fast as they could not be maintained by a population living by a losing vocation. Had the initiators not tried to divide and weaken the efforts for making agriculture economically remunerative, their activities could have been ignored. Some of these superficial 'face lift' programmes and projects were patently pernicious. A celebrity NGO succeeded in spreading the plantation of "Lucena" as a latter-day "*Kalpataru*". In fact, it proved to be a very pernicious weed that caused untold damage to agriculture in many parts of the country. Farmers value all life—human, cattle as also plant and have antithetical relations with wildlife-faddist NGOs. Some of these well-meaning people did succeed in bringing about some improvement in isolated spots. Their contention used to be, "if only this success is replicated hundredfold, thousandfold and millionfold, all the problems of rural and national poverty will cease to exist." This replication syndrome was as pernicious as the now debunked percolation thesis. Many NGOs thought the spate of farmers' suicides a lucrative opportunity for building up websites and statistics quite unconcerned about the stark human tragedy.

Yet another brand of less well-meaning activists insisted on maintaining that the poverty and the indebtedness of the farmers was largely due to their ignorance, personal wasteful expenditure on social functions that frittered away the substantial subsidies endowed by the government. Unlike the busybodies in NGOs, these activists had a certain basis in the agrarian community and were supported by the DALDA school of agronomy (Dandekar, Alagh, Lakdawala, Dantwala, Ashok Mitra, Thamrajakshi *et al.*). These leaders came largely from those who had displaced by the anti-*zamindari* and anti-*sahukari* legislation in the early decades of Independence, included the gentry that occupied positions of political power and had an interest in keeping their less fortunate peasant brothers permanently "needy" as also in hiding the anti-farmer animus of the government in power. They were obviously disinclined to admit the vicious role played by the government in imposing negative subsidies on the farmers. They advocated various kinds of subsidies to lift the farmers out of the penury. This brand of leadership continued to maintain that Indian farmer was so heavily subsidised that his class came to control the reins of political power. This school was the dominant school of opinion until the WTO documentation left it no feet to stand on.

In 1980s, a new realisation of the agricultural situation spread through the length and breadth of the country. Its proponents demanded nothing but freedom of access to markets and to technology for the farmers. The groundswell support that this movement received was unprecedented.

Soon followed a plethora of anti-market and anti-technology NGOs. Most of them masquerade in under some kind of an environmental mask. Though green outside, they were mostly disgruntled fellow travellers disappointed by the fall of the Soviet Union. They saw in environmentalism a new argument stronger than Marx's 'proclivity to crisis' argument against market-driven economies. Their *modus operendi* was to select any success story of any project that promised to be successful and start opposing it. They opposed Coca-Cola, computers, GM seeds, major dams, pesticides and what not. The very magnitude of the projects they opposed secured them a certain type of celebrity and, at least in some cases, generous kickbacks.

Those who opposed projects involving displacement of farmers scored significant initial successes. Unfortunately, they failed to appreciate the fact that agricultural land had ceased to be a paying asset and that most farmers preferred to leave agriculture at the first possible promising opportunity.

The leaders of such movements attained for themselves a certain celebrity status but the movements that they led invariably came to a dead-end.

The NGOs, for sometime, stoutly opposed the advent of computers. They claimed that the information technology (IT) would cause mass unemployment. Unfortunately for them, the onslaught of the computers was so massive that it simply lifted all opposition off the ground and dumped them in the dustbin of history.

The first entry of the genetically modified seeds could have been in the area of drought resistance. Unfortunately, it was in the area of big-money pesticides. The Bt cotton seed promised to wipe out the threat of the bollworm and rendered redundant the most substantial application of the pesticides. The pesticide manufacturers felt threatened and have pushed a large number of NGOs to mount massive campaigns against the new technology.

The "green above, red inside watermelon" environmentalism is unfortunately alive even today. They have got hold of some self-proclaimed farm leaders to claim that use of GM foods can cause emasculation amongst men and infertility amongst women.

The fact that the genetically engineered cotton seed has been a massive success has not deterred these busybodies from pursuing their lucrative campaigns.

Opposition to free markets naturally meant opposition to the World Trade Organization. The ministerial meeting of the WTO has been heckled by sizeable gatherings of motley crowds consisting of old fellow travellers, environmentalists and sundry haters of the United States including the terrorist fundamentalists.

The NGOs which startled with the lofty intention of doing some social services have gone astray because they lacked the mental capacity required for a detailed analysis of the problems of any community and have gone bust to a point where they have joined Al-Qaeda and old Kremlin forces in the pursuit of their anachronistic anti-globalisation and anti-technology planks.

---

4 May 2009.

62 Dangerous Prospects of an Agro-War

War is in the air. Even if there is no outbreak of hostilities, the acts of terrorism may continue as part of the proxy war. The armed forces are reported to have taken comprehensive measures to protect the Supreme Court building. There appears to be little preparedness against agro-terrorism. Agriculture is the soft underbelly of the country. The impending war should make the government and the people more conscious of the importance of agriculture.

Osama bin Laden, the mastermind of the September 11 attacks, is reported to have said in one of his interviews that the choice of the targets was influenced as much by the Media value as by the strategic importance. The attack and its aftermath have to be spectacular, he said. Most people in the US expected the Golden Gate Bridge to be the most likely target for subsequent terrorists attacks. But the terrorists attacked entirely differently—spreading anthrax germs through the postal service.

The Lashkar-e-Taiba (LeT) and the Jaish-e-Mohammed (JeM) that planned the attacks in India chose the Parliament House for the December 13 attack. It is reported that their next target is likely to be the Supreme Court building. Sansad Bhavan (Parliament House) is the symbol of democracy, a shining post-Independence achievement. The Supreme Court is yet another icon of democracy.

Most professional generals are known for their proclivity to prepare themselves rigorously for the last war. The hide-bound *junta*'s presumption is that the next war will be, more or less, a continuation of the last war. Whoever planned the attacks in India appears more like the professional army general rather than a terrorist like Osama bin Laden.

It would appear that those who targeted the Parliament House were more keen on showing links with the September 11 attack than on causing serious damage to India and its democracy. In the eyes of Indian terrorists, the Parliament House or the Supreme Court building would rank low in the priority list of sensitive targets as the terrorists would prefer to cause economic damage to the already doddering Indian economy. And the vital points of the economy are not the Bombay Stock Exchange or the Nariman Point in Mumbai. Even the total devastation of these so-called economic centres would leave the quasi-totality of the economy unaffected. Anti-India terrorism is more likely to be agricultural in nature.

India needs to beware of agro-terrorists rather than the kind of terrorism that shook the US. India's finest accomplishment, since Independence, lies in the fact that it became self-sufficient in food and is not only able to feed its teeming millions but has godowns overflowing with food grains. Hence, the harshest blow against India would be in its stomach rather than on the head.

The Green Revolution was made possible by the irrigation waters of the Bhakra-Nangal canals as also of many other river projects and the water lifting pumps they powered. These are the vital centres of the economy. Even a small damage to one of the major river valley projects is certain to cause massive destruction by flooding and inundation. It would also negate all the gains of the Green Revolution and set the country back by almost a century in the most critical and vital agriculture sector. These projects may be well-guarded against terrorist attacks, but that may not be enough protection against the enemy in the event of unlimited war.

India is still largely an agricultural country, centred around its countryside. Paradoxically, we have a professional army that attaches primary importance to technological sophistication. We are a largely populated country with poor capital recourses. Our army, on the contrary, is highly capital-intensive and has not even considered the possibility of a general mobilisation.

All the jingoistic enthusiasm for war is confined to political circles. The common man is watching in amusement as if the next war with Pakistan is another cricket test match. Only those families that have at least one of their members actually risking his life on the frontiers understand the stark reality.

The enemy is not likely to be impressed by pretensions of modernity and industrialisation. The enemy will try and hit where it hurts most, by attacking dams and canal works. It is more likely to try and organise locust swarms rather than the air raids.

New Delhi has been indifferent to the real Bharat. The threat of a serious war should force it to be more objective.

17 January 2002.

63 New Crop of Farm Champions

A number of self-appointed spokesmen are pontificating on agricultural issues and advocating their own brands of programmes. Since Independence, India has witnessed two types of farm leaders. One, the Chaudhari-Deshmukh type and two, those who demanded only freedom of vocation and technology. Now a new type of NGO elite is coming on the scene. It shares its mindset with the Chaudhari-Deshmukh type but not the latter's parochialism.

At least since the great depression of 1969, the terms of trade have been moving against Indian agriculture. The deterioration of the terms of trade was the hallmark of the colonial rule. Even after 1947, when acute food security prevailed, the prices of agricultural commodities moved unfavourably compared with those of agricultural inputs and articles.

The Green Revolution ended the era of food scarcity. Both farm production and productivity went up. The income and terms of trade of the farmers continued, nevertheless, to deteriorate. A species of farmers' champions cropped up who put the blame for the peasants' penury on the machination of the landlords and the moneylenders. The landlords took away the cream of the agricultural output and the moneylenders squeezed the farmers through fraudulent accounting, cruel rates of interest and feudal methods of loan recovery. This was the theme of the farm leaders of the epoch, generally caste leaders, who were interested in capitalising on farmers' woes to their political benefit.

Even these leaders of Chaudhari-Deshmukh brand could not deny that agriculture was unremunerative. That only added venom to the cruelty of the landlords and the moneylenders. But the unremunerativeness of agriculture came from the uncertainties of monsoons and weather, and the ignorance of the farmers who stuck to old methods of cultivation.

This brand of advocacy of farmers' causes was the predominant voice in the farmers' movements till the 1980s. It advocated government subsidies for agricultural inputs and massive assistance to agricultural research in governmental institutions and to the development of cooperative bodies in processing, marketing and financing. The *zamindari* and *sahukari* systems were abolished soon after Independence. Even the tenancy contracts were snuffed out. Land ceilings were imposed in three waves of increasing stridency.

Curiously enough, the beneficiaries of the abolition of the two structures were the *zamindars* and the *sahukars* themselves. The first obtained sizeable sums as compensation though the rates of compensation were fairly modest. This class of ex-*zamindars*, with the help of the lump-sums of compensation paid by the government, became the forerunners in the industry and commerce. This was also the class that produced Chaudhari-Deshmukh brand of farm leaders. More important, they dominated the political scene in the socialist era and were the most vociferous critics of the *kulaks* and the big farmers. The *sahukars* shifted their business to urban areas, prospered and gained political influence. The moneylender was replaced by a whole structure of government-supported and regulated cooperative bodies. In theory, the cooperative movement should have eradicated corruption and brought down the extent of rural indebtedness. Nothing of the kind happened. The rural indebtedness continued to mount. Paradoxically, the level of indebtedness was higher in regions where farm productivity had increased and the cooperative bodies had come up for processing and marketing. Everybody who left agriculture prospered thereafter, while those who remained in agriculture sunk into poverty and indebtedness.

The immiseration of farmers continued relentlessly in spite of increased production and productivity, the flourishing of the cooperative movement and a long list of so-called agricultural subsidies. This represented the big paradox in the economy. It should have set the alarm bells ringing that something was more seriously wrong in Indian agriculture than just vicissitudes of monsoons and tyranny of the landlords and the moneylenders.

The fact that State tyranny was the prime cause of the rural poverty was brought out by the leaders of the new movement of farmers in the 1980s. They presented a cogent economic argument. The distortion of agricultural terms of trade, the penchant for the so-called 'low-cost economy' and the advocacy of industrial and urban interests were the predominant features of the socialist era. They were not fortuitous accidents but a part of well thought-out policy to prevent the agricultural surplus kick-starting development of secondary and tertiary industries in the countryside itself. The motive was to promote development of primary capital required for the newly burgeoning licence-permit industry in the urban areas.

Stalin did it with tanks to help Soviet industry; Indian socialists used less bloody methods to the same purpose. The new movement of the farmers of the 1980s mobilised unprecedentedly large crowds of all layers of farmers in their rallies and agitations. They, however, failed to make an impact in the political arena and in the cooperative sector. Farm leaders with the socialist mindset armed by the DALDA school of economics ('Dalda Economics' and the anti-farmer bias", *Business Line*, February 28, 2001) continued to hold the reins of power.

A quirk of destiny came with the Uruguay round of WTO negotiations on Agreement on Agriculture (AoA). The documentation of the negotiations proved beyond doubt that the Indian farmer suffered from crass negative subsidies while his counterpart elsewhere benefited from massive positive subsidies. Not the leaders of the 'freedom' movement of farmers but a group of politicians who had a vested interest in continuing India's neo-colonial hold on Bharat presided over the ushering in of economic reforms in India.

The era of farmers' freedom appeared on the horizon when in a brief spell of one month, the Finance Minister announced an "era of farmers' freedom", the government of Maharashtra committed itself to abolition of the Maharashtra State Cotton Monopoly Procurement Scheme, the GEAC permitted commercial use of Bt cotton and the Union Commerce Minister lifted the quasi-totality of bans on agricultural exports. The farm leaders with socialist mindset—the Chaudhari-Deshmukh brand of politicians and the DALDA economists—are attempting to resurrect themselves. A large number of farmer-haters have started raising their heads in a clever advocacy of State control on agriculture.

These new champions of farmers have little standing in the agrarian community but they perorate from the pulpits of NGOs and five-star seminars. Their experience of agriculture is limited to tending kitchen gardens and amateur organic farming. They have been active surreptitiously for years. There are those who oppose dams, lest they usher in an era of modernity in the countryside. There are others who oppose farmers having a free access to such frontier technologies as information technology and biotechnology. Last but not the least, there are those who feel threatened by a market-oriented free economy based on competition.

If the mainstream farmers' movement of the 1980s made freedom the main theme, the new leaders are talking of the food security and the need to ensure right of livelihood for the most modest citizens. 'Market can never be just' is the burden of their song. "Market needs to be carefully and closely monitored", they add. When India is opening up its cloistered closed economy, some are bound to feel the compulsions of competition an unpalatable prospects. The new NGO leaders are capitalising on these fears and advocating an anti-WTO and Swadeshi programme. The anti-WTO NGO farms' spokesmen are arguably the most influential in this crowd. They have contacts with NGOs in the Western world that have reason to be disgruntled about the advent of freedom.

March 2002 was the red-letter month for the farmers seeking freedom. The NGO protectionists retaliated concertedly and in quick succession. They got the GEAC to impose conditions on the exploitation of Bt cotton seed. That makes one wonder why the permission could not have been given with all these conditions on the date of the application itself. They have plagiarised 'refuge' conditions from the American document. It would appear that the GEAC is unhappy about genocide of bollworms and would like to give them a chance to survive and multiply. Thankfully, those in authority of campaigns against smallpox, cholera and polio did not think like the GEAC *babus*. To the extent possible, the GEAC has underscored the point that the farmers cannot be allowed untrammeled access to technology.

The sugar barons of Maharashtra held an extraordinary meeting in Mumbai and declared that the WTO was responsible for the dire straits in which the sugar industry finds itself. The WTO did not impose licensing for sugar factories for political purposes. The WTO did not require India to import sugar from Pakistan. So, what have the sugar barons got against the WTO? Most of them know little about Marrakesh agreements. They simply dislike freedom and openness.

Abolition of the *zonebandi*, the draconian system of Sharad Pawar's invention that was designed to preclude all possibility of competition amongst factories and ordained that a cane producer must deliver his produce to an assigned factory no matter the price it was offering. NGOs from 13 Asian nations gathered in Kathmandu to demand that the WTO abdicate its agricultural mandate, since the Marrakesh regime will harm the poor countries. The Asian chief of the Food and Agriculture Organization (FAO) was present in Kathmandu. This must have been music to his ears. Since the 1980s, the FAO has been unhappy about the increasing domination by the WTO of the agrarian scene and would like to reassert the FAO's authority.

GEAC in Delhi, sugar barons in Mumbai and NGOs in Kathmandu represent the new NGO school in farm movement. The NGOs are telling the farmers that freedom can be dangerous and it is better to be guarded by benevolent, knowledgeable and paternal government. Unfortunately, benevolence, knowledge and honesty rarely go together.

---

22 May 2002.

64 Tilting at Imaginary Enemies?

The 'Whodunit' aspect of the September 11 attacks on the World Trade Center and the Pentagon is in the limelight again. The US President, Mr. George Bush's knee-jerk reaction was to put the entire blame on the Al-Qaeda and hold Osama bin Laden as the sole villain of the piece. The Western countries concertedly attacked Afghanistan, and practically razed the whole country to dust.

They have, however, failed in laying hands on the principal quarry, Osama bin Laden, and his close colleague, Ayman Al-Zawahiri. Having dug up all the mountains in Afghanistan without being able to find the 'mouse', the Al-Qaeda line of inquiry came to a dead end. A letter from a woman FBI agent, Coleen Rowley, raised the question whether there were any security lapses in the FBI and the CIA. Could the September 11 events have been avoided if the security agencies had reacted with sufficient alacrity and diligence to the warnings they had received as much as a week earlier?

President Mubarak of Egypt also announced that he had warned the White House about the likelihood of some major terrorist events in the near future. Coleen Rowley went on to observe that a 'witch-hunt' was unnecessary but the likelihood of having Al-Qaeda spies or moles in the FBI had to be carefully examined. The Senate committee has started holding seatings (in camera) on the security lapses, and Mr. Bush considered it worthwhile to address the nation on the measures he intended to take to avoid recurrence of September 11-like incidences.

It is quite clear that the terrorists and their allies are not all in Afghanistan or Pakistan. There is a likelihood that some of them are in positions of power fairly close to the decision centres in the American administration.

Americans are as patriotic as any other people. The fact remains, nevertheless, that even at the height of the Cold War, comprehensive investigations had to be launched to trace 'commies'. Nobody advocates another edition of McCarthy-like inquests; but there is reason to believe that the visceral hatred of the American way of life is not the exclusive prerogative of Muslim fundamentalist communities. There are large segments of American population which are unhappy about the economic recession and unemployment. Unable to fathom what hit them, the disgruntled Americans have concluded that the multinationals, globalisation and free trade are responsible for their miseries.

In the days of the Cold War, a large number of 'commies' were prepared to join the USSR intelligence and sabotage network against the American interests. Today, there is no Cold War; it is a unipolar world and there is no palpable enemy. Saddam Hussein and Osama bin Laden certainly do not come anywhere near being Kremlin-like centres of alternative power and philosophy.

In the unipolar world, the discontented citizen who despises globalisation finds that the most organised anti-market force pivots around the likes of Saddam Hussein and Osama bin Laden. This hidden, often latent, despair of the American way of life has percolated deeply in their society.

The discontented are looking for some opportunity to strike out and give vent to their pent up anger. They provide, through acts of omission and commission, help, comfort and solace to the enemy. Certain recent events give one a feeling that the threat is not over and that a groundswell of anti-globalisation forces is developing and reaching proportions of the immediate pre-September 11 period.

Only a few days back, over 40,000 anti-GM demonstrators paraded in Rome in front of the UN Environment Protection Agency's Conference on the subject of 'World Ecological Standards and Environment Pact'. There was no violence as at Genoa (August 2001). But the massiveness of the demonstrations shows substantial organisational and communications network at work.

The anti-biotechnology activists are scheduled to organise the biggest bash of the year—'Bio-devastation' in Toronto. An organisation called The Centre for Consumers' Freedom has brought out the dubious sources of funding for the Toronto conference and provided evidence that the anti-biotechnology activists have no grassroots support.

The Earth Conference in Johannesburg in September is expected to be another rallying ground for the anti-freedom motley crowd that includes sundry former communists, environmentalists, self-professed farm leaders and 'goody goody' NGOs which appear to have access to unlimited sources of finance and managerial infrastructure.

The funding of the anti-globalisation and anti-technology movement, though substantial, was limited to what could be trumped up by the chemical fertilisers and pesticides industry and other protectionist forces.

The 'Seattle' crowd needed more support than Osama bin Laden had the ability to offer. As a *quid pro quo*, it had the kind of deep-rooted network Osama bin Laden was dreaming to build.

The 'Seattle' crowd in India appears to be relatively quiet recently. It received two major setbacks. The Genetic Engineering Approval Committee permitted release of Bt cotton seed on March 26.

And second, on May 22, the Supreme Court refused to entertain the petition to review its earlier judgment permitting raising the height of the Narmada Dam at Kavedia. But the silence on the front is deceptive.

The anti-biotechnology forces are gathering strength. Last month, they held a *kisan* rally at Dharwar and prepared a detailed blueprint for sabotaging the spread of Bt seed in India. Bt cotton fields are to be attacked, and farmers will be cajoled into giving negative reports on their experience.

But the working machinery of the environmentalist crowd is very much intact, as evident from a recent event. There was a report about some environmental damage resulting from the Bt cotton that surfaced in China.

The report could be factual or fictitious. If, in fact, there was evidence of environmental damage, farmers and scientists would be interested in finding out ways and means of countering them.

The environmentalist lobby is not bothered about the remedial action; it kicks up a row at all important centres within a matter of 24 hours, demanding that the decision to release the seed be reviewed.

The US has become aware of the enemy within. It will certainly take some action in the near future. India is in the penumbra of a war with Pakistan. In the 1962 war with China, one was wary of fellow communists who shouted slogans of 'President Mao, our President'.

If the war with Pakistan breaks out at all, the 'Seattle' crowd in India—anti-WTO, anti-biotechnology and anti-Narmada Dam—will all need to be watched.

---

19 June 2002.

65 Through a Transformed Land

I was in Bharuch (Gujarat) to witnesses the deliberations of the leaders of the mainstream farmers' movement under the Kisan Coordination Committee (KCC) that concluded in the demand for scrapping the Genetic Engineering Approval Committee (GEAC).

Since then I have been moving across India—from the west, where the Narmada flows into the sea across Madhya Pradesh towards east where the great river rises at Amarkantak.

Adi Sankaracharya had undertaken this sacrosanct circumambulation in a mission to defeat the heresy of Buddhism. I have assigned myself a similar task—countering the opponents of free economy, trade and technology that have taken shelter in the arduous mountainous regions on the banks of the Narmada.

The northern banks of the Narmada lie in the districts of Bharuch, Narmada and Vadodara (Baroda)—all black cotton soil areas par excellence, inhabited mostly by tribals, Ranipars, Kolis, Bhils and Rathwas. Cultivation of cotton is not the sophisticated commercial activity here, as in southern Gujarat. Tribal farmers grow cotton in much smaller plots and used, till last year, the traditional practices and seed varieties. This *kharif* season there is a major transformation.

Most of them sowed at least five months before the KCC offered its protection to the Bt varieties frowned upon by the GEAC and the Union government. The Print and the electronic Media maintained a strict and deafening silence about the marvellous results of the impugned seed. This latter is not available in the normal agro service centres and seed shops. Somehow, the word went round that it was good and the largely illiterate tribals managed to get the seed from a virtually underground circuit.

The tribal farmers had obviously decided to switch to the unapproved seed as early as May-June 2002 and the KCC was only endorsing the farmers' spontaneous response and offered protection. The cultivation is so widely spread that it needed no protection. Not even the mobilisation of entire police and para-military forces could carry out even a minimally effective 'uproot and demolish' operation of the impugned seed.

Farmers who have not already shifted to the unlawful seed are determined to do so as soon as possible, regardless of whether the government permits its registration or frowns upon its existence. The cotton production in Gujarat, thanks to the opening offered by the illicit Bt cotton hybrid variety, will score a hefty lead as regards output, costs, yields as also quality over other cotton producing states such as Punjab and Haryana, that have not permitted Bt variety, and Maharashtra and Andhra Pradesh that are forced to use the much less beneficial varieties approved by the GEAC.

Traversing the newly carved out district of Narmada, it was a pleasure seeing the main canal of the Sardar Sarovar Project carrying hundreds of thousands of cusecs of water to the dry parts of north Gujarat, Saurashtra and Kutch. Two years back I had courted arrest, symbolically lifting a few buckets of water from the overflow and pouring it in the canal. The then Gujarat Chief Minister, Mr. Keshubhai Patel, had mobilised all the police and other para-military forces at his command to prevent the *kisan kar sevaks* from even symbolically transferring a few buckets of overflowing water into the main canal.

The *kar seva* took no position on the merits of the Sardar Sarovar Project or the contention of the Narmada Bachao Andolan, which were sub judice at that time. The objective was to bring out that the government had failed to construct a bypass tunnel—a safety valve that protects the main dam in the event of abnormal floods and that, had the bypass canal been constructed it would have been possible to take the waters from the overflowing Sardar Sarovar to the parched lands and thirsty people of North Gujarat, Saurashtra and Kutch.

At one stroke, the *kar sevaks* offended both the parties to the dispute. The Gujarat government felt 'caught with its pants down'. The Narmada Bachao Andolan activists were unhappy that the Sardar Sarovar water would actually reach the distant north which possibility they had stoutly rejected.

The Gujarat government mobilised all the forces to prevent the *kar sevaks* from reaching the site of the bypass channel and the NGO mounted an international campaign of vilification against the *kar sevaks* and the farmers' organisation Khedut Samaj in Gujarat. The *kar seva* was finally only a symbolic operation.

Fast flows the main canal now, as the government has completed the bypass channel, and the Sabarmati flows full at Ahmedabad, running into the Dhaulidhwaj reservoir at Surendranagar that will eventually provide water by various networks all over Saurashtra and Kutch. The *kar sevaks* suffered, but not in vain.

But the problem is not resolved. The Khedut Samaj's *kar seva* turned the spotlight on the drought in north Gujarat. The state government rushed in to a rescue operation abandoning the work of canals and sub-canals that would have benefited the region proximate to the Sardar Sarovar—Naswadi, Kawant, Chhota Udepur and Sankheda *tehsils* of Baroda district and Nadod and Tilakwada *tehsils* of Narmada district. The farmers in these regions, in particular the resettled ones, are unhappy and plan to start a campaign for attracting attention to their grievances. Narmada chapter one is over, the second chapter is just beginning.

From the newspapers I get to see on this forlorn route from time to time, I learn that both the Houses of Parliament have approved strict measures for reducing the size of bank NPAs (non-performing assets). There is no specific reference to the action envisaged on overdue or bad debts in the agriculture sector; there is no reference to the fact that agriculture has been, for decades, subject to negative subsidies that are the prime cause of the rural indebtedness and the farmer suicides.

The Prime Minister announced only the other day that there will be no coercive recoveries of crop loans from the farmers. The Finance Minister, Mr. Jaswant Singh's initiative completely bypasses the promise. Nor does it make any reference to the earlier initiative of Mr. Yashwant Sinha in the last Budget of a "one-time settlement" of agricultural loans.

I have seen in a couple of cases that agricultural assets, machines and implements seized by banks are rusting in bank premises as also cases of land taken over and auctioned in order to force repayment of loans. The new owners do not put land to agricultural use. That amounts to conversion of bank NPAs into farming NPAs. That does nobody any good. It might prove interesting if the banks take over agricultural land and assets of defaulters and try to produce some crops. That might make them better bankers and the economy a less dismal phenomenon.

4 December 2002.

66 The Narmada Oustees

Not Everything is Down the River

A little imagination at the right time could have saved lots of tears and crores of rupees in the matter of the Narmada Dam and the Sardar Sarovar Project.

Moving along the northern bank of Narmada, from Bharuch towards Amarkantak, I met throngs of peasants, mostly tribals, whose land had come under submergence of the Sardar Sarovar. They all looked lost and bewildered, as many more will, affected by other dams in Madhya Pradesh. Badwah is the highest point threatened by submergence as of now. The Kisan Coordination Committee (KCC)—the umbrella organisation of all non-political farmers' outfits—has announced a national farmers' rally to comprehensively review the situation of payment of cash compensation and the programme of resettlement of the peasants affected by the rising Sardar Sarovar and its backwaters. The situation is highly volatile and can explode any moment.

In the early stages of implementation of the project, the authorities offered cash compensation for the land coming under submergence. Calculated on the basis of land revenue assessment of the parcels acquired, the amounts offered were paltry. In many cases, the land revenue was paid not by the tribal peasants in whose names the land stood in the records of the revenue department but by the members of the community that had migrated from Gujarat and had ample resources at their command. In such an arrangement, the titular holders were the poor absentee landlords, while the actual exploitation was done by the moneyed tenants whose names did not appear on the revenue records at all—clearly a tenancy relationship gone topsy-turvy.

The authorities could not have taken cognisance of the informal relationship. But they negotiated with the nominal or titular tribal owners on the basis of land revenues paid by third parties. In most cases, the paltry sums of compensation were accepted by the tribal owners as a kind of windfall. For them, the land that was submerged had not been a source of pecuniary income in their living memory.

The real losers were the cultivators who stood to lose the land they were using but now left without a chance to claim any compensation whatsoever. This class turned to the only course of action open to it. It began providing moral and material support to the agitators of the Narmada Bachao Andolan (NBA) who, even while working on the environmentalist agenda of opposing the dam itself, demanded satisfactory compensation for the displaced. The tribal owners wanted heftier compensation; the moneyed tenants wanted the whole project scrapped. The NBA convinced the tribals to demand Rs. 2 lakh to Rs. 5 lakh per acre. The tribals thought the demand was far-fetched but hoped the NBA leaders could push it through rather than submit to voluntary drowning or *jal samadhi* in the rising waters.

The bureaucracy took advantage of the lukewarm interest of the titular owners in the matter and made them accept as compensation sums that were far lower than the estimated value of the land, calculated at the official stamp value—a hypothetical price presumed while calculating the amount of stamp-duty due in cases of actual sale or purchase. Further, the payment was made not in one lumpsum but in petty instalments. Even this trickle dried up soon enough. And what was collected went in weddings and such other expenses, and the tribals were left with nothing to acquire any income-yielding asset, even if they had the imagination and motivation.

Had this mode of compensation continued, the tribals would have lost interest in the matter and the NBA its gun-fodder. It, therefore, started demanding compensation in kind—land for land. This was well received by the tribals in the hope that they would get to cultivate after decades land in their own name. By now, they had developed a cultist faith in the NBA. The Andolan continued to promise *jal samadhi* rather than compromise on the opposition to the Narmada Dam.

Their demand-in-kind was accepted with unexpected alacrity by the Gujarat government.

Once the NBA and the *babus* entered, the resettlement plan became progressively generous. Those who held less than five acres—the minimum holding under law—were to be given a minimum of five acres. If the affected party had more than one major son and if the share of each son came to less that five acres in the submerged land, each was to be allotted five acres. Soon claims began to made on behalf of grandsons as well. Further, cash payments were made for acquisition of bullocks and agricultural implements. The package was further sweetened by a grant of Rs. 10,000 for construction of farmstead, and governmental help in levelling and improving the substitute land. This certainly was the best ever resettlement package offered to the project-affected people anywhere in the world. It was the combined interest of the bureaucracy and the agitators that brought about this wonder. All the same, credit must go to the NBA for drawing full advantage of the cupidity of the babudom.

This could have been the end of the resettlement issue for the Sardar Sarovar Project. That would not have pleased the actual exploiters of land under submergence. The NBA shifted the stand and opposed the dam on environmental grounds—their prime agenda. To keep the agitation's momentum, those effectively resettled in Gujarat were persuaded to go on protesting against the allocation on one ground or other. The workers of NBA went round the resettlement colonies exhorting their followers to demand relocation to more valuable land near Baroda and Ahmedabad that would have better resale value.

Then, the Supreme Court pulled the rug from under the feet of the NBA by approving increase in the height of the dam and ordering that the affected persons would have to settle for cash compensation if they could not be given alternative land that met their approval.

The clock has turned a full cycle now. Those who accepted cash compensation in the early stages are now thirsting for compensation in kind with full benefits in Gujarat. They are prepared to raise, by whatever means, money to return the compensation received earlier—though not with interest. Those resettled in Gujarat are far from content. They face a palpable hostility from the old inhabitants of the adjoining villages who resent the "son-in-law treatment" given to the resettlees and their perceptibly greater opulence and conditions as regards schooling, playgrounds, parks, water, electricity, roads, etc.

The Supreme Court judgment has taken the wind out of the NBA sails. There is no more talk of *jal samadhi*. The farmers are in bad state—mentally and financially.

Is there a solution to this imbroglio? There is. The affected farmers have themselves shown the way out. The submerged land remains under water for only a part of the year.

Right now, in November, one sees narrow strips of land where farmers continue to sow maize, grams, *jowar* and sundry vegetables during the period when the land is not under water but gets assured supply of water. One sees hundreds of pipelines jutting out of the riverbed lifting water to irrigate crops.

The point is that the land coming under submergence is not out of use. It can still be used for part of the year. A further advantage is that the banks of the Narmada both south and north are classical *parikrama* territory—the only exercise of circumambulation of a major river in the world. Scenically, the area is breathtaking with the pristine Narmada flowing between the Vindhya and Satpura peaks. The land marked for submergence on both the banks has great potential as tourist attraction, both Indian and foreign.

If a corporation of farmers is helped by the government to clean up the numerous bathing *ghats*, to provide clean cheap hotel facilities (of the ITDC type) and to provide clean drinking water, the enterprise could mop up massive revenues including in foreign exchange. The establishments could be franchised with the stipulation that the franchisees take care of the landscape and the pathways.

The total cost of the project would be much less than the amounts spent on resettlement and losses caused due to hold-up of construction because of the NBA agitation. The project-affected people will surely be glad to find an economic activity.

The million-dollar question is: Will the governments of Gujarat, Madhya Pradesh and Maharashtra show the necessary imagination and enterprise and will the agitators put the interests of those affected above their personal ambitions of fame and gain?

---

18 December 2002.

IX

WTO

67 India in the World Trade Organization

An Introduction

There was considerable debate in India if India should join the World Trade Organization (WTO).

Those opposed to Indian entry in the WTO were mainly non-governmental organisations (NGOs) that had apprehensions about:

- The kind of restrictions that might be put on the Indian sovereignty by the WTO,
- The consequences for the Indian industry, particularly the pharmaceutical industry of the provisions of the Intellectual Property Rights agreement, in particular by the regime of product patents,
- The obligations that may be imposed by the WTO on India to scale down its regime of subsidies to agriculture, customs duties as also the export regime.

As against this, the defenders of the WTO maintained that:

- India as the original signatory country of the GATT had little alternative but to join the Agreement on Agriculture (AoA) as well,
- India has been following, for long decades, a regime of negative subsidies on the Indian agriculture. In fact, the prices received by the farmers for their produce are, generally, less than the cost of production. In a regime that maintained that the prices received by the farmers should not be higher than the prices that would have been obtained in a free market ought not to disturb the Indian situation,
- India had the sovereign right to determine its bound duties for each item in the international trade,

- India did not have any subsidies on any of the items of agricultural export,
- Unlike in most international systems, the WTO provided for equal voting rights for all the member countries. It also had a Dispute Settlement System which could only be more favourable to the developing countries than the regime of Special 301 and Super 301,
- In this situation prevailing in the year 2000-01, Indian farmers will be quite content with the prices that were prevailing in the international market,
- Indian agriculture with its smaller holdings and lack of capital would, undoubtedly, be placed at a disadvantage in competition with the agriculture of the more developed countries where the size of holding is several times larger and in the capital and technology far more advanced. As against this, India had the natural advantage of abundant sunshine and adequate sources of water as also a hardy peasantry that had made it possible for India to become self-sufficient in food in spite of inimical State policies.

India had every interest in pursuing the negotiations under the WTO. There was no way India could prevail upon the richer countries to scale down their enormous subsidies. The stipulations of the Agreement on Agriculture that provided for a time bound scaling down of subsidies was the only thing that was going for the Indian agriculture.

India should, therefore, pursue the negotiations and with the help of the third world countries insist that the provisions of the Agreement on Agriculture in respect of domestic subsidies in the developing as also developed countries be strictly implemented.

After Doha Round, the WTO talks got derailed and the talks in Hong Kong, Singapore and Geneva have still not been able to bring them back on the rails.

The left-wing political parties and the NGOs are, of course, happy at the prospect of the crumbling of the WTO.

The stalemate in the WTO negotiations has warmed the coddle of the opponents to the very idea of free markets and in particular, of free multilateral trade as under the WTO. Little do they imagine or understand that the present imbroglio might actually pave the way for radical reforms in the administrative structures as also dispositions of the Marrakesh Agreements.

Even if the inter-governmental character of the WTO fails, that will not be the end of the free markets or of the multilateral trade. Forces of freedom and the comparative advantage of multilateral trade might push the principal parties to international trade *viz.*, traders, manufacturers and farmers to take over the negotiations and reformulate the dispositions of the WTO Acts, particularly, the AoA to make them more friendly to farmers rather than to macroeconometricians and international jurists.

2 May 2009.

68 Globalisation Rocks Farm Patriarchy

Agriculture in India, at one epoch held as a model of productivity, quality of the produce and technological sophistication both in production and post-harvest processing, started declining with the coming of the British, principally because the colonial rule meant the end of the autonomy of villages and that of agriculture. The State drew up revenue maps and fixed annual land revenue, swamped the Indian rural artisans with the mass-produced wares of the metropolitan industry.

After Independence, the government intervened even more comprehensively to promote formation of capital for the nascent socialist industries. It dominated the supply of inputs and distorted the agricultural produce markets against the interest of the agrarian community in favour of those of the urban industrial sector.

Phase one of liberalisation maintained the State-domination of agriculture in tact. The second phase—more particularly, the opening up of the international trade—is forcing the government to relax its stranglehold. The farm community might soon begin to breathe more freely.

The economic reforms appear to address another issue—the patriarchal stranglehold. Women might soon emerge as equal partners in agrarian community with equal rights in landed property as also in farm management.

Farm women lost their proprietary rights in agricultural land, probably over 3,000 years back, when men learnt the art and the science of harnessing the bullocks to the plough and the cart.

The women were reduced to the status of domiciliary slave labour putting in donkey's hours for household chores, animal husbandry and all post-ploughing work in the fields. They enjoyed no rights in landed property or farm incomes.

Occasionally, a father would make a gift of piece of land to his daughter at her wedding for her nominal maintenance. Women retained the moneys that came from sale of non-food grain produce such as vegetables, fruit and milk.

The daughters were given ornaments and the sons-in-law were endowed with cash and gifts in full settlement of the daughters' share in natal property.

The situation worsened after Independence. The pre-Green Revolution 'grow more food' campaigns, the tenancy and the land ceiling legislations resulted in near-complete erosion of women's ownership of agricultural land.

The land ceiling acts discriminated blatantly against daughters of the family. It became impossible to have any recourse to courts of law on grounds of abridgement of the fundamental rights because of the draconian provisions of the Schedule IX of the Constitution.

Women do most of the labour in the field but have few rights in property or income. The ever-increasing domination of the State machinery as also the cooperatives forced women to shrink back into a cloistered existence of hard labour of cooking, child bearing, child rearing, water fetching, fuel collecting and endless chores in the field.

Globalisation promises to break the patriarchal shell within the 'India'-dominated 'Bharat'. It demands increase in production, higher productivity and maintenance of high standards of quality.

The cooperative bodies have a poor track record in these areas; the governmental bodies abhor competition and openness and the open air of globalisation is anathema to them.

A new form of business organisation that may broadly be described as producers' corporations is on the horizon. The government cannot afford any mollycoddling of the cooperative bodies. The farmers will resist being forced into cooperatives while the city people use the corporate form.

Under the new form, farmers will pool together their fragmented holdings under the aegis of a corporate banner and will be given a proportionate share in the equity. The corporations will provide financial resources, technological know-how and managerial skills.

Farmers' corporations will enjoy a greater sense of confidence and loyalty from the farmers as they would have economic stakes in its prosperity. There is little chance of the producer farmer shifting loyalties as happens in the 'contract farming' regime.

The farmers' corporations are converting the immovable landed property into an easily transferable claim on dividends and appreciation. The male hegemony in the landed property got a certain sanction and support from various factors. Women were largely illiterate and preferred keeping away from public fora and courts and revenue offices.

Patrilocality—the social custom according to which married daughters shift to the matrimonial households—made it difficult for married daughters and widowed daughters-in-law to exercise any effective control over the immovable landed property. Finally, the high incidence of mother's death in child birth conferred on the male of the family a central role which made it difficult in law for women to maintain any claims on the ancestral property.

Things are changing very fast. The girl child's education is advancing by leaps and bounds; maternity deaths have become a relatively minor risk and women take part in *panchayat* activities in full equal right. The immovable character of landed property and the institution of patrilocality remain the last obstacles militating against equal property rights for women.

The farmers' corporations will convert the land into transferable scrip that can be held by any person irrespective of his or her geographical location. Married daughters in their matrimonial homes and widowed daughters-in-law staying in natal homes can hold equity shares and participate in the management as also earn dividends.

Globalisation offers an opportunity for ending not only the stranglehold of the State but also that of the patriarchal institutions. The unchaining of the rural women will unleash massive energy that could catapult India into the status of a global player in agriculture.

---

27 March 2002.

69 Two Nations, Two Agricultures

The conference of the US House-Senate on Farm Bill 2002 is reviewing the agreement announced by the negotiators in a news conference on April 26. The Congress will, most likely, approve the Bill and send it to the President, Mr. George W. Bush for his assent and signature. The President is expected to approve it without any modification. The Farm Bill, with its text extending over hundreds of pages, will come as a revelation to those dabbling with agricultural policy in India.

That the representatives of the House and the Senate convened a conference for negotiating the farm policy itself would surprise Indian politicians and economists. That the Farm Bill is drafted on the basis of an agreement reached with the farmers' unions would be unbelievable to the Krishi Bhavan satraps. The successive National Agriculture Policy drafts have been concocted in India in great secrecy with very little consultation with the state governments and no contact with the farmers' unions whatsoever.

Now that the negotiations on the US Farm Bill have come to a settlement, the draft bill is expected to be cleared in less than three months. That really is unbelievable. In India, no formal action has been initiated on the National Agriculture Policy document piloted by Mr. Nitish Kumar in 2001. The national policy document put together by Mr. Balram Jakhar, some years back, was simply allowed to lapse.

The US is among the top farm subsidy providers after Japan and the European Union. The amounts of farm subsidies given in the US total $300 billion. The Farm Bill 2002 provides for a further $173.5 billion—an increase of 70 per cent in the spending on agriculture.

Subsidy rates for some commodity crops will be hiked by 10 per cent in a single stroke this year.

$94 million are provided for a programme for apples alone, $500 million for sugar and a whooping $4 billion to subsidise peanuts.

Even the relatively better-off growers of rice, corn, cotton and soyabean get a bonanza. Of course, there is limit on the amount of benefits a single farmer can receive. The Senate had proposed a ceiling of $275,000 per farm per year. That was raised during the negotiations to $360,000. Corporate farmers have been given enough flexibility to circumvent even that limit which is the equivalent of nearly Rs. 18 lakh. This kind of support from the State is beyond the wildest dream of an Indian peasant who would be overjoyed if he had an assurance of a bare Rs. 18,000 per farm per year. The governmental support comes in various forms and modalities that fill up not only the famous WTO boxes—blue, green and red—but much more.

The Agriculture Ministry in India is contemplating abolition of the system of statutory minimum prices. The US Farm Bill introduces the concept of target prices and stipulates making up of the gap between the prices actually received and the target prices. This will take care of slumps in commodity prices resulting from not only seasonal but also cyclical fluctuations.

Agriculture is seen not only as a supplier of food, fibre, fuel and raw material but also as an important pillar of society. The concept of 'multi-functionality' introduced by the European Union has been picked up and funding of conservation and rural development has been substantially enhanced.

Liberal assistance has been provided for livestock and crop losses due to natural disasters in 2001.

The rates of marketing loans are proposed to be raised for the first time since 1981.

The dairy producers are offered an improved nationwide safety net to protect them against contingencies like the 'mad cow' epidemic.

All meats, fruits, vegetable, peanuts, etc. must show the country of origin on the labels. Only those food items can be labelled as originating in US as are made from plants and animals born, raised and processed in the country.

An elaborate system of trade promotion and food stamps for nutrition will ensure the wide availability of the American produce in the US and the world over.

The US Farm Bill could, in fact, shake the doddering sailboat of the ministerial negotiations of WTO that have crossed Doha and is trying to shore up at Mexico.

So far the US has been demanding that the EU and the Japan disclose in full the details of all support to agriculture. The idea was to get all members of the WTO to respect *de minimis* levels of 5 per cent for developed countries and 10 per cent for the developing countries. With this Farm Bill, the US, in one stroke, has given up all its moral authority to cajole other recalcitrant countries into falling in line with the stipulations of the Marrakesh Agreements. Mr. Pascal Lamy of the European Union is already howling protest that the US now pays three times more per farm than the EU. Even the French, normally in the forefront in mollycoddling farmers, would find it difficult to envisage munificence to agriculture on this scale.

What lies behind this Farm Bill? The developing countries, most of which have neither the fiscal ability nor the political will to subsidise their farmers on any significant scale, were hoping that the US and the EU can, somehow, be pushed to scale down subsidies to agriculture so that the international commodity trade can have a more level-playing field.

Even the public opinion in the US is shocked at the extent to which the government is venturing out to subsidise farmers. *The Wall Street Journal* has called the Farm Bill "A ten-year $173.5-billion bucket of slop". The criticism in other quarters is even more strident. The President of the National Farmers' Union is barely satisfied and has expressed the hope that the Farm Bill will be only the first step in the right direction.

Has Mr. Bush made up his mind to scuttle the WTO negotiations and revert to a new bipolar world in which China and the US can lord over the world on the lines of 'Super 301' and 'Special 301'? Is Mr. Bush overplaying his hand to pressure Japan and European Union?

It may come out that the whole exercise of the Bill is meant as a tactical ploy that would put other WTO members on the defensive. If the

US had to argue its case from starting point of present level of subsidies, it may end up somewhere very close to *de minimis* levels of subsidies. That would give rise to political difficulties.

The US administration was to start negotiations at levels of subsidies proposed in the Bill, that is, 70 per cent higher than the present level in the hope that at the end of all harsh negotiations, it may end not too far below the existing levels of subsidies and still keep the negotiations going. The US Farm Bill should alert the Government of India and its negotiators to the high polemical level of WTO negotiations.

The two largest democracies of the world are India and the US. India has two-thirds of its population eking out a bare existence in agriculture. Less than 3 per cent of the US's population provides food, fibre and fuel not only to the American people but also for all the needy of the world.

The US switched to the policy of farm support after the Great Depression of 1929 and became a world farm power in just one decade. The farmer in India suffered under the British rule and has been subjected to negative subsidies since Independence. The contrast is stark. The US Farm Bill should be made compulsory reading for Indian administrators.

8 May 2002.

70 Trading Blind-folded

The stated objective of the World Trade Organization is to minimise distortions caused by State interventions. As the former US President, Mr. Bill Clinton, said in his address to the World Economic Forum in Davos on January 29, 2000, open markets do create jobs, they do raise incomes, they do spark innovations and spread new technologies; they do, coupled with the explosion of international communications through the Internet, which is the fastest growing network in history.

The eight-year-old baby does not appear to have got over its teething troubles.

Free markets tend to bring about division of labour on the basis of the principle of comparative advantages. The partners in the free trade are not supposed to be identical clones; they are supposed to have distinct identities on the basis of their historical, social, cultural and geopolitical characters. The first round of difficulties for the WTO came with some countries wanting to impose uniformity in the structures relating to production the world over. They wanted the regulations on environment, even in developing countries, to come up to the standards of the developed countries.

They insisted that bonded labour and child labour should go forthwith and that labour laws should conform to international standards. Briefly, they wanted technology to remain the only source of economic advantage. That would have been derogatory to the principle of comparative advantage and defeated largely the basic objective of the WTO. Fortunately, all this has been kept in animated suspension, at least for the time being.

The second bout of troubles came with anti-WTO, anti-globalisation and anti-technology NGOs mobilising large crowds of demonstrators with the objective of scuttling the negotiations or, at least, change the environment of the negotiations.

A far more serious crisis is developing in the post-11 September 2001 era. The global campaign against terrorism has had its effects on the trade environment. For some time, one side to the war has been crying victory in a cacophony of jingoistic jubilation. The fact is that there is no winner in any war; there are, at least, two losers.

Maintenance of international agreements on abolition of weapons of mass destruction was, at least, one cause that led to the attack on Iraq. The application of the Bush doctrine is not seen to be uniform the world over. The US seems to have different standards about international probity varying from country to country.

The fact remains that the war in Iraq has brought to an end an era of international agreements that were based on voluntary disclosures by countries of their situation and implementation on international commitments. The anti-war feeling is now at a peek and the Seattle-like demonstrations can be expected to be even more boisterous hereafter.

Under the Agreement on Agriculture (AoA), member countries made certain commitments about market access (tarrification), domestic support and export competition. The WTO set the rules of the game, laid down timetables for implementation and mechanism of dispute settlements. So far so good.

Unfortunately, the rules of the game, particularly in the area of domestic support, dumping, sanitary and phytosanitary measures and non-trade barriers were drafted by people who lacked a fundamental faith in the efficacy of market forces to correct any mischief.

The WTO relied on a quasi-judicial mechanism of adversarial arguments. The WTO structures have, inevitably, being taken over by a new tribe of lawyers and jurists. Their arguments and jurisprudence are beyond the comprehension of a common citizen.

Access to the redress machinery of the WTO is not physically possible except through the agency of national governments. Consequently, there lies a real threat that the WTO agreements, far from diminishing the clout of the State, might actually make the State a more powerful agency than before Marrakesh.

The member countries of the WTO made their own declarations about the three basic programmes, that is, access, domestic support and export and they were accepted in good faith. It is only much later that the countries, particularly in the developing countries, started realising the subtly devious tricks that could be played by juggling green, blue and amber boxes.

The richer countries have, on their own part, started realising the importance of the multifunctional character of agriculture as also adverse effects of the Agreement on Agriculture access provisions, albeit short term, on domestic employment. The US, the European Union and Japan as also the Cairns countries are carrying on a highly polemical debate in a jargon that is understood less and less by the farmers world over who are the primary interested party.

The post-11 September 2001 scene has resuscitated the jingoistic nationalism of protectionists, even in countries that have traditionally stood for free trade and democracy.

Mr. Saddam Hussein was accused of surreptitiously developing and stockpiling weapons of mass destruction contrary to the spirit and the word of the international agreements. Major countries that were infuriated by Mr. Saddam Hussein's machinations are themselves trying to develop escape routes for withdrawing from the commitments under the URA.

The environment of international good faith and innocence stands breached and may stay breached for some time to come. Agricultural subsidies in richer countries are potent weapons of mass destruction as far as the peasantry in poor countries is concerned.

These latter accepted the Agreement on Agriculture conditionalities in the hope that that will create, at least, a moral force for making the richer countries accept and enforce them. The domestic support conditionalities of the Agreement on Agriculture are faulty, at least on three counts:

1. Keeping a fixed 1986-1989 period for hypothetical referral prices makes little sense, particularly during the period of long recession and changing exchange rates.
2. The richer countries have far greater capacity to play with rules and boxes of diverse colours than the poorer ones.

3. The Agreement's prescription would make more sense if it were based on comparison between domestic costs and domestic prices rather than between domestic prices and international referral prices.

The WTO agreements have been the subject of seminars, workshops and colloquia than any other subjects in recent times. The information on the factual situation in each member country, nevertheless, remains densely opaque. No one knows what and how many weapons of economic mass destruction are being accumulated by their partners in trade.

The UN system had to devise an inspection system and inspection mechanism for investigating cases of nonconformity with international commitments.

The WHO recently had to intervene in China for the investigation of the severe acute respiratory syndrome (SARS) situation. The WTO would need to establish a system of information gathering and inspection so that URA is rescued from the pedantry of the academics as also the legalistic arguments of the modern-day Shylocks. I agree that the time is still not ripe for the international system to devise an inspection mechanism that would be readily acceptable to all member countries. There will be harangues about encroachment of national sovereignty.

The WTO has survived those enthusiasts who sought to impose uniform production structures in all the three worlds. It is trying to extricate itself from the clutches of the jurists. It needs to develop a mechanism for overcoming the pedantry of the academics vulnerable to political influences.

---

7 May 2003.

71 EU: Realising the WTO Dream

On June 26, the day the ministers of Agriculture in Europe agreed to reform the 45-year-old Common Agricultural Policy, I received a number of calls from journalists in Europe and the US asking for my reaction. I was, of course, happy.

This was the development I had for years been hoping for, and opponents of WTO forecasting would never come.

I looked at all the newspapers that had arrived; none—not even the pink ones—carried any news about the EU decision that had sent shockwaves across the Atlantic. It was only on the Internet that some information was available.

None of the reports carried any positive reaction from any of the developing countries. There was something much deeper that did not meet my eye. There was a concerted effort to black out all positive reactions, particularly from the developing countries. My comments were also blacked out.

It is a long and complex story.

The agricultural systems, the world over, fall into three categories:

- The developing and poor countries attach a premium to industrial development and follow policies that favour industrial development at the cost of agriculture.
- The richer countries such as the US, Canada, the EU and Japan that have come a long way to industrial development and have only a relatively smaller portion of their populations dependent on agriculture, are more concerned about environmental health, sustainability and the social functions of agriculture.

They follow policies of giving massive budgetary supports to their farmers. Europe spends half of its budget—$50 billion—on agricultural support and the US Farm Bill approved last year entails a support operation of $300 billion for over a six-year period.

- Countries such as Australia, New Zealand, Brazil, Argentina, Canada, Indonesia, the Philippines—the Cairns group—have an agriculture sector that is largely export-oriented and therefore, have a built-in interest in getting the subsidies in the Quad countries scaled down.

India is a special case among the developing countries where pro-industry policies have assumed an anti-agriculture bias since decades and its farmers suffer from negative subsidies or net taxation.

The US and the Cairns group have been the prime movers of globalisation in agricultural trade under the aegis of the WTO.

The Agreement on Agriculture (AoA) of the WTO sets specific targets and a timetable for scrapping of import barriers and export subsidies, lowering of tariffs and scaling down of domestic subsidies.

The richer foursome Quad countries not only have had high levels of domestic support but also complex systems of reaching the farmers financial assistance.

These governments finance out of the budget various common services and infrastructural facilities. In addition, they give subsidies based on the quantum of production or quantum of production foregone as also export subsidies.

The delegates of the richer countries at the Uruguay round of negotiations cleverly introduced into the text of the AoA the main categories of subsidies as being minimally distortive of trade and hence, permissible as 'green' or 'blue' box subsidies. It is mainly the subsidies given in the form of price support that became targets for reduction.

The post-Marrakesh (1995) experience shows that the richer countries have serious social and political reservations about respecting their commitments under the AoA. They have been trying to dodge the commitments and fiddling with various coloured boxes, transferring subsidies from the amber box to the green and blue boxes.

At Doha (November 2001), the developing countries were keen on reviewing the performance on past commitments while the richer countries had plans for enlarging the agenda.

The Doha declaration succeeded in keeping the process of negotiations alive but it became quite clear that the WTO negotiations would be in trouble if the richer countries did not accept to scale down substantially their agricultural subsidies.

The Quad countries used their extensive apparatus for economic research and to claim that each of them was a pious saint fulfilling its commitments to the WTO in both word and spirit while the others were flagrantly violating them.

The voluntary declarations made by different countries ceased to be taken at their face value and it looked as if the WTO would have to develop, apart from its dispute settlement mechanism, a system of inspection and independent verification of the situation of each country as regards its international commitments (see "Trading Blind-folded" in *Business Line,* May 7, 2003).

The US Trade Act of 1974 had a provision requiring the President to determine, after conclusion of future agreement, whether any major industrial country had failed to make concessions substantially equivalent to the US concessions.

A similar legislation in 2004 would have been disastrous, not only for the WTO but also for all international agreements, particularly in the post-Iraq scenario.

The US Congress has already voted through over $190 billion of farm subsidies over the next decade and the US officials continued to maintain that despite this massive hike, the US farm subsidies were just about half of those in Europe.

The EU joined the GATT negotiations, as a union, only in the fifth GATT Round (1960-1962). The European Economic Community has followed policies on encouraging agricultural production over the last 45 years through massive subsidies related to levels of production. France, Spain, Portugal have largely been the beneficiaries while Germany has been carrying the fiscal burden.

It had serious difficulties taking unilateral initiatives in reducing subsidies as the farm community was addicted to them, the problems created by mountains of butter and lakes of wine notwithstanding.

It had additional difficulties because of the adoption of common currency and the prospective enlargement of the union by addition of 10 member countries to the existing 15.

The approach of the next ministerial meeting of the WTO at Cancun in September 2003 forced the ministers of the EU to take a bold step.

What they have agreed to do is to keep the total amount of farm subsidy in Europe constant at about $50 billion; but this amount will cover the enlarged union of 25 countries.

More important, they have agreed to delink farm subsidies from levels of production that have in the past resulted in overproduction and dumping in the developing countries.

This will be replaced by a single payment to farmers, conditional upon environmental considerations. There has been hue and cry in Europe itself. Milk producers in Ireland are protesting, environmentalists are unhappy.

It is feared that some of the member countries may find it necessary to continue the old system of production-linked subsidies, lest the farmers actually start abandoning land and farming.

The French—the major beneficiaries—have agreed to give the new experiment a trial and the German paymasters are willing to go along. That is quite an achievement.

Obviously, it would have been great had Europe done more to scale down subsidies. It is understandable it could not do more.

It needs to be appreciated that it has stolen march over both Japan and US in taking the first step towards the realisation of WTO dream; it has earned its passage to Cancun.

It is not meant to be a unilateral disarmament; it is a clear signal to other Quad countries that they should come forward with concrete measures for lowering hurdles that hamper free international trade in agricultural commodities.

In all this darkness, the European decision is like the light at the end of the tunnel.

If one of the Quads has got ready to reform its agricultural subsidies, it is only a matter of time before the others follow suit. Indian farmers, suffering from negative subsidies as they are, had put their hope in this kind of a breakthrough, and it has finally come.

The decision of the European agricultural ministers proves again that freedom will have its way, no matter how arduous and painful the hurdles.

---

9 July 2003.

72 Cancun: Keep the Wheels Moving

Nobody had heard of Cancun till the Doha declaration put it on the world map. Marrakesh, Doha, Cancun—the World Trade Organization (WTO) seems to be unwittingly doing its bit to improve people's knowledge of geography.

The provisions regarding the geographical appellations under the Intellectual Property Rights Agreement included scotch whisky and champagne bubbly wine but not Darjeeling tea or Ratnagiri Alphonso.

The sites of WTO ministerial meetings became particularly celebrated because each of them witnessed boisterous demonstrations by anti-liberalisation and anti-globalisation mobs.

The third ministerial at Seattle was scuttled because the ministers, in the circumstances prevailing there, could not agree on an agenda for negotiations.

The riots at Genoa (Italy) resulted in one death.

The Doha ministerial was not affected by the activities on the street; the possible reason being that the concepts of civil liberty are quite different in West Asia than elsewhere.

And now, another five-day ministerial conference is scheduled to begin in Cancun (Mexico) on September 10.

Trade negotiations are like a cycle ride. They have to be running to maintain balance and keep going.

The full agenda of freeing multilateral international trade will, possibly, never be completed. The negotiators advance a few paces and then realise that the agenda needs to be broadened if the whole process is to make any sense and bring the desired benefits.

The General Agreement on Tariffs and Trade (GATT) started at about the same time as the Bretton Woods Conference and the Los Angeles endeavour to create a United Nations.

It was on October 30, 1947 that 23 countries concluded the protocol for the provisional application of GATT. That was in Geneva (Switzerland).

The agreement entered into force on January 1, 1948. After that followed a succession of negotiation rounds—in Annecy (France) 1949; Torquay (England) 1950-51; Geneva (Switzerland) 1956; Dillon (Switzerland) 1960-1962; Kennedy Round 1963-1967; Geneva 1973-1979, called the Tokyo round; and finally, Uruguay 1986-1994. Each round of negotiations took longer than the previous one to finalise the Act.

The celebrated Uruguay Round started in 1986 and its agreements were signed at Marrakesh (Morocco) nine years later.

Basically, there is only one agreement to form a WTO but annexed thereto are 28 agreements—not counting understandings, protocols, decisions and declarations—forming a veritable forest of rules and regulations that would be the delight of any lawyer or an econometrician aspiring to make a career through undecipherable abracadabra.

That was not the end of the matter. When hundreds of jurists and experts, each nursing a separate vested interest lobby, come together, the discussions go on and on. Contentious matters cannot always be settled by clear agreements. Diplomats have evolved, over years, drafting gimmicks that give some satisfaction to all the parties concerned.

The WTO began operating in January 1995. Within the first three years, its members put their hands to agreements—not on the table at Marrakesh—on telecommunications, financial services and information technology.

The negotiations on the movement of natural persons were concluded in 1995 with modest agreement. Negotiations on maritime transportation failed. Those on telecommunication and financial services are at various stages of progress.

Negotiations to improve the WTO agreement on government procurement began in 1998 but failed quickly for obvious reasons.

Negotiations on agriculture and services—the toughest nut on the platter—were supposed to have started by 2000. However, the participants could not agree on the negotiating agenda in time. The first post-Marrakesh ministerial conference in Singapore (December 1996) made things more complicated by initiating studies on trade and investment, trade and competition as also transparency in government procurement and trade facilitation.

The second ministerial conference in Geneva (May 1998) took on the additional work of agreement on electronic commerce.

The third ministerial, in Seattle, closed without making any progress.

In the last ministerial in Doha (2001), there was no real progress in fixing the agenda or programme of action. The richer countries had a manifest interest in dodging concrete action on implementing the Marrakesh commitments and tried to broaden the agenda by bringing—if not to the table, at least on the radar screen—subjects like labour laws, environment, the four Singapore issues, matters relating to Trade Related Intellectual Property Rights (TRIPS) and public health.

The last has gained urgency because of the spread of AIDS in Africa and SARS in Asia.

As regards the implementation of Marrakesh commitments relating to freer access and lower domestic and export subsidies, the richer countries have made no substantive progress in implementation.

The European Union has made a sort of a symbolic gesture by delinking subsidies from income levels. Neither the developing countries nor the Cairns nations are enthused at that. Japan and the US realised the importance of their commitments at Marrakesh but have difficulty making pronouncements because of the impending elections in the US.

The richer countries are sitting in a conclave in Geneva to work out ways and means to ensure that the bicycle of trade negotiations does not collapse and that the negotiations proceed without ending in abject failure, which would be a serious setback to multilateral trade.

The Indian negotiators were ill prepared for the Uruguay Round. They indulged in some histrionics in Doha and convinced everybody at home about their triumph.

In the present situation too, New Delhi has no clear positions on the negotiations but, with the approaching general elections, would like to give voters the impression that India did not yield in Doha and Cancun more territory than the Congress did in the Uruguay round.

So, what are the prospects at Cancun? The basic proposition is simple. Multilateral trade unhindered by governmental interventions in the long run is good for all the parties concerned. Unfortunately, politicians are too short-sighted to bother about the long run.

If the trade negotiations were taking place between national chambers of commerce, industry and agriculture, most issues would have been resolved quicker. Once the governments became negotiating parties, inevitably came in the legalese, the 'whereas', 'wheretofore', 'notwithstanding' and the rest of the jargon and conveniently manipulated statistics and econometrics of pedantic.

The WTO has been so dominated by the jurists, the economists and the bureaucrats that they could, if they wished, continue the negotiating rounds till the cows—with or without foot and mouth disease—come home.

Outside, on the roads of Cancun, the scene may be quite different. Various anti-globalisation fora have made assiduous preparations to improve on their performance at Seattle. In the documents they exchange on the Internet, they have clearly called for derailing the WTO through people's mobilisation around Cancun, linking the WTO agenda to popular campaigners, elevating local struggles and impacting WTO decisions.

The wreckers are armed with detailed maps of Cancun, contact information with local groups, schedules of official conferences and receptions. They plan to observe a women's day, a biodiversity day and an anti-WTO day. The whole thing will reach a crescendo on September 15, which happens to be Mexico's Independence Day.

Inside the conference hall at Cancun, it may be like the American civil war. Unfortunately, there will be no Abraham Lincoln to bring light to the debates. There will be hundreds of John Wilkes Booths toting their guns. The only ray of hope is that the Booths can never really make the Lincolns disappear from the face of the earth.

---

3 September 2003.

73 Lessons from the Failure at Cancun

So, the much-awaited Cancun Ministerial of the WTO is over. And it seems that there was more excitement on the sidelines than at the talks themselves.

There were hundreds of demonstrators on the streets some distance away from the conference venue, most of them wearing ethnic headgear, masks and robes and adding considerably more colour to the proceedings than the epicentre of activity in the conference hall, where the tone was belligerent and aggressive from the word go.

Judging by the reports from Cancun it would appear that there is a general disappointment, both among the participants and the public, at the breakdown of the multilateral trade talks. As this means a further setback to the long-cherished dream of making the world a single free market with each country giving the other the treatment as given to the most favoured nations (MFN) and treating all goods and services as being on par with domestic products once they enter the national frontiers.

At the talks, there was widespread recognition that the Agreement on Agriculture (AoA) formed the main item on the agenda. In a way, the dozen or so new items that appeared on the radar screen sort of got pushed back to bring agriculture back into centre stage.

The main focus in the discussions on agriculture was the pattern of richer countries paying massive subsidies to their farmers.

This is, no doubt, fully understandable and even justifiable in the context of their economic situation—given the miniscule proportion of farmers in the population and high level of infrastructural and technological development.

But it is clear that if the rich countries' demands of free access to developing countries' markets are to be acceded, the subsidies will have to undergo a massive reappraisal in a relatively short span of time.

The heavy subsidies of the richer countries are the single major obstacle to the realisation of a global trade system governed by internationally accepted rules that do not permit abrasive, trade-distorting intervention from any member State.

The Indian team for Cancun had certainly fine-tuned its vocal chords. The Commerce Minister, Mr. Arun Jaitley, made his point forcefully. The rich countries must bring down their subsidies or else the prospects of successful negotiations would be bleak. Mr. Jaitley was, for the most part, suave and soft-spoken though, at times, he sounded a trifle loud for his complex and rather delicate mission.

Mr. Jaitley, of course, could ill-afford to play a Dattopant Thengadi who, only last week, attempted to hold a *kisan* rally at Ramleela Maidan in the capital and let out, in his speech, an outpouring of jingoistic abuse aimed at the *gore* (white) nations.

He said these "white nations" were pampering their farmers and depressing the prices in the domestic and international markets, directly affecting the economics of peasants in the poor nations.

His advice to the government was: Get out of the WTO even before Cancun Ministerial opens. He said: We will not be treated as equals by these white men in the WTO, so let's get out.

Mr. Jaitley's subtle pressure on the rich countries to scale down their subsidies in the manner acceptable to the developing countries is understandable.

As leader of a national delegation, and particularly as he assumed the unofficial leadership of a group of score or so nations, he was required to make some belligerent noises in the hope of producing a favourable psychological impact on the negotiators of the opposite side.

The rich countries were sure to be disappointed if the current round of WTO negotiations were stalled. But they could certainly have been expected to make substantive concessions to avoid such a contingency. The recent decision to allow patented medicines manufactured by non-patent holders into countries direly in need thereof is a good example.

International negotiations, however, do not proceed under exchange of ultimatums, 'walk-outs' or threats, as is routine in national legislatures.

Mr. Thengadi is demanding that the level of domestic support in rich countries be brought down, not to the minimum prescribed in AoA but to the level of domestic support in poor countries. Mr. Thengadi could not be unaware of the fact that the Commerce Ministry is on record as admitting that Indian farmers have a negative subsidy—domestic support or aggregate measurement of support (AMS), at least in the basic period of reference.

Whether the Indian negative subsidy is merely 18 per cent, as held by the Commerce Ministry, or 87 per cent as demonstrated by the farmers' organisations is an issue that can be easily resolved in a Cancun-like conference.

An American, European or Japanese interlocutor may ask politely: "Mr Thengadi, do I understand you correctly? Do you expect us to scale down the domestic support actually to minus 87 per cent? That is very interesting. By the way, does India actually impose such a massive negative subsidy on its peasantry? Would you not agree with me, Mr. Thengadi, that the poverty of Indian peasants is more directly related to India's negative subsidy rather than our positive subsidies?"

The moment of truth has come. The positive farm subsidies in OECD countries have worked in tandem with the negative subsidies of countries like India.

Developing countries might have scored a victory as, by sheer strength of their numbers, they succeeded in making Cancun a futile exercise. But whatever the perception of self-interest of various countries, ultimately, history will push them towards systems that are open and transparent.

Even if some of the extremist opponents of free trade managed to make Cancun futile, it is all not going to end in zero. The WTO will begin fresh rounds and improve its procedures. The trade negotiations will certainly recover balance and move on.

One only hopes the protectionists will not need a third world war to learn the lessons that World War II and the Iron Curtain apparently failed to bring home to them. At the end of World War I, the victors were foolish at Versailles and lost the peace in arrogance.

At the end of World War II, both the victors and the vanquished were sober, to say the least. After the fall of the Soviet Union and in the shadow of a world war against terrorism, indications are that, this time, the poor and the weak might let the prospect of peace recede through sheer pique at their poverty.

---

17 September 2003.

74 Get WTO Back on Talking Terms

The Doha Ministerial prepared a schedule for negotiations on the Marrakesh treaties. Most of the work that remained to be done was in the field of agriculture, investments and services. The Ministerial Conference at Cancun proved abortive as it could not finalise even a minimum common declaration, not even one relating to future programme of action.

Some kind of preparatory work was initiated at the Geneva headquarters of the World Trade Organization (WTO). Some hopeful noises were made by the United States, the European Union as also in Japan and the Cairns countries. There is little possibility that the Doha round of talks would be completed successfully as scheduled, by end-2004. In the next few months, a huge leap is required to meet the Doha timetable. As of today, that does not look likely.

The United States is caught up in the presidential elections. It is unlikely that the contenders—the President, Mr. George Bush or the democrat challenger, Mr. John Kerry—would venture to burn their fingers by taking a position that would help the Doha round of negotiation move forward.

The G-21 group that came together in Mexico is today even more disparate than it was on the last day of the Cancun Ministerial. The European Union has its hands full dealing with problems of expansion and the value of the euro. Suddenly, the WTO has become an unwanted baby that nobody cares for. Does it mean that all the work that since the end of the Second World War to establish a multilateral system of international trade has been in vain? The General Agreement on Tariffs and Trade (GATT) negotiations, beginning in the 1940s, plodded on wearily till the beginning of the 1980s.

No one involved in the negotiations was trying to score political or economic points. There were occasions when a whole round of talks would be devoted to marginal expansion of list of commodities or of categories of commodities covered by the GATT.

It was after the fall of the Soviet Union that many countries connected with the GATT Round appeared to have developed a penchant to bite more than they could chew. Thus, in the Uruguay Round the number of agreements, memoranda, etc., expanded nearly to 30. Even more questionable was the decision to include the Agreement on Agriculture (AoA) in the ambit of the Uruguay Round.

By Marrakesh (1995), it looked as if the whole system of the various specialised institutions of the United Nations had been subsumed by the WTO. No specialised institution could do a thing without risking some poaching on some area of the WTO competence. And the WTO continues to tread on the toes of the UN and its specialised institutions. The very word 'globalisation' creates an impression of something on astronomical proportions gobbling up nations and even the international community. This globalisation by WTO happened too close on the heels of the fall of communism.

A good number of persons and institutions that got out of breath keeping pace with the march of the WTO globalisation fell by the wayside but remained rabid opponents not only of the globalisation but also of market-based mechanisms both at home and abroad. These opponents organised themselves into radical groups with considerable clout and have been haunting all international negotiation ever since they tasted blood at the Seattle Ministerial Conference.

In the long history of international trade, there have been swings and slides—some times of roller coaster proportions. Nevertheless, freedom of trade and economy has made progress through cycles of mercantilism—from fully open *laissez faire* to completely closed communism—not because of the inclinations or otherwise of politicians and leaders.

Freedom has advanced because it goes to the fundamentals of all life and human societies.

The present impasse in the WTO and globalisation may be long and even a difficult one. But there is little doubt that some day, sooner rather than later, the world community will need to sit down and evolve a multilateral system of world trade that will be free, equal and viable. The basic principles of the GATT/WTO system are unimpeachably sound. One: Treat all nations outside one's national frontiers as being equal and therefore, most favoured. Two: Treat all commodities that have entered one's territory on parity. The difficulty comes when the bureaucrats start translating these principles into working rules capable of application.

The main bottleneck in the WTO negotiations comes in the sector of agriculture. It is in this sector that the member countries find it difficult to make concessions to others and bring about reforms at home.

The Agreement on Agriculture envisages: 1. Abolishing all quantitative restrictions (QRs) and replacing them with tariffs that would be governed by commitments on bound rates and the progressive reduction; 2. Abolishing subsidies, in whatever form, to export of agricultural commodities; 3. Scaling down domestic subsidies to farmers in keeping with agreed schedules.

Any agreement on trade presumes clear definition of qualitative and sanitary standards and grades, a dispute settlement mechanism and of remedial action. In the case of agriculture, the AoA was drafted to introduce concepts that were foreign to the communities directly affected, that is, farmers, and the procedures involved were so legalistic that they could be handled only by specialised international jurists.

When the next epoch of negotiations on multilateral trade in agricultural commodities comes around, the new scheme will have to provide for rules that are applicable uniformly in different countries with diverse systems that read like a code of conduct for literate farmers and not like complicated rules that can barely be understood by even specialists and experts.

One could elaborate by giving specific illustrations. I would give only a few. World over farmers understood what farm subsidies are. Subsidies were understood as an advantage conferred by the government that would not be available in a strictly market-based economy. Since in a free market system average cost would tend to be equal to the average revenue, subsidy also could be defined as the surplus the farmers get over and above their costs of production on State interventions.

The Marrakesh agreements introduced such concepts as the aggregate measure of support (AMS) and subsidy equivalent, not to talk of green, blue and amber boxes, that have barely made any progress in the negotiations.

Similarly, the system of CODEX adopted and the rules pertaining to sanitary and phytosanitary controls, dispute settlement and anti-dumping rules have created complicated disputes, whole bodies of jurisprudence that only the specialist international jurists can cope with. The drafting of AoA was influenced too much by econometricians and the legal pundits, and too little by the farmers for whom they were meant in the first place.

If the Doha round is resumed honestly and seriously, it will have to retrace its steps and streamline the AoA to clear it of many of the fatal faults. If the Doha round is given a quiet burial, these considerations will need to dominate the spirits of the next generation of the architects of multilateral international trade in agricultural commodities.

---

17 March 2004.

75 Now for the Non-Resident Farmer

Canada is rolling out the red carpet for Indian talent. No, not for software experts but for the wheat and paddy farmers of Punjab and Andhra Pradesh. The news will cause considerable consternation in India. So far, only doctors, engineers and software specialists were considered "importable" by the first world. But doctors and engineers have a declining market in the Western world.

The software engineers have a market that is widely fluctuating. There were times when they were courted and at others told to pack up.

Many non-resident Indians have done well and purchased luxurious houses, flats and mansions in the US and elsewhere in the Western world, but they could do this—become real estate owners—after slogging for a long while.

The farmers from Punjab, on the other hand, have the possibility of purchasing land in Canada and starting farming operations immediately on their entry into the host country. They would naturally enjoy the right of permanent citizenship given their property status. A large number of farmers from Andhra Pradesh have already migrated to Africa and Canada. It is the farmer from Punjab who is being assiduously courted now.

A large number of them are reportedly preparing to go, and are even thinking of selling off their land in India. The Punjab Agricultural University (PAU) has even started special courses that familiarise the intending immigrants with the agro-climatic conditions in the host countries.

People have long migrated from India. Hordes of labourers were shipped off to the Caribbeans and Africa as indentured labour to bring the virgin land under cotton and sugarcane. But for the first time, the Indian farmer would be migrating as proprietor farmers and landowners. Rich countries have faced, for some time now, the problem of keeping their land green and keeping people on the soil.

This was sought to be achieved by massive subsidies to agricultural inputs, exports and incomes. The subsidies have reached the order of billions of dollars. The agriculture subsidies put a heavy burden as much on the domestic consumers as on the taxpayer.

The rules of the World Trade Organization require that the rich countries such as the US, Canada, the European Union and Japan reduce their subsidies to agriculture. The domestic political pressures are still largely in favour of continuation of agricultural subsidies. But this is not expected to last long. Sooner or later, the taxpayer and the consumer will prevail and the agricultural subsidies will have to be seriously curtailed. Any reduction in agricultural subsidies would cause serious social strife if the farmers belonged to the rich countries themselves. The move to encourage immigration from third world of proprietary farming population to Canada would greatly facilitate the inevitable task of reducing agricultural subsidies without hurting the agricultural production and the environmental balance.

What would be the consequence of this migration in the third world countries? In Punjab, the immediate effect may be a fall in land prices. A large number of those who find it extremely difficult to sustain the pressures of new epoch of globalised agriculture propelled by genetic engineering, remote sensing and e-marketing in the environment of callous governmental policies would rush to get out of a vocation that, sooner or later, brings the farmer to the brink and in extreme cases, even suicide. In a way, the immigration would be a golden shake hand or a voluntary retirement scheme for the farmers who find their hard work and enterprise going unrecognised.

This might facilitate the redistribution of land and land reforms that the UPA government places so much value on. Indian agriculture will pass from traditional landholding communities to groups that have little experience or knowledge of agriculture as a vocation. The rural poverty will decline as measured by the index of property holding per head. But the production and the productivity will decline seriously.

The National Common Minimum Programme of the UPA government seeks to ensure employment through such plans as the Employment Guarantee Scheme. These latter will be immensely successful. In a not-so-distant future, we may see the richer countries, already well endowed in capital and technology in agriculture, also enjoying the benefit of skilled and hardy labour. On other hand, countries like India, poor in capital and technology, would lose their valuable human resource. The ill portents of farmer migration would be worse than the much feared brain drain. The non-resident Indian farm proprietor is bound to become politically influential in the host country. Consequently, even the political differences with India will narrow. In the WTO negotiations, the richer countries have serious reservations about welcoming manpower from the developing countries. The move to attract farm proprietors from the third world is a new and welcome step that would remove the stumbling blocks in the process of globalisation and make the rules of the world trade work more smoothly.

18 May 2005.

76 EU Constitution

Why France Voted 'No'

May 29, 2005 will be seen in the French, the European and the world history on a par with July 14, 1789—the day the French mobs stormed the Bastille.

The well-fortified and guarded prison of Bastille in Paris that the French kings and queens had used to lock up people had become the symbol of all acts bad of the autocrats. On July 14, 1789, a large number of French citizens stormed the Bastille and released the thousands of detainees. This marked the triumph of the French Revolution that proclaimed the message of liberty, equality and fraternity to the world. The history of France, it is said, is divided between two epochs: before and after Bastille. The history of the post-Second World War Europe will similarly be divided into pre- and post-May 29, 2005.

On that Sunday, the French voted massively against the ratification of the European Constitution, plunging the country into political disarray and jeopardising the idea of the European Union itself. With the victory for the *'non'* vote—55 per cent to 45 per cent—the founder and pillar of the EU turned its back on half a century of neo-European history.

Seven out of ten French turned up to cast their votes at the end of a furious campaign to break into the dreams of their leaders, especially the President, Mr. Jacques Chirac, to build a strong EU. It was also a setback to the Socialist Party and its first Secretary, Mr. Francois Hollande. The EU bosses in Brussels are preparing to switch to Plan 'B' that was kept ready for this eventuality. France is no more the rock of political certainty for the EU. The French people have suddenly realised that they do not have to be helpless spectators of the direction and the tempo of the advancement of the EU and are determined to use this newly discovered power.

Every one over the world has been watching the brave endeavour of the EU that brought together nations that fought two world wars and had every reason to hate one another. The EU started as a customs union but soon developed its own distinct economic and trade identity. The acceptance of a common currency, the euro, was the peak achievement. The EU began to be looked upon as a strong force to face the American hegemony in a unipolar world. It was preparing to expand by admitting as many as 11 new members, including the former Soviet Bloc countries and Turkey. It was the sheer diversity of the contemplated membership that warranted clear definition and strengthening of the EU institutions. The draft Constitution that was the subject of the French referendum sought to do precisely that.

There was nothing in the draft Constitution to upset the French. The demarcation of powers between the EU and the member countries' national institutions may have been slightly controversial, but nothing to merit an outright rejection. How does one, then, interpret the mandate of the French referendum?

Art Buchwald had commented that Nixon would not have been pushed out of power by the Americans if the beef prices had not sky-rocketed. People judge government policies not on the basis of charts and graphs but by their effect at the grocers. While the EU soared to ever greater heights, there was general discontent about French domestic policies. The massive *'non'* in the referendum was an expression of anger against the French Prime Minister who was sent packing by the President. Had he done it a week before May 29, maybe Mr. Chirac would have got an *'Oui'*.

The French and, as it came out a week later, the Dutch are worried about the nations standing at the EU gates. They cannot be accused of racism or communalism; after all, the French did run an empire in which the colonies were treated on a par with the ruling entity. But they are not sure of the orthodox church, East Europeans or the predominantly Islamic Turkey. With the voters surely not about to delve into the 200-page document, xenophobic politicians had a field day stoking the people's worst fears.

The British Prime Minister, Mr. Tony Blair, made his own contribution to get a *'non'* vote. Just on the eve of the referendum, he raised a controversy about the EU agricultural subsidies and demanded review of the structures of the Union's budget. Over 40 per cent of the EU budget goes towards agricultural subsidies of which France would be a major beneficiary. The contribution of the UK towards this end is reduced by grant of drawbacks. It would be difficult to say that Mr. Blair was prompted by his ally across the Atlantic; but it did suit well the US's position in the WTO negotiations.

Does the May 29 result mark a *'Finis'* for the euro-enthusiastic France? As the former President, Gen. Charles de Gaulle, said after a week-long riots by the 'Left Bank' students: *"Entente? Oui. Pas de Chi-chi."* (Understanding? Sure. Confused arrangements? No.)

This is not the end of the EU. It is not the end of multilateral trade arrangements either. Nor of the WTO. It is only the beginning of a new era of people-friendly structures for international relations.

After all, the capital region of France voted 62.5 per cent *'Oui'* and as the pre-Bastille saying goes, "Paris is France".

---

29 June 2005.

77 WTO Negotiations

The Potsdam Setback

> It is simplistic to think that the Potsdam failure signals the end of G-4 or of the Doha Round. For, the WTO negotiations will be resumed, sooner of later, as the advantages of free multilateral trade are too substantial and the desire for freedom too indomitable to be allowed to die.

Potsdam made history in 1945. Seven days after the surrender of Hitler's Germany, Joseph Stalin, first Winston Churchill and then Clement Attlee, and Harry S. Truman met at a conference from July 17 to August 2 to deliberate on the administration of the defeated Germany and Austria as also to re-draw a new world map after the end of the Second World War.

The Potsdam Agreement represented the first draft of the new world order. Later, after the fall of Japan, China's Chiang Kai-shek joined the leaders of the United States and Great Britain to sign the Potsdam Declaration. The task before the statesmen was formidably arduous. They did not have the benefit of any previous conferences between subordinate officials, resolutions or studies. The relations between the superpowers were so strained that they soon turned into Cold War. Yet, these statesmen crafted an agreement with the concurrence of all.

A folkloric story brings out the essential spirit of the 1945 Potsdam Conference. At the end of a gruelling day's work, the statesmen were sitting by the lakeside. There was a friendly wager as to who could catch more fish. Stalin took out his revolver and started shooting at the fish in the water. Truman got into the water and tried to catch the fish by fiercely moving his hands. Churchill took a teaspoon and started emptying the lake spoon by spoon with the conviction that one day the lake will be emptied and all fish will come to him. Finally, all joined Churchill in emptying the lake spoon by spoon.

Differing Perceptions

Sixty-two years later, in that very German town, Ms. Susan Schwab, Trade Representative of the US, Mr. Peter Mandelson, the European Union Trade Commissioner, Mr. Kamal Nath, India's Minister for Commerce and Industry and Mr. Celso Amorim, Brazil's Foreign Minister, abruptly ended the negotiations in the Doha Round of the World Trade Organization (WTO), two days ahead of the schedule.

"The failure of rich nations to accept effective cuts in farm subsidies and yet they asking for greater market access for their agricultural produce in the developing world resulted in the recent break down of global trade talks," explained Mr. Kamal Nath. "It is the end of the road for G-4. The G-4 is no more," he added.

The perception of Ms. Susan Schwab was quite different. "India and Brazil's fear of growing Chinese imports was behind the decision to help prompt the collapse of the G-4 trade talks in Potsdam," she said. "The Indian and Brazilian Trade Ministers were less flexible in their offers on their manufacturing tariffs at Potsdam than at previous negotiations. Although India has a small trade surplus with China, many in India fear it will turn into a deficit in the near future," she added. In her opinion, India and Brazil lacked flexibility in negotiations because of the process by which they reached a common negotiating position through G-20 and G-33.

Mr. Peter Mandelson was very clear that the differences emerged from the discussions on industrial goods and we would not be able to point to any substantive or commercially meaningful changes in the tariffs of the emerging countries.

From these statements, it is not very clear what the developing countries were defending in exchange for reduction in levels of domestic subsidy in the US and Europe. Were they keen on defending customs tariffs on industrial goods or agricultural commodities? It would appear that there is a difference in the perception.

Maybe, the G-33 was keener on resisting reductions in the tariffs on agricultural commodities while their leaders, India and Brazil, had greater stakes in resisting the opening of doors to import of industrial goods. Mr. Manuel T. Geershankee, the Philippines Ambassador to the WTO, reacted: "This is not statesmanlike for the G-4".

The tractation at Potsdam appeared to have one clear consequence: The US and the EU appear to have closed ranks. "Brazil and India offered no serious access to manufactured goods markets in return for the reduction in the US farm subsidies and European agricultural tariffs."

Trade-distorting Subsidies

Mr. Kamal Nath admits that the US offered to reduce its overall spending on trade-distorting domestic support to $17 billion while Brazil and India were pushing for an annual spending limit of $12-15 billion. The actual level of subsidy, at present, is around $10.8 billion. Evidently, the US was trying to hike the level of subsidies which was not acceptable to the developing countries. All the same, the gaps were fairly thin and certainly not unbridgeable.

Farm tariff is a politically volatile issue in a number of European countries, particularly France. Mr. Kamal Nath and spokesmen of the Congress party are making it look as if they were defending the tariff levels on agricultural commodities.

Mr. D. Raja, the national secretary of the Communist Party of India, did not appear over-concerned about the collapse of the Potsdam meeting. "The developed nations now clearly know that they cannot ignore the demands of Brazil, Russia, China, and India," he said.

It is a moot point if Mr. Kamal Nath, as a representative of the Indian government, which has maintained a policy of negative subsidies for its own farmers for the last 50 years, has the moral right to talk about the elevated levels of positive subsidies in any other country. Negative subsidies are as pernicious to the Indian farmer as the positive subsidies of the US or the EU. Only time will tell whether the unfathomable difference of opinion arose out of reduction by developing countries of tariffs on manufactured goods or on agricultural commodities.

The question that still remains is whether pressure tactics to the extent of letting the negotiations break down behooved a country like India, which aspires to be a global power. There is no disputing that the level of domestic subsidies for agriculture in rich countries is pernicious. But the more important question is: What is the best instrument for the developing countries to bring them down?

In the pre-WTO era, the US had nobody to answer to regarding its agricultural subsidy policy. If the WTO collapses, that would once again be the situation. Like the Super 301 and Special 301, the US could impose its will, given its preponderant share in international trade.

The only thing going for the developing countries was the fact that the US had accepted, in the Marrakesh Agreements, to scale down its policies on farm subsidies. It is wiser for the representatives of the developing countries to keep the instruments of Marrakesh intact and not let the US escape from their discipline. Nothing is gained by making theatrical announcements about the end of the G-4 or of the Doha Round. That may impress the Left and the NGO lobby. That might also give an impression, in some of the developing countries, that India and Brazil are valiantly fighting the battle in the WTO.

Pressuring the US

There may be a tactical advantage in pressuring the US by creating a stalemate at a time when any further progress will presume that the US Congress would renew the fast-track trade authority given to the Bush administration that expires in a week's time. That will also be good political gimmickry on the eve of the US presidential elections and the parliamentary elections in India.

The question is: Should these considerations be allowed to imperil the fruiting of the saplings of the world order that were so painstakingly planted in 1945 and so lovingly nourished through all the negotiations of GATT till Marrakesh and Doha.

If the Left parties, the *swadeshi* lobby and the NGOs that have opposed the WTO think that this is the end of GATT and the WTO, they need to be a little patient. All said and done, the G-4 was only a time-saving contraption adopted to facilitate negotiations. It did not have the formal plenipotentiary powers delegated by the member countries.

The WTO negotiations will be resumed, if not immediately, after the next administration takes over in the US. The advantages of free multilateral trade are too substantial and the desire for freedom too indomitable to permit the lofty objective of an open world as an alternative to world war to be permanently buried.

---

27 June 2007.

78 Multilateralism is Here to Stay

Will the collapse of the Doha Round lead to the end of multilateralism? Not necessarily, as there is every likelihood of a transparent, non-discriminatory framework for international trade emerging. In this system, nation States are likely to play a subordinate role.

Luckily for multilateralism, the end of the intergovernmental phase is marked by the emergence of information technology and e-platforms of the futures markets.

Wiser by the experience of the 1920s and 1930s, nations of the world after World War II rejected economic nationalism, beggar-thy-neighbour devaluation and tariff hikes by creating post-war economic institutions that fostered rules for a multilateral system of development and international banking.

In the bipolar world, multilateralism was more difficult to achieve. It was only after the fall of the Soviet Union that the Uruguay Round of the GATT negotiations succeeded in taking shape. For the first time, the nations of the world were ambitious enough to include even trade in agricultural commodities in the multilateral system.

Diversity in Agriculture

That was a fishbone that was bound to get stuck in the throat of the multilateral system. Industry and the financial institutions the world over had a certain degree of commonality. Agriculture, on the contrary, varies not only from country to country but also from region to region even within a country.

The agricultural interests of all the regions within a political nation are not necessarily similar. Often certain regions have greater commonality with regions in neighbouring countries rather than the neighbouring provinces within the country.

Further, the policies followed in respect of inter-sectoral terms of trade vary from country to country according to the geographical, social and historical circumstances. Briefly, national governments represented a highly heterogeneous bundle of interests and could not, by their very nature, be valid representatives of the whole political nation.

Till the end of the 20th century, the national governments were the only recognised players in international agreements. The United Nations and its specialised institutions provided the model for multilateral agreements. The GATT and the WTO had perforce to follow the model and developed an intergovernmental regulator for multilateral trade. The intergovernmental structure had its inevitable consequences.

The agreements had to be thoroughly legalistic to stand the test of legal challenges and interpretations. Apart from the jurists, yet another category of professionals which dominated the WTO agreements was the econometricians.

Fairly simple concepts such as agricultural subsidies were translated into complex measures like the aggregate measurement of support (AMS). The WTO became a favourite playing field of jurists and mathematical economists. The negotiating teams of most countries on the Agreement on Agriculture (AoA) were packed with lawyers and mathematicians rather than people who had practical experience in agriculture. No wonder the farmers had difficulty in understanding even the stipulations that went in their favour and took positions inimical to the WTO. According to all available indications, this epoch is coming to an end. The collapse of the Doha Round of the WTO negotiations would probably mark the beginning of a new epoch.

Agreement on Agriculture (AoA)

The AoA was the stumbling block in the WTO negotiations. The WTO has many accomplishments to its credit. Tariffs imposed by the richer countries have fallen dramatically to an average of 4 per cent. The WTO, with 151 members, is the most universal of international organisations. No member country has sought to distance itself after joining it. Disputes between the WTO members are almost always amicably settled. The twin principles of non-discrimination and transparency have come to be accepted as basic principles of multilateral systems.

The successes of the WTO were partly responsible for the problem that it is facing today. The WTO is essentially a democratic system with no nation enjoying a veto power or even a "first amongst equals" status. The dispute settlement mechanism worked in a manner that won the confidence of most members of the organisation.

The ministerial negotiations were, therefore, taken seriously by all participants. After Marrakesh (1995), even the more powerful States refrained from making commitments they had no intention of fulfilling. The richer countries stuck to their stand on providing hefty subsidies to the farmers and demanding easier access to markets in the developing countries. This stymied the Doha Round negotiations.

Global Warming

It was a cruel coincidence that the breakdown in the Doha Round negotiations coincided with the first and early experiences of the phenomenon of global warming/climate change. All countries, both in the South and North, are experiencing extreme vicissitudes in temperature and highly skewed precipitations.

The crop maps of the world are about to undergo major transformations. In India and other tropical countries, food grains production, as also that of milk and dairy products, will face a serious threat. Further, the entire technology of refrigeration is coming under serious criticism. It is likely that food grains production will be limited mostly to temperate and cold regions.

This is a double blow for the Doha Round negotiations. The situation in developing countries, especially those in warmer climes, are almost certain to deteriorate. The richer countries in the more temperate regions would find a new strength added to their fledgling argument about the need to protect agriculture, forests and the environment. While eventually technology should help postpone the disaster, the WTO negotiations have in the meanwhile received a fatal blow. Does it mean the end of the WTO and multilateralism?

The end of WTO does not necessarily mean the end of multilateralism, much to the disappointment of the WTO-baiters. It is only fading out of the intergovernmental phase of multilateralism in trade. This is probably a good thing.

The trader is the intermediary between the producer and the consumer. National governments ought to have, at best, a marginal role in the operation. The role of the government in trade, at best, is that of a traffic cop. Unfortunately, in most cases this cop happens to be a corrupt one interested in self-aggrandisement rather than regulating traffic. This phase of intergovernmental multilateralism was also accompanied by rather outdated systems of transport, finance and settlement.

Role of IT

Luckily for multilateralism, the end of the intergovernmental phase is marked by the emergence of information technology (IT) and e-platforms of the futures markets. At present, the futures markets are mostly a national phenomenon. It is, however, only a matter of time before the national platforms get interlinked leading to a global e-marketing system. Even in India, some of the recent government decisions had reference to the Chicago Board of Trade futures quotations.

It is perfectly conceivable that a multilateral system of transparent and non-discriminatory trade system may emerge out of the 'de-statisation' of the multilateral system of international trade.

The emergence of intergovernment institutions for global systems was an unfortunate necessity, given the historical background of the two world wars and two depressions. The failure of the WTO might actually mark the beginning of true multilateralism.

---

17 October 2007.

X

Budget

79 Good Luck, Finance Minister!

With recessionary conditions, a glut in the market, fewer takers for industrial and white goods, and even less demand for farm commodities, the Finance Minister is a much harried man. Forced to keep both the fiscal deficit and the rate of inflation within strict limits, and increase investment in infrastructure areas, Mr. Sinha needs to turn unpleasant to chart a way out of the crisis. Will he dare to?

AS 'B-day' approaches and the Finance Minister starts packing his briefcase preparatory to the presentation of the 2002-03 Budget, no doubt he is a harried person. Mr. Yashwant Sinha needs all the good wishes and sympathies that may be offered.

The recession has set in. There is a glut in the market. There is little demand even for agricultural commodities. Industrial goods and even white goods find no takers in spite of alluring discounts and swap offers. Even major companies are being forced to reduce their establishments.

There is little that the Finance Minister can offer to Parliament that will bring cheers. This time the most hostile reaction would come from the harassed urban middle-class housewives.

It is a pity. For only the harried housewives can appreciate the woes of Mr. Sinha. A poor housewife knows what it is to have all her children simultaneously demanding attention and proclaiming their hunger and other woes in every way possible. She should have sympathy for the Finance Minister who is besieged by supplicants from all sectors asking for relief and support.

The infrastructure and energy sectors are paralysed and need immediate investments of crores of rupees. The Railway Ministry alone needs over Rs. 40,000 crore just to ensure safe travel, if not punctual and comfortable. To add to all this is the war-like situation following the December 13 attack on Parliament. The Pakistani President, Gen. Pervez Musharraf, has announced his intention of increasing the expenditure on armed forces in geometric progression. Mr. Sinha would need to pay immediate attention to the requirements of defence as also to the economic recovery in the context of opening up of multilateral world trade.

Textbooks on public finance draw a distinction between a housewife's budget and that of a State. The housewife has to manage all her and the household's expenses within the limits of a given income. Finance ministers, on the other hand, tend to draw up a fancy wishlist of expenses to meet the political exigencies of the day. Having arrived at the gross total of expenditure, they start looking for revenue resources to meet them.

The distinction between family and the State budgets is no more valid. The Finance Minister today is forced to keep both the fiscal deficit and the rate of inflation within strict limits. He can no more have indiscriminate recourse to the printing press. He is, therefore, in a situation very much like that of a housewife who faces a multitude of pressing demands and strictly limited resources.

If anything, Mr. Sinha is in an even more unfortunate situation; a housewife is normally not bothered about hostilities from neighbours. Mr. Sinha very much is.

A housewife can, as a general rule, count on the sincere will and assiduous effort on the part of householder to maximise income and minimise wasteful expenditure.

Mr. Sinha cannot. Mr. Sinha's plight is like that of a poor housewife with numerous children, a drunkard and lazy husband, belligerent neighbours and no kitty anywhere.

It must be said to the credit of the Finance Minister that he is carrying on bravely. The inflation rate is well under 2 per cent. In spite of the recession, the fiscal deficit would still be contained around 5 per cent.

It would certainly require a wizard of a Finance Minister to present the Budget that would be a comfort to the politically doddering NDA at the Centre.

What are the options?

There is no question of returning to the old socialist misadventure; the international community will not accept it and the popular opinion will not take it. It might actually affect adversely India's defence capability.

A return to the statist system might, at best, postpone by a few years the economic catastrophe. What is needed is not 'less reforms' but more reforms 'with greater conviction'.

Fortunately, food stocks are abundant. There is no threat of a generalised famine. Foreign exchange reserves are swelling to a dream-like size. And, the people at large are prepared, as they were in 1965 under the leadership of Lal Bahadur Shastri, for sacrifices in the face of terrorism from across the border.

The Finance Minister needs to take courage in his hands and carry the government with him. Gone are the days when a comely, patient, suffering and self-sacrificing housewife could move her husband to give up his bad ways and turn industrious and hard-working.

More direct tongue-lashing and effective measures are called for.

The Finance Minister will need to turn unpleasant to chart a way out of the present crises. The important question is: will he dare and will the Prime Minister let him?

---

27 February 2002.

80 Appeasing the Aged

Budget 2003 will be remembered most for the recognition Mr. Jaswant Singh has given to a new political constituency—senior citizens. This obviously means the recognition of the increasing political clout of this community. For, in terms of numbers, senior citizens could, very shortly, become a larger political entity than farmers and even women. Soon, their voice could count much more than that of the traditional depressed castes.

The date was February 28. The year 2003. As the Sansad clock struck 11, the invariably punctilious Mr. Manohar Joshi, Speaker of the Lower House, entered the Lok Sabha, duly heralded by the officials, and took his seat. Without further ceremony, the speaker called upon the Finance Minister to present his Budget 2003-04.

Till this point, everything seemed to follow the annual set pattern of Budget presentation. Then things seemed to go haywire. Most journalists assigned on Budget duty either in the House or outside were seated in the Press section or in front of the television or radio sets all prepared to take copious notes about all the salient points in the first Budget speech of the new Finance Minister.

Over the years, the journalists have evolved their own worksheets for taking notes on the Budget speech. The sheets have printed on them figures of the last Budget estimate, the revised estimates, the actual realisations relating to each budgetary head leaving a blank spaces for the new budgeted figures. Using a worksheet makes jotting of notes much easier. When the Finance Minister rattles off figures relating to the previous years, journalists get enough respite to catch breath.

For years, Finance Minister after Finance Minister has started his Budget speech with introductory remarks, which invariably contain some profusely laudatory remarks about the boss, the Prime Minister, followed by some preliminary remarks about the general situation and special problems facing each important sector of the economy.

The inventory starts with the gross domestic product and goes on to cover foreign exchange position, balance of trade, balance of payment, industry, agriculture, infrastructure and so on. It is during these preliminary remarks that the Finance Ministers generally prepare the ground for the announcement of some major proposals and innovations.

The preliminary remarks often contain such profound banalities as, "Agriculture is the cornerstone of the Indian economy" and "Prime minister so and so's government is fully determined to give the hard working peasantry of the nation its unstinted support".

Generally, the introductory remarks represent a resume of what is already contained in the Annual Economic Survey distributed only a couple of days before the Budget presentation.

Following the scintillating victory of the Indian side against Pakistan in the World Cup, the Finance Minister quickly announced that all money earned by the team and by individual players will be exempt from income tax.

Mr. Jaswant Singh is clearly a cricket lover. The manner of his Budget presentation showed that he enjoys the finer points of the game. He opened his Budget speech with a googly. Unlike all of his predecessors, he started the speech by making a list of the principal objectives: eradication of poverty, growth of employment, lifetime concerns like health, education and housing and proceeded to outline the projects affecting these concerns.

That sounded more like an August 15 speech made by a Prime Minister from the ramparts of the Red Fort! The journalists felt quite lost, started looking at one another with big question marks written large on their faces; some of them kept aside their worksheets and started jotting down the notes on plain papers, some started drooling on the worksheets.

Then Mr. Jaswant Singh made a quick about-turn and fell into the standard Budget pattern of listing out expenses and proposals for raising revenues. In the final analysis, Finance Ministers have to talk of expenditures and revenues though they may start by talking of national objective to mark a difference of style.

It was a clever trap. Those in the opposition parties could not raise mayhem saying that there was nothing in the budget for the poor or the unemployed and the employees. The employees who have benefited from concessions in income tax and welcomed the revival of the leave travel concession would not agree with the Opposition in that case.

The fact that some five million families will be added to the Antyodaya Anna Yojana would make it difficult for even a hard-boiled Leftists to say that the Finance Minister had no concern for the poor and the starving.

The industrialists and businessmen have generally said that the Finance Minister is possibly casting a wider net and is only preparing the necessary foundations in his long-term projects and programmes. Mr. Jaswant Singh's Budget 2003-04 will be remembered, in spite of all, for long years to come, not because of the changes he made in the structure of income taxation, in excise duties nor for the changes in the tax structure for petroleum; nor will it be remembered for the hike in prices of urea and Diammonium Phosphate (DAP); this Budget will be remembered for the recognition Mr. Jaswant Singh has given to a new political constituency—that of the senior citizens.

The ascendancy of the senior citizens has been happening in different countries over years. Populations the world over are becoming increasingly aged as an outcome of both birth control measures and the large number of welfare schemes for keeping the elderly alive, if necessary on life-support systems.

The number of senior citizens who are above the age of 55 years and who are predominantly dependent for their livelihood on one or the other governmental welfare measures has been steadily increasing over the years and has grown to scales unknown in history.

Their voice has to be recognised, even in minor matters such as decisions relating to the Unit Trust of India or the interest rate payable on savings and general provident fund accounts.

For the first time, a Finance Minister has recognised that India has not only a large proportion of senior citizens but also probably the world's largest population of senior citizens.

In terms of pure numbers, senior citizens could, very shortly, become a larger political entity than the farmers and even women. They are already approaching a level where their voice could count much more than that of the traditional depressed castes in India.

Mr. Jaswant Singh has showered a number of advantages on the senior citizens. A new special pension scheme has been announced for them. Senior citizens have been given a 20 per cent deduction in income tax. Tax on their income from the Unit Trust of India units will not be deducted at source.

Further, the Finance Minister has also announced a large number of measures that would result in reduced cost of health services as also of instruments and apparatus that are required by the old, by the diabetic and by the invalid.

What are the portents of this recognition to senior citizens as a special interest group? It obviously goes with the recognition of the increasing political clout of this community. Most influential political leaders belong to this category, it would have the support of a built-in majority in all legislatures of the republic.

The fact that this is happening just about the time when the Dalit lobby is trying to raise its sights into even further concessions makes it even more significant. It could effectively break the Bhopal Declaration lobby; this latter is already divided about the reservations for women. It might find itself further divided on account of concessions given to the senior citizens.

The 2003-04 Budget has little to commend itself unless something brilliant comes out of this box as years go by and if Mr. Jaswant Singh continues to hold the finance portfolio.

The special treatment of the senior citizens could add a new dimension to the fiscal politics of India and might stay on much longer than most things kicked off in recent Budgets.

---

12 March 2003.

81 Poll Politics 2004

With the country getting into election mode, political parties are readying to do their best, or worst, to grab control of a liberalising India that wants to be a superpower.

The coming year promises to be one long festival of polls, to the Lok Sabha, various State Assemblies and if they happen, elections to the Panchayat Raj institutions. The Election Commission (EC) had put the Lok Sabha elections on its planner some time in September when the term of the present, 13th, Lok Sabha expires.

September is generally a good month to hold elections. The monsoons are nearly over; the major agricultural operations have been completed; women do not have to trudge long distances for firewood and drinking water; the festival season is approaching; the examinations are still a while away; and the weather is generally pleasant all over the country.

The historical accident of two successive short-lived Lok Sabhas brought general elections around the time of polls to the State Assemblies; Panchayat Raj elections happened round the year.

The scattered schedule of the various elections facilitated security arrangements, as the deployment of forces could also be staggered. It also suited, in a way the leadership of various political parties as they could participate in the electoral campaigns in the states to build up their following and to consolidate it for the national hustings.

But saner citizens were hoping all elections would be held simultaneously so as to effect substantial savings in expenditure and minimise the periods around every polls when governments become inoperative.

Once the polls are announced, the governments are discouraged from making any new policy initiatives or announcing projects that could be seen as an attempt to bring undue influence on the electorate. But governments have fine-tuned ways around this Election Commission diktat. They all become suddenly conscious of the good work they ought to have been doing all along. Like a pupil in the examination hall, after the ten-minute warning bell, they get into a tizzy of activity or, at least, pronouncements.

The ability to guess the date of the polls is a prized faculty. Those in the ruling party have a big advantage in setting dates to suit them. Just about a month back when the vote of no-confidence was brewing in the Lok Sabha, the Leader of the Opposition, who is also the president of the party that held power in 14 states, for all purposes looked set to be the next occupant of the Prime Minister's *gaddi*.

Then came the mini-general elections—the Assembly polls in five states, importantly four in the Hindi belt—and that changed the whole situation overnight.

Even before the polling, one heard whispers from the BJP circles that Mr. Atal Bihari Vajpayee would go for early polls if the party won two of the four Hindi belt states. But the BJP bagged three, and the party was euphoric even as Congressmen sank into unwarranted despair. It was a foregone conclusion that the Lok Sabha polls would be advanced.

Though the actual proroguing was still some time away, the parties got into election mode. Any ruling party would have rushed with announcements of bonanzas to woo the voter. The BJP did so too. Then came the moves to secure allies. The Congress President, Mrs. Sonia Gandhi, got busy on her telephone, calling on neighbours. The NCP chief, Mr. Sharad Pawar, toyed with the possibility of aligning with the BJP-led National Democratic Alliance. For the BJP, this had the blessings of the Shiv Sena strongman, Mr. Bal Thackeray, himself. To sweeten the bait, the Centre announced a loan package of Rs. 1,600 crore for the ailing cooperative sugar factories of Maharashtra. But the Baron of Baramati was not satisfied, and he quickly turned around and started opening channels to 10 Janpath. Clearly, this time there would be no bars to political gimmickry or chicanery.

Meanwhile, the BJP national executive endorsed the advancement of elections. What were the major considerations? The big win for the party in the mini-general elections and the despondency in the Opposition? Could not be. There have been umpteen instances in recent years when two successive polls have produced diametrically opposite results.

Could it be that the triumph of three women Chief Ministers made the male politicians on both sides have a second look at the Women's Reservation Bill, which was to come before the last session?

The ruling NDA was foresworn to seeing it through and the Congress was rearing to go for it. The threat that the trend would continue and produce a woman Prime Minister—predicted by some influential astrologers too—was frightening. The BJP started to build up a campaign of hypnotising the nation into a stupor of 'feel-good' and 'Bharat as the latest super-power'. On cue, the Finance Minister, Mr. Jaswant Singh, produced on January 9 a series of measures benefiting the young and the privileged, the well-to-do senior citizens and India inc. Students would get cheaper loans; the moneyed elderly higher rates of interest on their savings. There were sops for rural housing and agricultural loans (already announced earlier).

But in a government where the right hand does not know what the left hand is doing, the Ministry of Commerce struck a strident note by announcing a ban on the export of onions, the politically sensitive vegetable. The onion producers of Nashik and Pune districts of Maharashtra protested strongly. Once bitten by the onion producers, who stymied BJP elections in five states, the Prime Minister came forth to announce a new TV channel and phone facilities for the farmers.

Whenever a State is vested with economic powers, corruption is inevitable; so is the rigging of elections. This has happened in socialist India all along. In a liberalising India preparing to be a superpower, political bigwigs are readying to bid for control for the next five years.

---

21 January 2004.

82 Budget: No Good Harvest, Really

Though the Budget appears to set store by the farm sector, it is still far from redeeming the promises made in the Common Minimum Programme.

The consensus at the conclusion of the 2004 Lok Sabha elections was that while 'India' might be shining, 'Bharat' was not. Everybody expected the new UPA government at the Centre to take bold measures to improve productivity in agriculture as also the living standards of the farmer. This expectation was heightened by the fact that the National Common Minimum Programme of the UPA government specifically promised to:

- Eliminate all measures that had the effect of depressing agricultural prices, and
- Lighten the burden of debt and interest charges on the farmers.

Further, on June 18, a new credit policy for agriculture was announced and on June 24, the Prime Minister, Dr. Manmohan Singh, promised a 'new deal' for the farmers. All this had heightened the expectations in the agricultural community about the UPA government's first Budget. Unfortunately, the Finance Minister, Mr. P. Chidambaram's Budget came as an anti-climax for the farm sector.

If in Andhra Pradesh, the Congress-led alliance scored in the elections by promising free power supply to farmers, in Tamil Nadu, the ruling AIADMK did the same to contain the hit the party had taken in the polls. The all-India Kisan Coordination Committee (KCC) made a radical change in its traditional anti-subsidies position and demanded free supply of power across the country.

This year the monsoon showed great promise only to deceive. In early June, the Meteorological Department forecasted early and abundant monsoons. The rains did arrive early but in fits and starts. In several states, the first sowing did not even reach the germination stage. In many others, even the second sowing was wasted. The farmers need new seeds to replace those wasted.

All this together brought farmers to the brink and drove many to suicide. It was expected that the United Progressive Alliance (UPA) government would come up with a massive and comprehensive package to help farmers in despair.

The Finance Minister has promised an initial expenditure of Rs. 100 crore this year for the maintenance of traditional water sources. This is to be followed with an annual expenditure of Rs. 3,000 crore for the next five years. This is both "too small" and "too slow". The farmers need immediate relief—by way of supply of water and seeds.

The National Common Minimum Programme made promises on these aspects. But the Budget has done little on them.

Post-Independence, successive governments followed policies that tended to depress agricultural prices. These policies resulted in the imposition of negative subsidies on the farmers of the order of 87 per cent.

Japan ensures that its farmers get in the market 90 per cent more than the cost of production. The European Union provides its farmers an income 65 per cent higher than their cost of production. In the US, the positive subsidy to the farmers is of the order of 35 per cent.

In 1989, the then Minister for Commerce, Mr. Pranab Mukherjee, submitted a statement to the World Trade Organization that Indian farmers actually had a negative subsidy. According to one calculation, the extent of negative subsidy was as high as 87 per cent in 1996-97. While after that the government did take some measures to lower the negative subsidy, much remains to be done.

After the promises of the National Common Minimum Programme, it was hoped that the UPA government would abolish the Essential Commodities Act and introduce farmer- and consumer-friendly marketing and warehousing systems.

Some of Mr. Chidambaram's predecessors had initiated some measures in this direction. But the latest Budget has no mention of steps to abolish measures that depress agricultural prices. This militates against the National Common Minimum Programme.

Further, while the Finance Minister has claimed a large increase in the funds made available for extending credit to farmers, he has completely overlooked the fact that merely supplying additional funds to the commercial, regional rural and cooperative banks does not help the farmers, most of whom have become, over time, ineligible to get loans on account of their inability to repay loans.

Credit availability makes no sense unless agriculture becomes remunerative enough. This is possible if, and only if, the farmers are assured remunerative prices for their produce. The Budget fails to provide any solace in this vital matter.

The Finance Minister has categorically rejected any possibility of a "write-off of agricultural loans". He appears to have a mistaken notion of what constitutes agricultural indebtedness. Farmers have neither a contractual obligation nor a moral responsibility to repay the loans taken from public sector institutions. Government policies that depressed agricultural prices but ensured that farmers were unable to perform their part of the contract—of repaying loans.

In fact, if one were to draw up a balance sheet of what the farmers owe the government and vice-versa, the farmers will emerge net creditors; particularly, if one takes into account the incomes lost on account of State policies, both in agriculture and commodity markets, and the amounts held by farmers as shares and deposits in various cooperative societies.

According to an expert committee, the loss in income caused to the farmers on account of governmental policies alone could total Rs. 300,000 crore over the last 20 years. Compared with this colossal sum, the amounts owed by farmers by way of loans and electricity bills are insignificant.

The Finance Minister relies on such schemes as the Employment Guarantee Scheme (EGS) for providing employment for 100 days in a year to at least one member in every family. He has cited the example of Maharashtra for the success of the EGS. But the reality may be otherwise. The scheme does not seem to have created any tangible asset. There are allegations that muster rolls are tampered with for claiming wages, and that most workers get wages at half the rates without working at all. In fact, in Maharashtra the EGS is derisively described: "EGS—half you, half us".

The Finance Minister has cited the success of the Anand cooperative model and plans to create similar state cooperative societies for the development of horticulture and fruit crops. But the success of the Anand model, which incidentally is not a state-wide cooperative society, is due to a combination of factors, including the liberal supply initially of milk powder and butter oil from the European Community.

Mr. Chidambaram earns quite a few brownie points on economic reforms, but none on the agriculture front, which was crying for attention.

---

21 July 2004.

83 Clouds Gathering for February 28

What will the Budget that the Finance Minister, Mr. P. Chidambaram, presents on February 28 look like? Will he produce another "Dream Budget"? One only hopes that it would, at least, not be a "nightmare budget". If there are some silver linings to the 2005-06 Budget, it might be confined to the corporate sector. The representatives of the corporate sector have had extensive confabulations with the Finance Minister, who would certainly not like the soaring market to collapse.

The United Progressive Alliance government's second Budget would necessarily be a coalition exercise with notable influence from all the three major components of the UPA. Whatever that means for the corporate sector, it offers little hope for agriculture and the farmer.

Successive Congress governments have followed policies of low-cost economy, which effectively means keeping the prices of food grains and raw materials depressed. This was supposed to be good for the consumer; though it was even better for the industrialists who could keep the wage rates low thanks to the low food prices and also make profits on account of the availability of cheap raw materials.

The second major influential element of the UPA is the Left, particularly the Communists. The Left's thinking on agriculture is based on the premise that agriculture is a hugely profitable business and that those who had large landholdings were essentially moneyed landlords who fleeced the masses of landless labourers. The Left's single-point programme has been confiscation of the land of the landlords and their redistribution among the small holders and the landless. Pending such revolution, they insist on two more things. First, massive facilities for education and health for the farm labour and their families; and second, a punitive income tax on the so-called agricultural "haves". So insistent are some of the Left parties on the idea of an agricultural income tax that they have apparently even threatened to quit the UPA if the Finance Minister does not accept it in this very Budget.

The third element of the UPA consisting of cow-belt communalists is unlikely to try and disturb the precarious balance between the land-owners and the peasant masses.

The agriculturists have already got two ominous signals. The Agriculture Minister, who also happens to be in charge of the Consumer Affairs, appears to have swung wholly in favour of the consumers, though they are by no means as badly placed as the farmers, many of whom are on the threshold of committing suicide. The minister has banned export of food grains, though India still has substantial stocks, on the plea that there have been reports of malnutrition and starvation from various parts of the country. Experience shows that banning of export or import of agricultural commodities has never improved the availability in the domestic market. On the contrary, free exports have always promoted a buoyant commodity market and higher production levels.

Farmers have never really opposed the imposition of income tax. In fact, they would welcome the privilege of paying the income tax provided they have the income to do so. If there is no income tax on agriculture, it should not be forgotten that it suffers under a massive transaction tax in the form of negative subsidies. The real reason why no Finance Minister has so far thought of imposing an income tax on agriculture is that the bureaucracy in the income tax department opposes it. Used to getting income tax returns at their doorsteps, the officialdom cannot countenance the idea of going to remote villages and work out the actual income farm-by-farm. In fact, the whole controversy is pointless.

An income tax on agriculture can bring about a major change in the economy if the proceeds are given directly to the village *panchayats* instead of keeping the local bodies dependent on handouts from the Central and state governments. With a stroke of pen, one can do away with difference between agricultural and non-agricultural incomes and make every assessee pay tax on the basis of his taxable income.

The Left is trying to deepen the divide between the poor and the less poor in the countryside. It appears more interested in scoring points against its traditional enemy—the village well-to-do. No farmer would grudge the farm labour being provided life insurance, housing, medical facilities and free education. However, if one expects that in the closed economy and society of village it is possible to make such perks available to farm labour when the farmers' families themselves are nowhere near enjoying them, one is only playing politics.

The Left continues to emphasise land reforms. It argues that the land reform legislation has been entirely futile. This may partly be true in some states. But it cannot be denied that it has been amply effective in several major states.

In fact, the states that are relatively more advanced in agriculture are the ones where land reforms have succeeded and the rifts in village society have disappeared.

During Emergency, large tracts of land were handed over to the landless. Before that, tenancy legislation saw massive shift of ownership of agricultural land.

The fact remains that the landless who received land have hardly shown any interest in cultivation, much less in improving productivity. Most Leftists are wary of the idea of paying any compensation to the landholders for the land taken away from them. Confiscating land without compensation would be politically impossible.

There is, however, a sensible and easy way of bringing about land reforms so that the land is transferred from the inefficient and the reluctant cultivators to the more efficient producers. If the government takes measures to develop a land market which enables quick selling and buying of land, it would not only bring about a better distribution of holdings but also boost the long-sagging investments in agriculture.

Faced with such difficult problems, the Finance Minister is more than likely to bypass them. He is certain to bypass all measures to reduce expenditure and improve the productivity of the working force. Tax restructuring is easier and gains a Finance Minister more brownie points and international accolades.

A Finance Minister who introduces VAT is more likely to go into history books than the one who slashes dramatically the governmental expenditure.

---

23 February 2005.

84 Budget: Another Political Statement?

The Budget speech by the Finance Minister, Mr. P. Chidambaram, made many people happy. A few, however, grumbled about the fringe benefit tax and the cash withdrawal tax. But these are only minor points on which the minister can afford a roll-back. In fact, they were probably introduced as a diversionary tactic. The major policy announcements lie where they are least likely to provoke any opposition. These are: A whole list of munificent allocations, particularly in favour of the disadvantaged sections, including the scheduled castes, the scheduled tribes, the minority community and to some extent, the weaker sections of Bharat.

This spate of compassion and activism, of course, has its origins in the rhetorical tradition of the Congress party itself. In the Nehruvian epoch, of the immediate post-Independence era, the party brushed aside Gandhiji's ideals and economics and promised an era of modernity and prosperity on the lines of the erstwhile USSR. It flopped. Indira Gandhi held out a more practical promise of eradicating poverty. That did not work either. Had the nation tried the Gandhian approach, even if it had flopped it would not have created the kind of massive dissatisfaction that the failure of the Nehruvian model did.

The Nehruvian misadventure vetted appetites that it could not satisfy. That gave rise to a large number of social and political movements that cried out for justice for the various disadvantaged sections. These included the traditional Marxist-Leftists of various hues and colours and the numerous casteist outfits that used the Marxist jargon, with the difference that they emphasised the caste contradictions, rather than those that Marx highlighted.

The Leftists lost the race, and were confined to a few pockets and issues such as environmentalism, anti-globalisation, anti-MNCism and protectionism. The caste-based politics received a big push with the then Prime Minister, Mr. V. P. Singh, accepting the recommendations of the Mandal Commission. That made creation of employment and reservations in jobs on the basis of caste far more important than economic growth. The casteist outfits easily outdid the traditional Left in gathering mass support.

The National Democratic Alliance (NDA) made a brave attempt to create a political alternative on the basis of the consolidation of the majority community rather than economic and historic contradictions, but failed. The Congress won in the 2004 elections but could not muster the required majority without forming an alliance with the Left and the casteist forces. But surely the party is looking to come to power on its own steam. Thus, the second and perhaps the real Budget of the Congress-led government makes a determined effort to wean away the support of the weaker sections and the minority community to weaken the Leftists and the casteist allies in the United Progressive Alliance (UPA). This not so-secret design explains the dubious claims about having over-fulfilled the targets in respect of supply of credit to farmers and food-for-work programme and the apologia for having dragged its feet on rural employment guarantee bill. But for the coming fiscal and beyond, there is a long list of alluring projects.

The reinforcement of Antyodaya Anna Yojana, the mid-day meal scheme, Sarva Shiksha Abhiyan, Rajiv Gandhi mission for drinking water and sanitation, separate budgetary chapters for the development of the scheduled castes and the scheduled tribes and the separate budget for women, special educational and social schemes for the minority community, creation of a backwards region fund and last but not the least, the Bharat Nirman. The long-term purpose of the schemes is to alienate the disaffected sections from the allies in the UPA so that the next time around, the Congress would be able to win the seats they had lost to their allies. This was urgently required because of the fast-approaching elections in West Bengal and Kerala where the Congress would be pitted against its Leftist allies and it has to win not only votes but also hearts.

There is yet another design behind this Budget that is far more significant. The Congress ushered in the Nehruvian socialistic pattern of society. It was again the Congress that admitted to the failure of the misadventure and launched the economic reforms and the move towards liberalisation. It was again the first to realise the political risk involved in an endeavour that emphasised individual initiative and enterprise rather than governmental patronage.

The former Prime Minister, P. V. Narasimha Rao, who initiated the economic reforms had started having doubts about the whole enterprise and talked of a "middle path". At the Congress conclave at Ramtek, the party started a shift towards a more welfare regime. The NDA ended up with the same dilemma. It realised the long-term advantages and the inevitability of liberalisation and managed to restrain the *swadeshi* and the *Hindutva* forces within its ranks to push ahead economic reforms. That produced growth but also the electoral disapproval. The Congress(I) and the UPA are unwilling to take that kind of risk and are trying to evolve a pragmatic mix of reforms and the so-called human face. The Prime Minister, Dr. Manmohan Singh, tied to the Leftists to run in a three-legged race, had to re-strategise. What is the new strategy?

The first element of the new strategy is the "management of the Left" so that the roll-back is not construed as a victory for the anti-reformists. The Budget performance reveals many telltale signs of this.

- The soft-pedalling of the question of foreign direct investment by not referring to any specific percentages;
- The ignoring of the high-pitch demands of the Left for imposing an income tax on agriculture as also for a second bout of land reforms.
- The shelving of the proposal for a review of labour laws that was hinted at in the Economic Survey, to soften the blow.
- The conceding of the wishes of the Left in respect of interest rates on provident fund.

The UPA has also made up its mind to make the government a more active instrument of development. The political leadership and the bureaucracy are not happy playing the role of a mere animator or an enhancer, there are several phrases in the Budget speech that emphasise the leaning towards decisive intervention by the State in favour of the poor. The Finance Minister referred to Dr. Amartya Sen, the Nobel Laureate, as also to Saint Thiruvalluvar to lend the support to his new policy line.

The implications are very clear. Dr. Amartya Sen does not question the overall validity of Arrow's theorem that collective decisions are *a priori* irrational. He, however, argues that an exception ought to be made in favour of people suffering from dire poverty, malnourishment, unemployment and social discrimination.

He advocates effective organised action against these curses of humanity. This argument comes in handy for communities that lack the enterprise and the determination to make a plunge towards freedom and liberalisation. The real question is: Is not effective collective action a contradiction in terms?

The UPA government is going the way of Nehru in 1951 and Indira Gandhi in the 1960s. 'Dangling carrots' is the name of the game. The government makes promises, very clear in its mind that it will never be called to answer for them.

There is no evaluation system, which puts the blame for inadequate performance or even abysmal failure squarely at the door of the guilty parties. If Nehru and Indira Gandhi failed, why should one think that Ms. Sonia Gandhi will be able to do better?

What one should ask the Finance Minister, the Prime Minister and the Planning Commission is for minimum failure standards. It is all right to say one crore hectares will be brought under irrigation or that 60 lakh additional houses will be constructed for the poor.

But simultaneously, there should be an undertaking that if less than 50 lakh hectares are brought under irrigation, failure will be accepted. Similarly, if the number of houses constructed is less than 30 lakh, no attempt will be made to protect the guilty parties.

Once again, the government is assuming an activist role in the place of an animator or enhancer. This will soon result in a new avatar of the licence-permit-quota *raj*, and enhance corruption as also desperation.

The President, Dr. A.P.J. Abdul Kalam, in his address before Parliament, maintained that freedom was development. The Finance Minister is countermanding him by giving the government a role restrictive of individual freedom and enterprise.

---

9 March 2005.

85 Outcome Budget

Exercise in Futility?

The budget exercise consists of putting together the Budget estimates of the preceding year, the revised estimates for the preceding year and the Budget estimates for the year ahead. Expenditure, expenditure, expenditure! And then the Finance Minister proceeds to find funds to meet the list of estimated expenditure, as compiled by the various ministries and vetted by the Prime Minister.

Of course, then come the estimates of revenues and proposals for raising them.These piles of monetary figures have a real content. Somewhere in each ministry, or at the state or district level, lie specific projects and plans for work.

It is on the basis of these physical plans that a ministry compiles its Budget Estimates, which get included in the General Budget.

In his Budget speech this year, the Finance Minister, Mr. P. Chidambaram, said: "I must caution that outlays do not necessarily mean outcomes; the people of the country are concerned with the outcomes." That looked an impressive pronouncement and the people at large had the impression that something startlingly new was being attempted.

The Finance Minister promised to put in place, together with the Planning Commission, a mechanism to measure the development outcome of all major programmes. Subsequently, the Prime Minister wrote to the ministries stressing the importance of converting financial outlays into physical outcomes, with fixed quarterly measurable and monitorable targets to improve the quality of implementation of development programmes.

The ministries have attempted this exercise and worked out the targets of intermediate outputs/outcomes in respect of the planning programmes/schemes being implemented by them.

The Finance Minister presented the results of the exercise in the form of a voluminous document to both the Houses of Parliament. From next year, this Outcome Budget will be a part and parcel of the regular financial budget. The Finance Minister emphasised that the exercise had been complex and involved:

- Standardising unit cost of delivery;
- Benchmarking the standards/quality of outcome and services;
- Capacity-building for requisite efficiency at all levels in terms of equipment, technology, knowledge and skills;
- Ensuring flow of right amount of money at the right time to the right level with neither delay nor parking of funds;
- Effective monitoring and evaluation systems; and
- Involvement of the community/target groups/recipients of the service, with easy access and feedback systems.

Quite impressive and high-sounding. However, if one goes through the compilation put together by the Finance Ministry, one wonders what the whole hullabaloo is about?

There are, no doubt, some positive bits of information:

- Subsidy outlay on LPG and kerosene of Rs. 3,600 crore;
- Expenditure to enhance refining capacity at State-owned oil companies of Rs. 6,163 crore;
- Money to be spent on revival of sick public sector units put at Rs. 400 crore;
- The government will slowly reduce support to restructuring sick units;
- The National Highway Development Programme outlay at Rs. 8,800 crore;
- Golden Quadrilateral Project to be completed by December 2006;
- North-South East-West Highway Corridors to be completed by 2007;
- Outlay for repayment of aircraft loan put at Rs. 308 crore; and
- Expenditure for the setting up of rural parks at Rs. 200 crore.

There is more information of this type. As for agriculture, the whole exercise appears to have been wasted. The Budget had promised an integrated scheme of oilseeds, pulses, oil palm and maize at Rs. 200.40 crore. The outcome? The state governments at times do not fully use their allocated funds for lack of matching grants!

Yet another scheme was integrated development of tree-borne oilseeds. The outcome? Non-availability of the right planting material, unfavourable weather conditions and non-availability of cultivable wasteland.

In respect of the National Agricultural Insurance Scheme, the Outcome Budget mentions figures of *kharif* 2004. Even the figures of *rabi* 2004-05 are not available in the exercise of the 2005-06 Outcome Budget.

On the all-important, Farm Water Management project for increasing crop production in eastern India, the outcome is: the Department of Agriculture and Cooperation has recommended transference of this scheme to the state governments!

As for the Technology Mission on Cotton, the deliverance will be realised by the end of the year because of the inability of the state governments to contribute their matching share in time!

There is little point in continuing this roll-call. It is quite clear that the ministries referred to the files of physical projects they had to begin with and submitted some sort of a progress report.

In the pre-Budget period, the physical projects were converted into financial terms and, in the Outcome Budget they are being re-converted to physical terms, keeping in mind the actual release of the funds.

The people do want to know the outcome in physical terms. But they never wish to have physical planning of the type that the erstwhile USSR used.

One wonders whether, in the last days of planning, when the State limits its role to engendering a conducive environment for the economy, if this exercise in pseudo-physical planning makes any particular sense.

This year's Outcome Budget exercise was limited only to the Plan expenditure, where possibly it had some utility.

The Finance Minister promises to extend this exercise to even non-Plan expenditure from next year onwards. At a time when the need of the hour is to substantially slash governmental expenditure, one wonders if the exercise of the Outcome Budget is worthwhile.

---

7 September 2005.

86 What is on the Farmer's Wish List?

Come February and scribes start playing the guessing game. What could be going on in the mind of the Finance Minister? Under what kind of pressures must he be from the Left and the Right? More important, would he like to go down in history as a liberal ushering in economic reforms? Or, would he rather be remembered as the messiah of the masses? What importance does he attach to being honoured as the best Finance Minister? And what importance does he give to the advice of the various people he consulted before starting to work out the Budget?

In this guessing game, every scribe's conclusion is largely coloured by his personal and class interests. I have visited the families of so many farmers who committed suicide in Vidarbha recently and thought so often about what their last thoughts might have been that I am reminded of the fable of the match-girl.

A little girl sells matchboxes for the livelihood of herself and her grandmother. One day, she is caught in a snowstorm. All frozen and hungry, she tries to keep herself warm by lighting matches, one after another. As she lights each stick, each of her most ardent wishes come true. First, a warm shelter, then some hot food and then the presence of her beloved mother, who is no more.

This column is devoted to some of the dreams the dying farmers must have had at the end and hoping they will have some place in what the Finance Minister, Mr. P. Chidambaram, has termed would be a "Sweet Dream Budget".

This year, the Finance Minister did not consider it worthwhile meeting the representatives of farmers and left the work to the Ministry Secretary.

The UPA leaders like to believe that their coalition represents an alliance of the proletariat and the salaried middle class, that is, the *aam aadmi*—a politically astute posture that pays rich dividends at the hustings. The National Democratic Alliance over-highlighted the role of the employer and the producer and was rebuffed in 2004. The UPA government is now trying to placate the unproductive and the inefficient, hoping that this will get them votes, if not performance and prosperity for the country.

There has been a major change in definitions since the days of Indira Gandhi. Then the poor were identified by economic criteria and by the nature of their economic activity. The slum dwellers in the cities, the landless labourers in villages and the small and marginal farmers constituted the bulk of the BPL (below poverty line) masses then.

Now, things have changed. The BPL is no more a secular concept; it has become caste- and creed-based. The poor are those born into certain communities.

The priority list of beneficiaries includes the scheduled castes, the scheduled tribes, other backward castes and the minority communities. In UPA economics, all help is to be targeted at SCs STs, OBCs and minorities under the slogan of 'alliance against communalism' (read Hindutva).

Note that this four-fold definition of poverty is like the Hindu caste system, based on birth. It does not include the farmers who are driven to suicide in their thousands.

Cooperative Credit, the Serial Killer

The years 2004 and 2005 will be known for farmer suicides. After much prevarication and obfuscation, the experts and the state governments concerned have admitted that most of the suicides were motivated by despair about being able ever to repay the loans and the humiliation heaped on them by the recovery officials of the cooperative banks.

It has also been established that the high incidence of suicide among the cotton farmers is because the product-specific negative aggregate measure of support—an indicator of the level of negative subsidies—has been worst over the last 30 years.

The cooperative banking system is said to be responsible for driving the farmers to suicide in two ways. First, these banks apparently flout the Supreme Court directive—partially endorsed by the directives of the Reserve Bank of India—that the farmers should be charged interest only once a year and that they should not be charged compound rates except in the case of overdue repayments. Second, while the commercial banks as also the private moneylenders have limits on the degree of coercion they practice in the recovery of loans, the cooperative banks have no such restraint.

For too long, the formal credit sector has been the preferred mode. The village moneylender has been despised as a latter-day Shylock and sought to be replaced by the formal banking institutions. However, experience shows that none of the formal credit institutions has the flexibility that is essential to serving the farm sector with all its vicissitudes and uncertainties.

While there is some truth to the stories about the cruelty of the moneylenders and their rates of interest, these were not really outrageous considering the high incidence of their NPAs. But the Government of Maharashtra has declared all their loans void.

This appears aimed at eliminating all competition for the politically strong cooperative sector. But it is necessary that the private moneylenders be allowed to operate rather than being treated as outcasts.

The predecessor NDA government, as also the present UPA regime, announced that the rate of interest on the farmers' loan will not exceed 9 per cent. In reality, no lender abides by this limit.

Under these circumstances, a farmer driven to suicide would want—if he had the match-girl's matchbox—from the "Sweet Dream Budget" of Mr. Chidambaram:

- Strong measures to ensure that the Supreme Court directive on charging and compounding of interest is fully implemented by the cooperative credit institutions.
- A scheme allowing private moneylenders to operate exactly like other credit institutions under an appropriate regulatory authority.
- His children do not to pay more than 9 per cent interest.

(While the government claims that the availability of credit to farmers since 2004 has increased from Rs. 80,000 crore to Rs. 1,30,000 crore, on the ground there appears to be little perceptible change.

The UPA government has been trying to increase the funds available for agricultural credit and also making large quantities of funds available for the restructuring of the cooperative network. However, these funds, apparently, go to the more organised farmers and to the politically strong cooperative movement.)

- The state governments and the cooperative set-up do not devour the funds given by the Centre to restructure the cooperative institutions.

What of the family of the farmer who commits suicide?

Inputs for the Future

The dying farmer's first wish would be that his son and his family get water, both for drinking and irrigation. The farmers are facing a serious problem in respect of all the major inputs—water, power and seeds.

The Finance Minister has often talked about resuscitating the waters sources and tanks and of 'Bharat Nirman'. He had said so even in the last Budget speech. But nothing has happened.

The load-shedding for 12-14 hours a day and the voltage fluctuations are causing serious hardship to the farmers, especially when motors and pumps get damaged.

The farmers face serious difficulties in obtaining quality seeds. There is total confusion, what with the government-approved seeds being both costly and ineffective while the cheap and effective Bt seeds have not been approved.

The son would only want the Finance Minister to remember that his father was driven to suicide because he did not get quality power and inputs.

In the fable of the match-girl, she is found frozen to death, hungry and forlorn. That was what has happened to the farmer and that could well be the fate awaiting the son if finance ministers continue to do what they have been doing the last 58 years.

---

22 February 2006.

XI

Case Studies

87

Paddy MSP

Politics, Economics and Common Sense

Used to an ever-increasing MSP, farmers this year were taken aback with the Centre deciding not to raise it. Much is wrong with the MSP, that has caught farmers in a wheat-paddy trap. Politics, rather than economics or common sense, dictates the decision.

This was bound to happen sooner or later, and it has happened. The ruling coalition at the Centre does not have a reliable majority in Parliament. And the majority of states are ruled by the party in the Opposition. The state governments owing allegiance to the leader of the Opposition at the Centre take instructions from Ms. Sonia Gandhi rather than from the NDA Prime Minister.

The NDA government takes decisions that the Opposition governments in the states cannot stomach; and the state governments take policy lines that do not match with those of the Centre. Sooner or later, the Congress Chief Ministers would have had to face a situation where they could not support the Central policies and keep quiet about it.

The Punjab Chief Minister, Capt. Amarinder Singh, was the first to offer a *dharna* on the question of the MSP for paddy right in front of the Prime Minister's residence. He was taken into custody and charged under Section 144 of the IPC and released without any further ado.

Mr. Ajit Jogi, another Congress Chief Minister (of Chhattisgarh), had to show the world that he was as concerned about the MSP for paddy as his Punjab counterpart.

Ms. Sheila Dixit, the Delhi Chief Minister, has warned the Home Minister that she will have to take the path of agitation if he does not withdraw his Ministry's diktat.

And Mr. S.M. Krishna of Karnataka, confronted, on the one hand, by Veerappan and on the other, enraged by, drought-affected farmers, has declared his intention to flout the injunction of the Supreme Court to release Cauvery waters to Tamil Nadu. He has gone on a *padayatra* that could only provoke further disturbances.

Most politicians of the vintage required to reach the chief ministerial *gaddi* have a background of leading agitations. When they find themselves caught between the devil in New Delhi and the deep turbulence of mass hostility, the easiest option is to make a theatrical gesture of resisting the impugned orders through a personal *satyagraha*.

Those interested in the democratic institutions of the country would be perturbed at this development. That the phenomenon of *satyagrahi* chief ministers is limited to economic causes is great comfort. If the divergence of opinion spills over to non-economic issues, the situation could be highly explosive.

The Tamil Nadu Chief Minister, Ms. Jayalalithaa, has announced her intention of filing a contempt petition against Mr. Krishna. It is a safe bet that somebody in Tamil Nadu will soon try and organise *ryot* uprisings that would match those in Karnataka.

If the chief ministers take to deliberate disobedience of the law to vindicate their positions and to counter the policies of opposition, India could be on the brink of conflicts between and among states. Karnataka and Maharashtra may break into hostilities on the border dispute. So, possibly, would Punjab and Haryana, on the Yamuna-Sutlej canal dispute. Karnataka and Tamil Nadu have a common interest in Veerappan and therefore, may not break into violent conflict immediately, even on the Cauvery water issue.

Even on economic issues, the rebellious chief ministers appear more concerned about their political image and the electoral mileage they can draw. The Centre itself appears to be working against its own interests. There is reason to believe that somebody is subverting the policy structures to put the Centre in trouble and the nation in jeopardy.

Let us examine the question of paddy MSP that infuriated the suave Punjab Chief Minister enough to offer a *dharna*. By announcing the MSP, the Centre commits itself not to let the price sink below that level. The announcement of the MSP has to take place before sowing. The idea is that it should help farmers decide the crop pattern.

The MSP for paddy should have been announced the latest by early June. But no announcement was made till 15 days after the new harvest started arriving in the *mandis* of Punjab and Haryana. As misfortune would have it, both these food-granary states suffered from an unprecedentedly severe drought. There was a wave of sympathy for the victims of the failed monsoons. The chief ministers concerned presented demands for assistance of thousands of crores of rupees for drought relief.

The paddy farmers had no reason to believe that the state governments, even while waxing eloquent on the misery of the peasants, would leave them in the lurch. They did whatever they could to protect the paddy crop from the effects of the dry spell. Some sank new tube wells; some deepened the existing ones. New and bigger power motors were installed. That electricity was free in Punjab at that time permitted reckless expenditure, which they would not have made had the power been priced.

Fertiliser prices were also hiked. In brief, the cost of production of paddy-2002 was at least Rs. 100 more per quintal than last year. The farmers, as also the state governments, were expecting a hike in the MSP of that dimension—Rs. 660, instead of Rs. 560, per quintal for A-grade paddy.

The Centre and the Food Corporation of India (FCI) together made the situation worse. If somebody in the government forgot to announce the MSP, the FCI ought to have started the procurement to match the *mandi* arrivals. It did not. It was a tense fortnight for the farmers as the FCI did not commence procurement at all on the pretext that the revised MSP had not been announced.

Had the FCI commenced its operations at last year's MSP, the frustration among the farmers would have been less severe. The simmering discontent of the Punjab peasantry exploded when, towards end-September, the Centre announced that there would be no increase in the paddy MSP from last year's levels.

Mr. Prakash Singh Badal of Punjab, Mr. Om Prakash Chautala of Haryana and several others from Andhra Pradesh—all allies of the NDA—

sought a meeting with the Prime Minister, who characteristically directed that the farmers be paid Rs. 20 per quintal more than last year; but this was not to be treated as an increase in MSP.

The hike could not be assigned either to the "Green Box" or to the "Blue Box". It was directly linked to the quantity actually procured and would certainly qualify as product-specific aggregate measure of support (AMS), in WTO parlance. The government desisted from calling it an increase in the MSP lest it become a precedent.

This three-legged hopping of the government and the knee-jerk bravery of state governments are tragic, particularly because the two together lost a golden opportunity to make the right moves to resolve two chronic maladies. One, the wheat-paddy trap, in which northern farmers have landed themselves since the advent of the Green Revolution; and second, the poverty of post-harvest infrastructure, for which, generally, the FCI is blamed.

After the prolonged good fortune of 14 monsoons, India's food godowns are bursting. There is little scope for export because the international prices of food grains are low. The situation in oilseeds and edible oils is exactly the reverse. The production is poor, and 60 per cent of India's edible oil requirements are met through imports.

The solution to this paradox is clear. Following the oil technology mission of Rajiv Gandhi days, farmers need to be encouraged to shift a part of their irrigated lands from food grains to oilseeds. This could have easily been done had the government taken the farmers into confidence, and explained to them the inevitable unremunerativeness of producing food grains and announced an attractive hike in the MSP of oilseeds.

It would have taken a massive PR exercise to make farmers put up with a *status quo* in paddy MSP. However, the job was not impossible. Had the government marshalled the courage to scrap the inefficient FCI that gobbles enormous funds without delivering any tangible benefits for either the farmer or the poor consumer, they would have given it three cheers.

Further, the government should have allowed the emergence of warehousing companies that construct silos and godowns and accept food grains for storage, paying farmers, say, 70 per cent of the market price and issuing warehousing receipts that are negotiable instruments. This would have released them from the stranglehold of inefficient FCI operations and simultaneously tackled the problem of abundance of food grains and shortage of oilseeds.

Not that conceptual inputs were lacking. Several committees made recommendations to this effect; but they were all brushed aside and the whole issue has come to be centred on the MSP.

The fact is, whether MSP is increased, reduced or kept unchanged, the FCI will come out the victor; the only losers are the nation, its farmers and its poor masses.

---

9 October 2002.

88 Enough Politics, Some Sugar Economics Please

Normally, these announcements are made by the Minister of Agriculture. Occasionally, the privilege has been given to the Minister of State. But on December 19, the Prime Minister himself got up in the Lok Sabha to announce that the SMP for sugarcane has been increased by Rs. 5 from Rs. 64.50 to Rs. 69.50 per quintal.

He was intervening in a debate on agitation by the sugarcane producers of Uttar Pradesh. The hike, however, applies to all the states, though the UP cane-growers will get an additional bonus of Rs. 4 per quintal. The SMP applies to sugarcane with a recovery of 8.5 per cent.

The region through which I am traversing (on a circumambulation of the Narmada to counter the opponents of free economy, trade and technology) right now has no access to the English language pink papers. All that the citizens in this area get to read are Hindi newspapers, which do little justice to economic news. The Hindi newspaper I read, *Nai Duniya*, a widely circulated and respected daily, reported that the Prime Minister mentioned that the new rates would apply to sugarcane with recovery of 6 per cent. I am sure there is some mistake somewhere.

For long the SMP has been fixed with reference to a recovery of 8.5 per cent. If indeed the Prime Minister has announced that the new price of Rs. 69.50 (or Rs. 73.50 in case of UP) will apply to a basic recovery of 6 per cent, there indeed has been a massive hike that is hardly warranted by the circumstances.

If the additional price, that is, premium for higher percentages of recovery has remained unchanged at Re. 0.76 per quintal for each one-tenth per cent increase, the hike announced by the Prime Minister would effectively amount to not just Rs. 5 but to more than Rs. 23 per quintal (Rs. 27 in the case of UP) for a general recovery of 8.5 per cent. Even if the hike were limited to Rs. 5 per quintal in all the states and Rs. 9 in UP, there would arise serious points of concern.

The cane producers of Maharashtra, even earlier than those from UP, have been on the warpath for weeks now against the cooperative sugar factories that do not pay them as advance price even the pre-December 20 SMP as calculated for each individual factory. Every cooperative factory in Maharashtra has its own recovery percentage, which is determined, among other factors, by the efficiency of plantation, cultivation and extraction management of the factory concerned.

Similarly, each factory has different levels of costs on account of harvesting and transport. If the definition of the SMP is strictly interpreted, each factory must, under law, pay within two weeks for the sugarcane it receives a sum that corresponds to the SMP applicable to the appropriate level of sugar recovery minus the corresponding amount of harvesting and transport costs per tonne. The average sugar recovery and cost of harvesting and transport in Maharashtra for the sugar season 2001-02 were 11.86 per cent and Rs. 180 per tonne respectively. The average SMP for sugarcane thus payable in Maharashtra would be over Rs. 700 per tonne. The specific price applicable to each factory may vary from Rs. 650 to Rs. 1,000 per tonne.

The Maharashtra government has ordained that no factory should pay more than Rs. 560 per tonne without obtaining a clearance from the Director of Sugar. The order amounts to incitement to commit a crime, and the farmers are furious. These latter think that rather than hiking the SMP, the Centre ought to take stern measures to ensure that the prevailing SMP is actually paid by the sugar factories and take action against state governments that abet breach of law.

The cane producers of Kolhapur, Sangli and Satara districts had effectively stopped supply of sugarcane to the factories in southern Maharashtra and forced almost all of them to make the minimum initial payment of Rs. 750 per tonne. The minimum price payable under law would be much higher in the case of these factories.

The champions of the sugar cooperative empires maintain that it is impossible for the factories to pay the SMP as they have large stocks of unsold sugar that also cannot be disposed off under the prevailing circumstances of world-wide recession unless the government comes forward in a big way to take the dead stock off their hands or to help them to dispose off the surplus stocks.

The farmers, on the other hand, hold that the factories that cannot pay the SMP had better close down than carry out the illegal business of purchasing sugarcane at prices lower than the SMP.

The first question is, if the Prime Minister's announcement is intended to have any effect on the ground at all. The government has announced a build-up of additional 20 lakh tonnes of sugar stock, and kept aside an amount of Rs. 786 crore to ensure the payment of arrears to cane-growers. These measures will not even begin to meet the real dimensions of the problem.

The sugar industry in Maharashtra has survived for too long on the bonanzas handed out by the government. It is time the sugar industry set its house in order, took objective stock of the situation of each factory, made serious efforts to salvage those that can be saved and let those that have no justification for their existence except the political linkages sink.

The million dollar question is: Is the government in Delhi prepared to take stern legal and penal action against those who contravene the statutory provisions relating to the payment of the SMP and those who abet such contraventions? If it is not prepared to do that, the contemplated handing over of additional funds and building up of additional stocks might actually worsen the situation by discouraging factories from taking any effective measure to step up efficiency and better management.

There is little to indicate that the measures announced by the Prime Minister are meant to do anything except provide a temporary political respite for the ruling NDA. The enlargement of the buffer stock will not begin to touch the fringe of the problem. The allocation of Rs. 786 crore towards clearance of arrears of cane payment is apparently intended only for UP. That sum would, again, make no dent to the situation in Maharashtra.

The farmers in UP are agitating albeit at a much lower key. But UP is, after all, UP, and cane producers there are better represented in Parliament. UP being much closer, the rulers in Delhi have been traditionally panicky in their reactions to demonstrations from that state than those from, say, Maharashtra or Tamil Nadu. Also, the leaders of UP cane-growers have been knocking at the doors of Parliament.

It is, therefore, understandable that the Centre's decision is influenced by the situation in UP than that in Maharashtra. Another reason may be that Maharashtra is under a Congress government while UP is under a BJP ally.

The recent round of sugarcane agitation is far from over. That was merely an opening salvo. UP is readying for the next round. Gujarat will not be too far behind. The situation of the sugar industry in India as a whole threatens to become much worse before it starts becoming better.

---

1 January 2003.

89 A Bitter Cup for Sugarcane Farmers?

The Centre has set up a committee to study the sugarcane pricing situation. While appointing the panel was a good idea, the committee itself seems to have a weak structure, with mills and farmers finding no representation. Nor does the panel have a watertight plan of action to find a solution acceptable to all interests.

Farmers have been agitating on sugarcane prices in Uttar Pradesh, Punjab, Haryana and Maharashtra over two years. The agitations have by and large been non-violent so far, though the police actions have drawn comments from the Human Rights Commission.

At present, the SMP for sugarcane fixed by the Central government stands at Rs. 730 per tonne of sugar recovery of 8.5 per cent. For every additional 0.1 per cent recovery, there is a premium of Rs. 8.50 per tonne. The SMP is decided by the Union Cabinet on the basis of recommendations made by the Commission on Agricultural Costs and Prices.

Some of the northern states also declare an SAP, which is higher than the SMP. In the southern states, where the sugar recovery is higher, farmers are denied even the SMP.

Some time back, the Centre had announced the release of Rs. 600 crore to make up the gap between the SMP and the SAP in three northern states. The southern states were, naturally, aggrieved, though nothing came of it.

Farmers in Uttar Pradesh are agitating for better prices and arrears for the sugarcane delivered over past few years. In the south, where the sugar industry is predominantly in the cooperative sector, farmers are demanding that the mills pay at least the SMP.

The millers claim that in the present depressed market, huge unsold stocks caused mainly by large imports from Pakistan do not permit payment at even the SMP. Cooperative sugar factories in Maharashtra are on the verge of bankruptcy. It is time, therefore, that the whole situation of the sugar industry and the sugarcane prices was reviewed in order to make structural alterations and fine-tuning.

The Union government has finally moved to create a six-member committee to look into the issue in its entirety and suggest changes in the sugarcane-pricing regime. The group is headed by Mr. T. Haque, Chairman of the CACP. The members are all government officials. Neither the millers nor the farmers are represented on the panel. The recommendations of the committee can worsen the situation rather than improve it.

It is for the first time that the methodology of the working of the CACP is being reviewed by the Chairman of the Commission himself. The long tradition has been that such reviews are carried out by experts from outside, as Messrs S.R. Sen, C.S. Jha, C.H. Hanumantha Rao have done in the past.

A more appropriate thing to do would have been to create a committee with representation from the Central government, state governments concerned, the millers from both the cooperative and private sectors, and the sugarcane producers. That would have inspired confidence in the exercise.

The mandate of the committee reads as if the government has already made up its mind about the changes in the sugarcane pricing system, and is expecting the CACP Chairman to provide arguments for what it intends to do in any case. Further, it looks as if the government is preparing to abandon the system of cost plus the MSP that has been in vogue since the 1960s.

The Haque Committee proposes to study whether the pricing of sugarcane should be fixed on the basis of sugar prices received by the mills. This is an idea that could have come only from the millers—both private and cooperative.

Sugar cooperative barons in Maharashtra are crying themselves hoarse that it is impossible to pay the growers the SMP, given the present sugar prices in the market. If the cane prices are linked to market realisations rather than inputs made by the producers, that will be the end of whatever safety net existed since 1960s under support price mechanism.

Under the present system, the SMP is supposed to be announced before the sowing season. More often than not, it is announced only at the beginning of the crushing season. If the SMP is fixed on the basis of realised market prices of sugar it can be done only a year or so after the crushing season is over.

That would defeat the very purpose of the SMPs that indicate to the farmers the minimum price they can expect well before the sowing season.

Further, in a large number of cases market realisations may permit a negative SMP. Hence, the government would be obliged to prescribe some minimum positive SMP that the farmers must get.

The entire purpose of introducing the element of market realisation would be frustrated.

Alternatively, if the SMP were fixed on the basis of sugar prices of the previous year, it would fail to provide any guidelines to the sugarcane producers.

From the press communiqué issued by the Centre, it appears that the Haque Committee has the mandate to examine the possibility of fixing different rates of SMPs for different states.

This would make some sense if the differences in prices are linked to the percentage of sugar recovery. As a result, the SMPs in Bihar, Orissa, Uttar Pradesh, Punjab and Haryana would be lower than those in Gujarat, Maharashtra, Andhra Pradesh, Karnataka and Tamil Nadu.

There is much to be said for a differential system of SMPs for sugarcane. However, if the principle of differential support prices were to be extended to wheat and paddy the consequences could be disastrous.

It would also appear that the Haque Committee intends to take into account market realisations by the millers obtained through diversification of activities as well.

Thus, sugarcane producers will be paid a higher price by a mill that earns profits in the sale of molasses, ethanol and chemical byproducts.

It makes some sense, but the methodology for the purpose will be complex and controversial and not transparent enough to sort out the sugar industry's decades-long problems.

Appointing a committee for a comprehensive review was a good idea. But the Haque Committee seems to have too weak a structure and none-too watertight a plan to produce the desired results.

---

26 November 2003.

90 Malady of Yavatmal

Cotton Turns a Killer

Why are cotton farmers of Maharashtra's Vidarbha region, where the annual farm turnover is often in six digits, driven to committing suicide? More than the incidence of spurious pesticides or defective seeds, as in Andhra Pradesh, it is the state monopoly procurement scheme that has pushed them deep into debt and, now, the harsh process of loan recovery.

Yavatmal is one of the better-endowed districts of the Vidarbha region of Maharashtra. Thanks to bountiful rains, it has large tracts covered with lush green forests. It is a major cotton-producing district. So much so that in the days of the Raj, the British companies considered it worthwhile to construct a whole railroad for the transport of cotton. The meter-gauge track meanders throughout the district criss-crossing roads and thick forests.

At the dawn of Independence, *Ijaradars* dominated the social, cultural, economic and political life of Yavatmal.

The term '*Ijaradars*' literally means those who wear trousers. In real terms, it means petty landlords with holdings of around three to five hundred acres. Thanks to the bountiful nature, they lived an opulent life; drought and starvation were unheard of.

Fifty-odd years after Independence, the Yavatmal scene has changed completely. According to official statistics, in this district, 154 farmers committed suicide since 2001—17 in 2001; 38 in 2002; 52 in 2003; and 47 in 2004 till end July.

All but nine of those who committed suicide were in debt taken from credit institutions or private moneylenders. The amounts outstanding were mostly in five digits—certainly not a burden that can be considered unbearable in a community where the annual farm turnover is often in six-digits.

In the neighbouring cotton-producing districts of Marathwada, there have been several cases of farmers committing suicide; but not quite as many. In Satara, Pune, Solapur and Jalgaon districts, the first suicides happened towards the end of July 2004.

What explains the relatively high incidence of farm suicides in Vidarbha? First, it is the cotton farmer who is affected.

In Andhra Pradesh, where there have been farmer suicides on a large scale, it is again the cotton farmers who are the principal victims. But, unlike in Andhra Pradesh where the victims have been primarily from the landless section, in Vidarbha they are land-owning cotton farmers.

Further, the incidence of spurious pesticides and defective seeds is, unlike in Andhra Pradesh, negligible in Maharashtra. There is, obviously, something about cotton that takes the toll of those who produce it.

The aggregate measurement of support (AMS)—that is, the difference between the prices actually obtained by the farmers and the price they would have obtained in a hypothetical free market—is the worst in the case of cotton (-258.51 per cent in 1996-97). Clearly, the negative AMS or the negative subsidy is the prime cause of farmer suicides in India.

The cotton farmers in Vidarbha, unlike the tribals in the adjoining Amravati district, are unused to starvation and famine. This year some 9,000 cases of child malnutrition and starvation came to light in the tribal Chikhaldara tract of Amravati district.

The cotton farmers of Vidarbha have not been driven, in living memory, to break stones or do earth-work in famine relief camps.

The drought this year came as a severe shock. Truant monsoons destroyed two successive sowings—a phenomenon the farmers had never encountered.

And even before the onset of monsoons, the loan recovery officials had launched their operations. These included gentle persuasion, threats, humiliation, seizure of household goods, bicycles, tin roofs and auctioning of land.

This year, the recovery officials were particularly severe and brutal. The year 2003-04 was particularly good for Vidarbha farmers. The cotton crop was bountiful and the sale price high, thanks to the suspension of the Maharashtra Cotton Monopoly Procurement Scheme operations (so also with soyabean.)

The farmers had earned more money than they ever did in a long, long time. The recovery officials of the lending banks, cooperative societies and commercial banks, and the moneylenders saw an opportunity. This was a good time to clear loans and settle accounts.

The recovery method became particularly severe and coercive, bordering on the extortionate this year. It is alleged that houses of farmers were entered and belongings of farmers taken away. Activists of a farmers' organisation have even filed police cases of unlawful entry and robbery. All to no avail.

The farmers were driven to suicide, first in trickles and then in waves, as suicide became a thinkable proposition. The accounts of the Yavatmal District Central Cooperative Bank showed that the amount of loans recovered this year was the highest in the last five years.

The situation of the cotton producers in Vidarbha was even worse because of the monopoly procurement by the Government of Maharashtra since 1971.

The prices obtained by the farmers under this scheme were much lower than those prevailing in Madhya Pradesh, Andhra Pradesh and Gujarat.

Over 30 years, cotton farmers have sunk deeper and deeper into debt. If there is one single villain of the cotton farmers' suicides in Maharashtra, it is the State Cotton Monopoly Procurement Scheme.

---

4 August 2004.

91 Quandary of Cane, Cotton and Onion

Farmers were promised policies that eliminate price-depressing moves and lighten the burden of loans and interest. But the Maharashtra government is trying to revive the Cotton Monopoly Procurement Scheme, the *zonebandi* system for sugarcane and a pointless liberalisation of onion trade. Are these policies really farmer-friendly?

Dussehra, in Maharashtra, marks the auspicious day for launching enterprises. The Maratha armies used to celebrate the festivities of Dussehra at home and then proceed northwards for conquests. The tradition still continues.

The rival forces of the Congress(I) and the Nationalist Congress Party (NCP) mutually agreed upon a ceasefire in the fight for the chief ministership of Maharashtra. Chief ministers might come and go, but October 23 will certainly not be remembered as the day the Congress and the NCP resumed hostilities. It is more likely to be remembered as the day on which the state government resumed purchase of cotton, ostensibly under the Maharashtra State Cotton Monopoly Procurement Scheme (CMPS), which lay in suspension since last year. In fact, the purchase will be under the aegis of Cotton Corporation of India (CCI). The farmers will be paid by CCI at the minimum support price (MSP), as in any other state.

There is no clear indication if private traders will be allowed to make purchases from the farmers. If it is presumed that the orders issued last year remain in force till they are formally revoked, the private traders will be legally permitted to enter the market, though under the present situation of depressed market prices, they may have little economic incentive to do so.

The joint manifesto of the Congress and the NCP, for the Maharashtra Assembly elections, had announced that the new government would resuscitate the CMPS and had even a guaranteed a minimum price of Rs. 2,700 per quintal.

There are two evident contradictions here. The National Common Minimum Programme (NCMP) of the United Progressive Alliance (UPA) clearly promises that all measures that have the effect of depressing prices of agricultural commodities will be eliminated. The assurance of resuscitating the CMPS goes contrary to the letter and spirit of this element of the NCMP.

Further, last time the Centre granted a fresh lease of life to the CMPS, it had clearly stipulated that the guaranteed minimum price under the CMPS should not exceed the MSP fixed by the Centre.

Many critics had then raised the point whether it made any sense to continue the CMPS and if it would not be much simpler to wind it up and allow both CCI and the private trade to operate as in all other states. CCI intervenes in the market to ensure the MSP all over India. If that is all the CMPS in Maharashtra was allowed to do, it had lost all the justification for its existence.

Last season, the Maharashtra government stopped making the Cotton Monopoly Procurement a prestige issue and permitted the entry of both CCI and the private traders, and the latter offered a hefty Rs. 1,000 above the MSP. The assurance of a price of Rs. 2,700 in the electoral manifesto of the Congress-NCP alliance goes against the Centre's directives that the guaranteed minimum price should not exceed the MSP, which stands at Rs. 2,010 a quintal this year.

It may be recalled that last season's guaranteed minimum price was Rs. 2,500 a quintal when the private traders were offering as much as Rs. 2,900-3,000. This season, the market price appears stuck at less than Rs. 2,000. The new government will have to bear a loss of anywhere between Rs. 5,000 crore and Rs. 6,000 crore if it complies with the electoral promise. If it does not, the political price might be heavier. In Vidarbha alone, over 500 farmers committed suicide last year. The figure might double if the cotton prices are allowed to fall with the market. So much for the white gold—cotton—situation in Maharashtra.

Now, for the pungent gold. A few days earlier, the Central Cabinet announced that onions were deleted from the list of commodities that come under the purview of the Essential Commodities Act. The Finance Minister, Mr. P. Chidambaram, who made the announcement, said the move would benefit exporters and farmers.

The liberalisation of the onion market is some indication of the government's intention to go back on the policies followed for over a quarter century of banning export of onion immediately after the harvest and lifting it four-five months later after the stocks pass into the hands of the traders. During this quarter century, much water has flowed under the bridge.

The WTO regime frowns upon all quantitative restrictions in international trade. And, restrictions on export of onions are contrary to the spirit of the new rules of the WTO game. The Centre has removed onions from the list of essential commodities not in pursuance of any reformist policies in agriculture or in pursuance of the NCMP; it was forced to do so as, otherwise, its restrictions would have invited complaints from other nations.

Finally, the issue of sugarcane—the sweet gold. The SMP of sugarcane is Rs. 730 per tonne for a recovery of 9 per cent with a premium of Rs. 8.6 per tonne for additional 0.1 per cent recovery. In the prime sugarcane-producing region of southern Maharashtra, the recovery is, generally, above 12 per cent.

That should earn them Rs. 900 per quintal. This is subject to deductions on account of harvesting and transport costs as the factories carry out these operations at their own cost. All told, the farmers have been demanding a net price of, at least, Rs. 1,000 per tonne.

The state government persists with a state advised price of Rs. 560 per tonne. Sugar factories across the border, in Karnataka, are offering Rs. 1,050 per tonne with no deductions on account of repayment of loans or contributions to diverse funds. The Assembly elections in Maharashtra had stopped the sugar cooperative factories from moving against this encroachment across the border.

Soon after Dussehra, once a new Chief Minister assumes charge, the sugar barons of south Maharashtra—all NCP loyalists—will surely move to stop the transport of sugarcane to Karnataka factories.

In fact, they will urge the Maharashtra government to bring back the despised *zonebandi* system to protect their fiefdoms by imposing monopoly procurement.

The Congress-NCP feud over the chief ministership coincided with the prime sugarcane harvesting season. Maharashtra's sugar barons were worried that, by the time the new chief minister is sworn in, the Karnataka factories may have taken away much of the harvest and have, thus, start declaring prices well above Rs. 1,000 per tonne, braving the wrath of the new government and Mr. Sharad Pawar. The UPA government at the Centre has promised to take pro-farmer measures by eliminating price-depressig policies and lightening the burden of loans and interest. On the ground, it is trying to bring back the defunct CMPS and the *zonebandi* for sugarcane and tom-tomming about a pointless liberalisation in respect of onions.

Clearly, the government lacks a policy on the subject. It would be forced to give up its second misadventure in CMPS under pressure of international market forces. In any case, the state fisc cannot bear the burden of cotton monopoly purchases. Similarly, the market forces will, sooner or later, drive the rickety cooperative sugar factories in Maharashtra to bankruptcy.

Mr. Sharad Pawar and the Centre are aware that liberalisation is good for agriculture and the economy. They know equally well that liberal policies will hurt the cooperatives, which provides their political stay.

The position of the Left on the economic reforms in agriculture is not known as yet. Whoever the new chief minister of Maharashtra, he/she cannot escape this quandary of the white, sweet and pungent gold in the state.

---

28 October 2004.

92 A Case of the Fence Eating Crop?

The crisis that has been brewing in the sugarcane growing regions of Maharashtra has reached a stalemate. The Maharashtra government has been insisting, all along, that no factory should pay more than Rs. 850 per tonne of sugarcane. There is general acceptance that this year the final price for sugarcane will be much higher than the SMP, given the fact that sugar, molasses and bagasse prices are on the upswing. There is also no denying that the cane growers in most other states are getting more than Rs. 1,100 per tonne.

All the same, the Maharashtra government firmly refused to hike the advanced price above Rs. 850. One day, during the agitation, the Maharashtra Chief Minister, Mr. Vilasrao Deshmukh, spoke to representatives of farmers and said it may be possible to pay an advance price of Rs. 1,200—subject, of course, to the approval of the Cabinet. The Cabinet never met; or it never came to approve the assurance given by the Chief Minister.

Two days later, it came out with a formula that the advanced price should be limited to Rs. 850 per tonne, and that the factories could pay such additional price as may be justified by individual transactions. This was considered signal enough for the sugar factories to offer to pay, when the cane was delivered, Rs. 850 per tonne in cash and a post-dated cheque, encashable in six weeks, for Rs. 350 per tonne.

The farmers have resisted harvesting for six weeks now. This is a brave act in a year of devastation by flood. The river waters are shrinking and the load shedding is so severe that it has become extremely difficult to irrigate the sugarcane crop to keep it ready for delivery to the factories.

The farmers can be said to have made a tactical retreat, which speaks well of the acumen and statesmanship of their leaders. There are, however, political parties, with only marginal interest in the agricultural economy that are now rushing into areas from where traditional farm organisations are retreating.

One can say that the question of sugarcane prices for the 2005-06 season is settled for the time being. That does not, however, mean all the issues are settled. For the last four years, the Maharashtra cane-growers got an advance price, which was substantially lower than the SMP. The sugar prices are abnormally depressed, it was argued. But this year they were not. Why not make up this year for the last four years?

Prices of sugar and other products are booming and it should be possible for a reasonably efficient sugar factory to pay about Rs. 2,000 for a tonne of sugarcane. But it cannot be done. Why? NABARD (National Bank For Agriculture And Rural Development) does not allow it! NABARD is said to have issued instructions to the sugar factories that any unit paying more than Rs. 850 as advance price per tonne of sugarcane will automatically lose the advantage of the credit package it is preparing.

Everyone in the government and from the sugar factories spoke as if he had personally seen a copy of the NABARD circular. NABARD officials maintain that this circular was based on the findings of the committee that went into the financial structure of a number of factories and that both the report and the circular were made available to all sugar factories.

There are others who maintain that the NABARD circular mentions the price of Rs. 850 as a minimum advance price, and not a maximum price. It was even hinted that the Union Ministries of Finance and Agriculture initiated the idea.

If it were true, that would hardly make sense. NABARD was established as a development bank for providing and regulating credit and other facilities for the promotion and development of agriculture, small industries, cottage and village industries, handicrafts and other rural crafts and allied economic activities in rural India.

It does not get into any direct financing itself. It is essentially a refinancing organisation. It has supervisory functions that include inspection and offsite surveillance of the rural financial institutions.

As a bankers' bank, NABARD would be fully justified in making an on-the-spot or off-site inspection of the rural banks as also industries that they finance. But does its mandate permit it to decide the maximum price at which sugar factories buy and sell? Would the Reserve Bank of India do that for any industry?

It would appear that a NABARD committee examined the financial situation of a number of cooperative sugar factories in Maharashtra. It came to the conclusion that the situation was not only serious but also precarious. Licences had been issued where none was justified. Decisions regarding the opening of a factory and its capacity were highly political.

In several cases, managements were found grossly inefficient and most of the factories could be salvaged only with great difficulty. Corruption and malpractices were rampant. In addition, the decisions on the price to be paid for sugarcane were influenced by political factors and have not augured well for the industry.

On the basis of these findings, the government should have moved to undertake a general inspection of all the factories and the holdings of movable and immovable property of those who owned them. This would have permitted the government to classify the existing factories among those salvageable and those that were bound to sink.

NABARD, functioning as the banker, would have taken that course. Unfortunately, it did not. It trained its guns on the most vulnerable, and ordained that they should not be paid more than the SMP calculated for a basket-case factory.

The farmer has till now looked upon NABARD as a friend. It seems he will have to have second thoughts about it.

---

30 November 2005.

93 Sugar: A Bitter-Sweet Policy

Even as there is call for the government to exit businesses, it remains interested in many, often for reasons political. The most regulated sector in agriculture is 'sugar'. From licensing of mills to the specifications of gunny bags to be used for packaging, every thing is dictated by the Sugarcane Control Order, 1966. The government's 1998 decision to de-licence the sugar industry is pending before the Supreme Court. A number of matters relating to levy sugar, the statutory minimum price (SMP) and the state advised price (SAP) are pending before various courts. Now, sugar mills have also been co-opted for co-generation as also ethanol production. And, under the new United Nations' norms for co-generation, the industry is also to take up Clean Development Mechanism (CDM) projects.

In this context, every aspect of the sugar policy needs to be reviewed.

Cane Area

The government retains the power to reserve any area where cane is grown for a sugar factory, considering the availability of sugarcane and the crushing capacity of the unit. The limit of 15 km as the minimum distance between two factories has been held by the court to be directive in nature and not mandatory. While the sugar industry no more requires compulsory licensing, it would help the growth of a healthy industry if the assessment of sugarcane availability were left to the discretion of the entrepreneurs.

The power of *zonebandi*—reserving cane areas for sugar factories—is with the state governments rather than the Centre. The restriction of 15 km was fixed in the context of open pan technology. The sugar industry unnecessarily carries the whole of the sugarcane load, from the field to the factory. This can be easily avoided by doing the crushing and primary crystallisation near the field itself and then going to refineries, each of which can serve a radius of 40-50 square km.

The SMP for the sugarcane is decided on the basis of a number of considerations. The general dissatisfaction about the SMP fixed by the Central government is widespread.

Price Conundrum

The statistical averaging method used by the Commission of Agricultural Costs and Prices (CACP) results in some hilarious but very wrong computations. The costs attributed to labour, pesticides, manure, power and irrigation have been often quite bizarre. Recently, the Minister of State for Agriculture in Maharashtra admitted that the actual cost of production of sugarcane in the state was about Rs. 300 a tonne higher than the SMP.

Further, the cooperative mills also deduct from farmers' dues various amounts for their trusts, and various deposits including some non-refundable ones. The SAP given by Punjab, Haryana, Uttar Pradesh, Uttarakhand and Tamil Nadu is much higher than the SMP.

Quota and Free Sale

The Centre also has the powers to take away a certain percentage of the sugar produced, as levy sugar at a price to be determined by it. Different levy prices are fixed for different zones. In principle, they are determined by the cost of cultivation of sugarcane and the cost of production of sugar. In practice, however, the levy prices fixed have no rhyme or reason. There is a suspicion that the government follows a hidden policy of equalisation of incomes per hectare for different zones. It may be noted that while fixing the MSP and procurement prices for other commodities, no attempt is made to equalise net incomes per hectare for a given crop.

The Centre also uses tariffs on import of sugar and restrictions on exports as also releases of monthly quota of free sale sugar in a manner not consistent with the interests of the sugar industry or of the sugarcane producers.

There have been instances of monthly quota releases of free sugar and the restrictions on exports and imports being manipulated to score political brownie points. At times the free sale sugar is converted into levy sugar on various pretexts. But rarely the other way around.

All producers of sugar are required to use new jute bags for packaging. Given that the sugar deteriorates on exposure to moisture, jute bags are, obviously, not the best. The jute industry has remained moribund for decades and shown no inclination to modernise. It appears to pressure the Centre to make the use of jute sacks mandatory for food grains and sugar. Some years back, a move was made to allow other packaging material to some extent. The present UPA government has ordered use only of jute bags, perhaps on pressures from allies.

The Tax Burden

The sugar industry is subject to heavy taxation. The current rate of the excise duty is Rs. 71 a quintal. Including VAT (value added tax), the levies come to Rs. 143 a quintal. Ironically, even the members of the cooperative sugar mills have to pay a hefty purchase tax though there is no sale or purchase involved.

The reasons why politicians seem keen on tightly regulating the sugar industry becomes clear from recent experience. In the 2006-07 season, sugar exports were banned as long as the farmers held the sugarcane. Once the mills seemed on a roll and the cane supply appeared assured, export of sugar was allowed. But only for a short time. Assembly elections in five states and the continuously rising inflation made the government announce a ban on export of all politically sensitive commodities such as sugar, onion and wheat.

The sugar industry needs to be deregulated entirely. The Food Corporation of India (FCI) must be kept out of the levy sugar and PDS network.

A new Sugar Industry Policy is required in order to ensure that the industry is de-politicised and gets into a position where chemical products from molasses will give the major value-addition and sugar will become a byproduct. The industry will be able to take up co-generation and production of ethanol and take its place amongst major modern industries instead of a mofussil agro-processing industry.

---

21 February 2007.

94 Why are Wheat Farmers Angry?

Farmers of Uttar Pradesh and Punjab staged demonstrations in front of Parliament, now in recess, to demand a better price for wheat. Before Parliament went into recess, the Agriculture Minister had announced a bonus of Rs. 100 a quintal. The bonus takes the procurement price to be paid by the Food Corporation of India (FCI) to Rs. 850 a quintal. There was considerable thumping of treasury benches as if the declaration of bonus was an astonishingly generous act.

Clearly, the farmers do not think so. Mr. Prakash Singh Badal, the recently installed Chief Minister of Punjab, was urged to announce a further bonus of Rs. 100 a quintal on behalf of the state. Mr. Badal has not responded because the Rs. 100 Central bonus had itself come in response to his own proposal. He could not offer a second bonus without letting it out that he was not fully conversant with the situation in Punjab when he had made the first proposal.

In 2006, farmers in Punjab were a happy lot despite a mediocre harvest. The Centre had for once acquiesced to rein in the FCI by allowing private traders to enter the wheat market. Farmers got around Rs. 1,000 a quintal though the official procurement price was Rs. 750 a quintal including a bonus of Rs. 50 above the minimum support price (MSP). The Agriculture Minister was visibly happy about what he had done for the wheat farmers.

Inflation Attack

Then followed two things: One, the Minister had to go back on his assurance given in Parliament that it would not be necessary to import any wheat in the ongoing year. Second, the farm prices, particularly of food grains, started rising, and the UPA government came under attack for the rising inflation.

Consequently, the government announced its intention to import just about 5 lakh tonnes of wheat for the Public Distribution System (PDS) in the south. But, by the time the year ended, the government had imported 55 lakh tonnes of wheat at a price higher than what the private traders in India were paying the farmers.

Inflation continued unabated and the Left allies of the Congress grew restless. They blamed the purchases by private traders as also the dealings on the futures markets for the mess. The Leftists wanted the FCI to be restored to its glory and all non-FCI purchasers kept out of the market. In October 2006, the futures price of wheat for April 20, 2007 had reached Rs. 930 a quintal.

Banned or Not?

There was some confusion whether the government had actually banned private trading in wheat and rice. Spokesmen of the Forward Markets Commission denied any such ban. The Agriculture Minister added to the confusion by declaring that there was no such ban. However, commodity exchanges such as National Commodity Derivatives Exchange (NCDX) were not permitting any new trade.

On February 27, 2007, farmers announced their resolve to give the maximum possible quantity of wheat to the NCDX platform; on February 28, the futures market was banned. The Forward Markets Commission decided to suspend taking open positions on the futures markets for wheat and rice.

On March 17, a farmers' gathering at Moga in Punjab reiterated the decision to bypass the FCI procurement of wheat. The very next day the private traders lined up, bid more than the government procurement price and started offering as much as Rs. 1,000 a quintal in Punjab.

On March 30, the Agriculture Minister tried to explain away the issue by declaring that the government had not asked the private traders to abstain from entering the market. That hardly cut ice, because everyone knew by then that the government had asked the private players to let the FCI have its fill first before entering the market. The district police officials in Moga were frankly admitting that they had instructions not to allow private trade in wheat for 45 days after the opening of the season.

Myopic Policy

The Punjab wheat farmers along with their counterparts in Haryana and western Uttar Pradesh are annoyed at the myopic policy. The FCI is supposed to ensure that market price of wheat does not go below the MSP. As a procurer, it has structural difficulties in purchasing wheat at a price higher than the procurement price.

This year it can offer nothing more than Rs. 850 a quintal. The private traders are wooing the farmers, offering Rs. 1,000 a quintal. The government has already announced its intention to import wheat this year. The wheat farmer is angry at what he sees as the government's attempt to corner him by stymieing free trade, blocking the futures markets and forcing him to sell his wheat to the FCI at an unconscionably low price. He finds it difficult to understand this.

The FCI is not exactly known for its efficiency. When it offers Rs. 850 a quintal of wheat to the farmer it operates through the *arhatias* and pays for costs towards auction fee, market fee, rural development fund, infrastructure cess, labour charges, *kachchi adat* and *pakki adat* taking the gross cost of procured wheat to Rs. 971.55 a quintal. The total cost of its operation varies from 11.5 per cent in Punjab to a mere 1 per cent in Bihar and Gujarat. "Why should the government be spending Rs. 971 a quintal of procured wheat and keep the share of the farmers limited to Rs. 850?", the farmers are asking. In Punjab and Haryana, whichever the party in power, the *arhatias* rule the roost. The MSP-FCI-*arhatias*-PDS racket is said to be unbreakable.

In anger the farmers, who are at a loss to know what the government is doing, have decided to take matters into their own hands. On April 11, that is, on the eve of Baisakhi that marks the opening of the wheat season, they plan to make a declaration of their intention to boycott wheat *mandis* and demand a price of Rs. 1,000 a quintal or, in the alternative, want the ban scrapped on the private trade and the futures markets. It promises to be a hot summer in the wheat land of India.

---

4 April 2007.

95 The Travails of Wheat Procurement

It was by coincidence that I read the news about the Agriculture Minister, Mr. Sharad Pawar's statement abandoning all plans for import of wheat on the very day I received a typed demi-official letter from him stoutly making a case for import this year of some 50 lakh tonnes of wheat. In hindsight, the letter makes tragi-comic reading.

The gist of the letter is as follows:

The Minister of Agriculture had stated how kind the UPA government had been to wheat farmers as it hiked the minimum support price (procurement price) by Rs. 230 (*sic*) per quintal—of which a full Rs. 100 was increased in the current year alone, as against its predecessor, which had increased it by only Rs. 50.

The Minister admits, not in words but in a statistical table, that in spite of its tightfistedness the NDA government had satisfactory procurement and was never required to import wheat; while the UPA government, in spite of its munificence and a bonus of Rs. 100 per quintal, could garner only 19 lakh tonnes of the total increase of 55 lakh tonnes production in the current year and was forced to import.

The Paradox

What explains the paradox of good procurement response to a "grudging" NDA government and the poor response to a "generous" UPA government? The answer is self-evident. The NDA prices were more in tune with the market realities, while Mr. Pawar's generous bonus of Rs. 100, taking the procurement price to Rs. 850 per quintal was based on a wrong reference to the Chicago Board of Trade (CBOT) quotation.

The minister states that the CBOT price for March 15, 2007 was Rs. 744 only and that approving a bonus of Rs. 100 was a sign of prudence.

What he does not mention is that the CBOT price of March 15 had no relevance to the procurement operation in India, which takes place in the months of April and May. He, further, failed to notice that the CBOT price is, necessarily, as in the US, free on board (FoB), not to be compared with the procurement price, which obviously is c.i.f. The cost of insurance and freight comes to Rs. 50-100 depending upon the port at which the cargo is disembarked.

If the minister has taken into account the April-May CBOT prices and also the c.i.f. factor, the indicated procurement price would have been around Rs. 1,150 per quintal, justifying a bonus of Rs. 400 per quintal. This became clear at the beginning of the procurement season when the private traders offered around Rs. 1,100 per quintal, which was consistent with a sensible reading of the CBOT data.

The minister, in his letter, for once praises the NDA government for following open market policy, which benefited farmers and takes credit for having continued that policy in 2006-07. But he adroitly skips the issue of why the open trade policy was abandoned in the current year. If the government had not suspended taking open positions in the wheat futures market on February 28, 2007, the minister could have had the advantage of referring to the National Commodity and Derivative Exchange (NCDEX) sentiments for fixing the procurement price rather than using the irrelevant CBOT quotations.

On the other hand, the CBOT quotations would have been relevant in deciding on the two international tenders invited by the government after it decided to import over 5 million tonnes. If on this occasion as well, the minister had referred to the CBOT prices, which showed a buoyant sentiment, he would have, in the national interest, decided to accept the bid of $263 per tonne. Instead he chose to refer to monthly report of May 24, 2007, of the International Grain Council (IGC), which works under the aegis of the UNCTAD, which predicted a fall in wheat prices as a result of an increase in production. The tender was consequently scrapped.

When fresh tenders were called, the empowered group of ministers decided to import at $389 per tonne based on various reports of further decline in prices. The CBOT readings were to the contrary. The crop estimates for the coming year are optimistic. The UPA government has denied itself the use of an untrammelled domestic futures market.

Unanswered Questions

It is only by coincidence that the decision of the government to give up all plans for import seems justifiable. Certain questions remain unanswered though:

How come the international market was rife with rumours that India was in the market for import of at least 2 million tonnes?

Why did the minister talk recently of the need to import for even the next year, thus adding fuel to a market already on fire?

How come the minister based his decision on three different sources of information on three separate occasions in the same year? Was it a case of finding a source of information that suited the decision taken in advance?

Is it clear to the policymakers at least in September 2007 that CACP based procurement prices are exorbitantly expensive and that the domestic futures markets are the best guidelines for farmers to take decisions regarding sowing and marketing as well as for the government?

---

19 September 2007.